CITY OF BRISTOL COLLEGE

COORDINATED AWARD

PHYSICS for AQA

Patrick Fullick

Heinemann Educational Publishers
Halley Court, Jordan Hill, Oxford, OX2 8EJ
Part of Harcourt Education
Heinemann is a registered trademark of
Harcourt Education Limited

© Patrick Fullick, 2001

Copyright notice

All rights reserved. No part of this publication may be reproduced in any material form (including photocopying or storing it in any medium by electronic means and whether or not transiently or incidentally to some other use of this publication) without the prior written permission of the copyright owner, except in accordance with the provisions of the Copyright, Designs and Patents Act 1988 or under the terms of a licence issued by the Copyright Licensing Agency Ltd, 90 Tottenham Court Road, London W1P 0LP. Applications for the copyright owner's written permission to reproduce any part of this publication should be addressed to the publisher.

First published 2001

ISBN 0 435 584 200

05 04 03

10 9 8 7 6 5 4 3

Edited by Margaret Shepherd

Designed and typeset by Gecko Ltd

Illustrated by Harvey Collins, Martin Fish, Steve Lach, Joe Little, Andrew Quelch, John Storey, Geoff Ward, Tony Wilkins

Printed and bound in Italy by Printer Trento S.r.l.

Acknowledgements

The authors and publishers would like to thank the following for permission to use photographs:

2: Mark Powell; **3**: Mark Powell; **6**: Mark Powell; **9**: (*all*) Mark Powell; **12**: T Mark Powell, B Mark Powell; **14**: T Peter Gould, B Peter Gould; **15**: Peter Gould; **18**: Peter Gould; **21**: Mark Wagner; **24**: Corbis; **30**: Science Photo Library/Henry Groskinsky/Peter Arnold Inc.; **32**: Commotion; **34**: T Science Photo Library/Jeremy Burgess, B Corbis; **35**: MIRA; **36**: Actionplus; **40**: SPL/Martin Bond; **42**: T Corbis/Gunter Marx, B Mark Powell; **43**: Corbis; **44**: Environmental Images/Phil Brown; **46**: Science Photo Library/Alfred Pasieka; **47**: Peter Gould; **48**: Science Photo Library/Phil Jude; **49**: Science Photo Library; **51**: Mark Powell; **54**: Science Photo Library/Martin Dohm; **55**: TL Science Photo Library/Chris Taylor, TR Science Photo Library/Jesse, M Science Photo Library/Dept of Clinical Radiology, Salisbury District Hospital; **58**: Corbis; **60**: Corbis; **64**: Science Photo Library/J.L. Charmet; **65**: TL Corbis, TR Science Photo Library/John Thomas; **68**: T Corbis/Bettman Archive, B Science Photo Library/NASA/Goddard Space Flight Centre; **69**: Science Photo Library/NASA; **70**: M Science Photo Library/Jerry Schad, B Science Photo Library; **72**: The Kobal Collection; **73**: EPL/Leslie Garland; **78**: Science Photo Library/Dr R Clark & M R Goff; **80**: (*both*) Art Directors and TRIP; **81**: Science Photo Library/Alfred Pasieka; **82**: (*both*) MLC Marshmead. Photo courtesy of Methodist Ladies' College, Melbourne; **83**: Environmental Images/Martin Bond; **85**: Mark Powell; **86**: SPL/Martin Bond; **89**: Environmental Images/Trevor Perry; **90**: Environmental Images/Robert Brook; **91**: T EPL/John Novis, B Science Photo Library.Martin Bond; **92**: Science Photo Library/Tom McHugh; **93**: TR Science Photo Library/Hank Morgan, ML Science Photo Library/NASA; **96**: OSF/Richard Packwood; **97**: T Science Photo Library/Novosti, B Science Photo Library/John Mead; **107**: Peter Gould; **108**: Science Photo Library; **109**: TR Mark Powell, ML Science Photo Library; **110**: Science Photo Library/Sheila Terry; **111**: Science Photo Library/Chris Knapton; **114**: TR Science Photo Library, BL Science Photo Library; **115**: Corbis; **120**: Corbis; **121**: L Science Photo Library, R Corbis; **122**: Art Directors and TRIP; **125**: T Science Photo Library/BSIP, Beranger, B Beaumont Veterinary Practice/Ginny Stroud-Lewis; **126**: (*both*) Science Photo Library/Will & Deni McIntyre; **127**: NRPB; **128**: Science Photo Library; **129**: Science Photo Library/Hotel-Dieu e Montreal/J Leveille; **132**: Art Directors and TRIP; **133**: TL Science Photo Library/David Parker, TR Cambridge Veterinary College, B Science Photo Library/Tim Beddow; **136**: Science Photo Library/Space Telescope Science Institute, NASA; **139**: SPL/Argonne National Laboratory; **140**: Science Photo Library/Paolo Koch; **142**: Science Photo Library; **143**: T Science Photo Library/US Dept of Energy, B Environmental images/Graham Burns.

Picture research by Ginny Stroud-Lewis

The publishers have made every effort to trace the copyright holders, but if they have inadvertently overlooked any, they will be pleased to make the necessary arrangements at the first opportunity.

AQA examination questions are reproduced by permission of the Assessment and Qualifications Alliance.

Tel: 01865 888058   www.heinemann.co.uk

Introduction

Physics – the science which looks at everything around us, whatever its scale – from the tiny particles that make up atoms to the entire universe in which we live. The world of physics is often strange, and sometimes unbelievable. In this book you will find out more about the physical world, and how interactions involving matter and energy shape everything around us and all we do.

This book has been written to support you as you study the AQA Coordinated Science GCSE. As well as lots of facts and clear explanations with diagrams and photos to illustrate the science, there are some other features which will add interest and depth to your learning.

- **Science people** introduces you to some of the scientists who have worked out the science we now take for granted.
- **Ideas and evidence** looks at the way ideas about physics have developed and grown over the years.

At the end of each double page spread there are questions to help you check that you have understood the material you have just read, and at the end of each chapter there are GCSE style questions which will allow you to test your knowledge for the exams ahead.

Studying physics will give you an increased understanding of the world around you and the way that things behave. I hope this book will help you in your studies, and help you enjoy physics throughout your course.

Contents

Chapter 1: Electricity

1.1	Electricity and circuits	2	1.7	Energy from electricity	14
1.2	Simple circuits – some explanations	4	1.8	Using electricity safely	16
			1.9	Keeping safe – circuit breakers	18
1.3	Current, voltage and resistance	6	1.10	Static electricity	20
1.4	Current-voltage relationships	8	1.11	Using static electricity	22
1.5	Energy in circuits	10	1.12	Electrolysis	24
1.6	Electricity from the mains	12	1.13	End of chapter questions	26

Chapter 2: Forces and motion

2.1	Distance, speed and time	28	2.4	Frictional forces	34
2.2	Changing motion	30	2.5	Falling freely	36
2.3	The link between force, mass and acceleration	32	2.6	End of chapter questions	38

Chapter 3: Waves

3.1	The behaviour of waves (1)	40	3.7	EM waves and communications	52
3.2	The behaviour of waves (2)	42	3.8	Sound waves	54
3.3	The behaviour of waves (3)	44	3.9	Seismic waves	56
3.4	Light waves	46	3.10	Moving plates beneath our feet	58
3.5	The electromagnetic spectrum	48	3.11	Effects of moving plates	60
3.6	The effect of electromagnetic waves on cells	50	3.12	End of chapter questions	62

Chapter 4: The Earth and beyond

4.1	The Solar System	64	4.5	Is there anybody there?	72
4.2	Gravity grabs the planets	66	4.6	How did it all start?	74
4.3	Artificial satellites	68	4.7	End of chapter questions	76
4.4	A star is born	70			

Chapter 5: Energy resources and energy transfer

5.1	Transferring heat energy	78	5.7	Electricity from wind and water	90
5.2	Less energy by design	80	5.8	Using solar and geothermal energy to produce electricity	92
5.3	Designs for energy efficient living	82	5.9	Electricity on demand	94
5.4	More about conduction, convection and radiation	84	5.10	Electricity and our environment	96
			5.11	Getting it right	98
5.5	Energy transfers – useful and useless	86	5.12	Energy calculations	100
5.6	Electricity from fuels	88	5.13	End of chapter questions	102

Chapter 6: Electricity and magnetism

6.1	Magnets from electricity	104	6.5	More about electricity distribution	112
6.2	Using electromagnets	106			
6.3	Electricity from magnets	108	6.6	Tesla – unsung genius of electrical power	114
6.4	Electricity – from the power station to your home	110	6.7	End of chapter questions	116

Chapter 7: Radioactivity

7.1	Introducing radioactivity	118	7.7	How long?	130
7.2	Unravelling the radioactive mystery	120	7.8	Using radioactivity	132
			7.9	The structure of atoms	134
7.3	Radioactivity all around us	122	7.10	Developing a model of the atom	136
7.4	The effects of radiation on living things	124	7.11	Atoms and radioactivity	138
			7.12	Using radioactive decay	140
7.5	Working with radiation	126	7.13	Nuclear power	142
7.6	Radioactivity and medicine	128	7.14	End of chapter questions	144

Data sheets 146
Index 148

1.1 Electricity and circuits

Simple circuits

Anyone investigating the behaviour of batteries and lamps soon finds out that a lamp will only light if each terminal of the battery is connected to each side of the lamp in a complete circuit. Figure 2 shows a circuit made up of a battery, a lamp and a switch. (Notice how the term 'battery' here is used in a slightly different way to that generally used in everyday life – when talking about electric circuits, a battery is something made up of two or more cells.) A circuit diagram shows the symbol for a battery made up of two cells, together with the symbols for a lamp and a switch.

↑ **Figure 1:** You can't see it, hear it or taste it – but it's definitely there! These young children are investigating electricity using safe equipment.

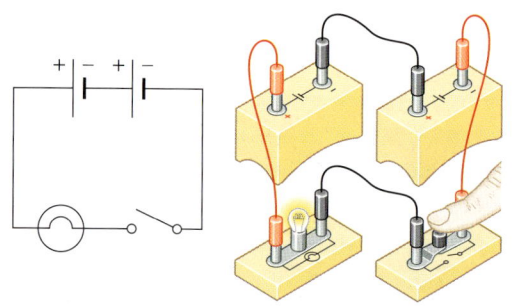

← **Figure 2:** When the switch in this circuit is closed, the circuit becomes complete and electricity flows.

Simple investigations show that increasing the number of cells in the battery increases the brightness of the lamp. Increasing the number of lamps decreases the brightness.

Making measurements

Making measurements will help us understand what is happening in a circuit. To make these measurements we use two different instruments: an **ammeter** and a **voltmeter**.

An ammeter measures the size of the current flowing through it at the point in the circuit where it is connected (between the battery and one of the lamps, for example). Ammeters measure current in **amperes** (A), often shortened to **amps**. Using an ammeter we can show that increasing the number of cells in the circuit (for a fixed number of lamps) increases the current and the brightness of the lamps. On the other hand, increasing the number of lamps in the circuit (for a fixed number of cells) decreases the current – and the brightness of the lamps also decreases.

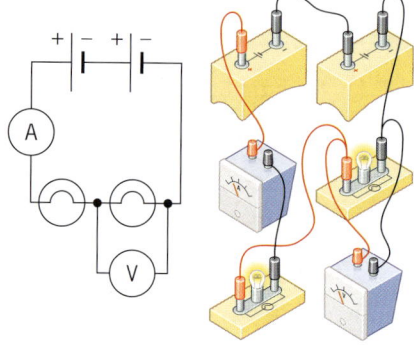

↑ **Figure 3:** Investigations in which we make measurements are an important way of understanding all kinds of situations – not just those involving electric circuits.

The voltmeter is always connected across one of the components in a circuit (a lamp, for example) and measures the **potential difference** (p.d.) across it in **volts** (V). Potential difference is sometimes called **voltage**. Connecting a voltmeter across the battery in our circuit shows that the greater the number of cells in the battery, the greater the potential difference across it. Connecting a voltmeter across one of the lamps shows that the larger the potential difference across it, the larger the current flowing through it.

When connecting ammeters and voltmeters into circuits it is important to connect them the correct way round. Notice how the batteries in Figures 2 and 3 are marked with a '+' and a '−' sign. This shows the **polarity** of the battery, which tells us the direction that electric current flows around the

Electricity

circuit, that is, from the positive ('+') terminal of the battery to the negative ('−') terminal. Ammeters and voltmeters must be connected into a circuit so that the **red** terminal of the meter is nearer to the positive terminal of the battery, and the **black** terminal is nearer to the negative terminal.

Wiring up car lights

Sabrina wants to see more clearly when she is driving her car, and she thinks that an extra pair of lamps on the front of her car would help. The instructions on these lamps are:

These two driving lamps are designed for use in cars with a 12 volt electrical supply. They should be connected as shown in the diagram. It is particularly important that the correct fuse is used – for the bulbs supplied with these lamps, a 10 amp fuse should be fitted.

Notice several things about the way that the lamps must be connected.

- Current flows from the positive terminal of the battery through the two lamps. It returns to the negative terminal of the battery through the metal body of the car.
- The lamps are connected in parallel – so if one lamp 'blows' the other remains on.
- A fuse is connected into the circuit. This is an important safety feature used in all electrical supplies. You will find out how fuses work later in this chapter.
- Although it does not matter which way the current flows through the lamps, some electrical equipment (a CD player, for example) may be damaged if it is connected to the power supply so that current flows the wrong way through it.

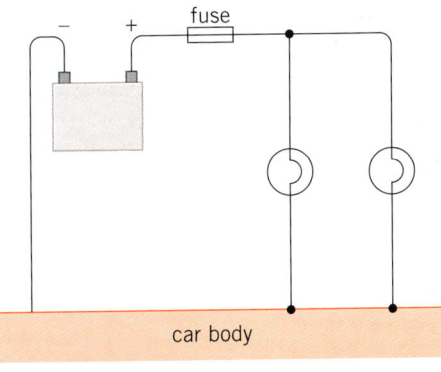

↑ **Figure 4:** The circuit diagram supplied with Sabrina's driving lamps.

Science people

Like many units used in science, the unit of electric current is named after a famous scientist – in this case, the French scientist and mathematician André-Marie Ampère, who lived about 150 years ago. The volt is named after the Italian scientist Alessandro Volta, who lived about 200 years ago.

Questions

1. Copy the circuit in Figure 5, adding to it to show how you would connect an ammeter to measure the current through the lamp.

2. Copy the circuit in Figure 6, adding to it to show how you would connect a voltmeter to measure the voltage across the battery.

3. Look at the circuit diagram for Sabrina's driving lamps (Figure 4) and answer the following questions.

   a What can you say about the potential difference across each lamp?

   b If the two lamps are identical, what can you say about the current through the two lamps?

   c Current flows from the lamps back to the negative terminal of the battery through the car's metal body. Why is the car wired like this, rather than using another wire to carry the current back to the battery? (Hint: there are lots of electrical circuits in a car!)

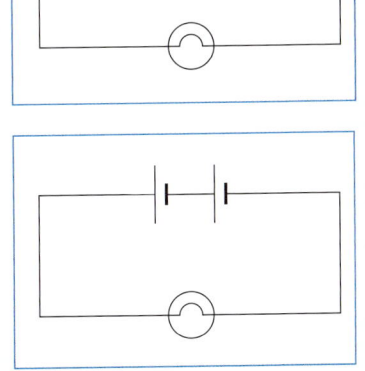

Figure 5 →

Figure 6 ↑

Key Ideas

- A complete circuit is needed for a current to flow.
- Current is measured in amperes, using an ammeter connected in series.
- Voltage is measured in volts, using a voltmeter connected in parallel with a component.
- Current flows round a circuit from '+' to '−'.
- The same current flows through each component in a series circuit.

Electricity 3

1.2 Simple circuits – some explanations

Why should increasing the number of cells in a circuit increase the current through it? Increasing the number of cells in the battery increases the potential difference across it. Potential difference is a measure of the battery's ability to push current through the circuit, so increasing the number of cells increases the current and makes the lamps brighter. The lamps however push against the current and tend to stop it flowing – we call this behaviour **resistance**.

To help us to understand what is happening in the circuit, we can use a **model** of the circuit. Scientists use models when they want to simplify things they are studying – this helps them to make predictions, which they can then test using experiments.

Electricity flowing through wires behaves like water flowing through pipes. Water can be pumped through pipes using a pump – this is like electricity being pushed through wires by a battery. A piece of narrow pipe tends to decrease the rate at which the water flows – so this is like a resistance (a lamp, for example). Increasing the number of cells in a battery would be like making the pump work faster – this would pump more water (electricity) around the circuit in a given time. Connecting more lamps into the circuit would be like making the water flow through more of the pieces of narrow pipes – making the water (electricity) flow more slowly round the circuit.

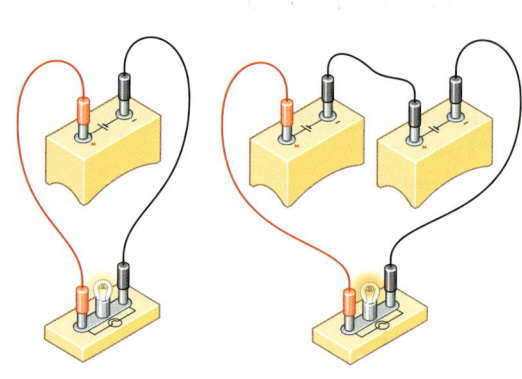

↑ **Figure 1:** Increasing the number of cells increases the current, making the lamp brighter. Increasing the number of lamps decreases the current, making the lamps dimmer.

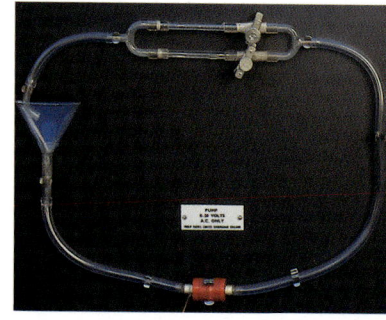

← **Figure 2:** A water circuit can be a helpful model for an electric circuit.

Ideas and Evidence

Scientists use models all the time to help them to understand things better. Sometimes a scientific model provides a different but more straightforward way of representing something – a circuit diagram is an example of this. This sort of model makes it much easier to draw a circuit than it would be if we had to draw a picture of the circuit as it would appear in a photograph. At other times a model might be a smaller or larger representation of something – like a hard sphere representing an atom or a collection of different sized and coloured balls representing the Sun and planets in the Solar System. This type of model helps us to imagine what something looks like on a scale that we are familiar with – neither too large nor too small. In the water circuit, we imagine the water flowing through the pipes like electricity flowing through wires. Just as water in the water circuit does not leak out of the pipes, electricity does not leak out of the wires in the electric circuit. The pump pushes water around the water circuit, and narrow tubes tend to stop the water flowing – while in the electric circuit, a battery pushes the electricity while a lamp tends to stop it.

Because they represent the real thing, all models have their limitations. A circuit diagram tells us how the different components in a circuit are connected, but does not tell us what the circuit will actually look like when it is connected up on the laboratory bench. A model of the Solar System may help us to think about how the planets are arranged relative to each other and to the Sun, but may not tell us about their relative sizes. A water circuit can help us to understand the behaviour of electric circuits in many cases, but not all. We shall meet the water circuit model and other models for electric circuits throughout this chapter.

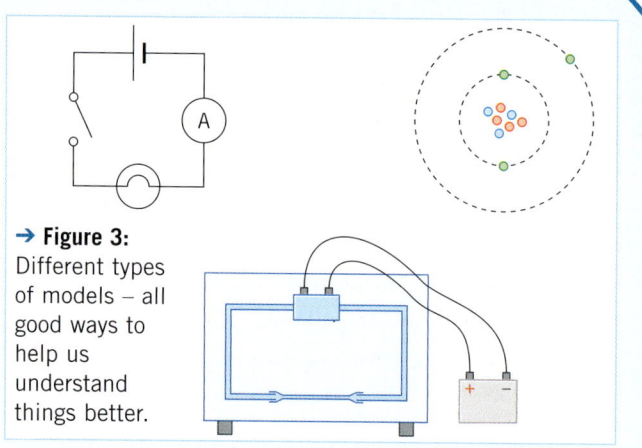

→ **Figure 3:** Different types of models – all good ways to help us understand things better.

Electricity

Resistors in series

We can use special electrical components called **resistors** when we want to make a circuit that contains resistances that are known accurately. Figure 4 shows one cell and two resistors, R_1 and R_2 connected in series so that current flows first through one resistor and then the other. The water circuit reminds us that electricity cannot leak out of the wires in the circuit, so the same current must flow through each part of the circuit. We can find the total resistance of the circuit like this:

total resistance of circuit = resistance of R_1 + resistance of R_2

The potential difference across the cell is shared by the resistors so that

p.d. across cell = p.d. across R_1 + p.d. across R_2

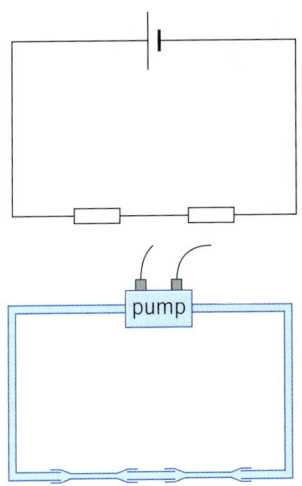

→ **Figure 4:** Two resistors connected in series – and the water circuit model of this electric circuit.

Example

Three 3 ohm resistors are connected in series across the terminal of a 4.5 volt battery. Calculate:

a the total resistance of the circuit

b the current through the circuit

c the potential difference across each resistor.

a The total resistance of the circuit is the sum of the individual resistances,

$(3 + 3 + 3)\,\Omega = 9\,\Omega$

b We know that

potential difference = current × resistance,

so we can write

4.5 = current × 9

Dividing each side by 9 gives us

current = $\frac{4.5}{9}$ A = **0.5 A**

c The p.d. across the battery (4.5 V) is shared across the three resistors. Since the three resistors each have the same resistance, the p.d. is shared equally between them, so

the p.d. across one resistor = $\frac{4.5}{3}$ V = **1.5 V**.

? Questions

1 Bernard thinks that his torch is not bright enough. He thinks that if the bulb was connected to three cells in series instead of only two cells, it would light more brightly.

   a How will the current through the bulb change if Bernard uses three cells instead of two?

   b How will this affect the brightness of the bulb?

   c What might happen to the bulb?

2 Four 2 ohm resistors are connected together in series with a 12 volt battery.

   a What is the total resistance of the four resistors?

   b What is the potential difference across each resistor?

3 How could

   a an ammeter   b a voltmeter

   be represented in a water circuit?
   (Hint: think carefully about what the ammeter and voltmeter measure.)

Key Ideas

- A potential difference (voltage) provides a 'push' to drive current around a circuit.

- Components resist a current flowing through them.

- Models can help us to understand situations better. In a series circuit total resistance is the sum of the individual resistances.

Electricity

1.3 Current, voltage and resistance

The relationship between voltage, current and resistance

The current through a component in a circuit (a lamp, for example) is affected by both the potential difference and the resistance. If we measure the potential difference across a component in a circuit and the current through it, we can calculate its resistance by using the relationship

potential difference = current × resistance
(volts, V)   (amperes, A) (ohms, Ω)

Resistance is measured in **ohms**. A component has a resistance of 1 ohm if a current of 1 amp flows through it when there is a potential difference of 1 volt across it. The symbol Ω is sometimes used instead of the word ohms.

↑ **Figure 1:** Resistors are used to reduce the size of electric currents in electronic circuits. The resistors on this circuit board are the components with the coloured stripes.

Resistors in parallel

Figure 2 shows two resistors arranged in parallel so that the current flowing round the circuit from the cell splits in two to flow through the resistors. The water model for the circuit tells us that the current must split in such a way that the total current through the circuit is equal to the sum of the currents through the two resistors:

total current through circuit = current through R_1 + current through R_2

The two resistors have the same potential difference across them, so the current through each resistor will depend on its resistance – if R_1 and R_2 both have the same resistance, the current will split so that half of it goes through R_1 and half of it goes through R_2. But if the resistance of R_1 is twice that of R_2, R_2 will have twice as much current flowing through it as R_1.

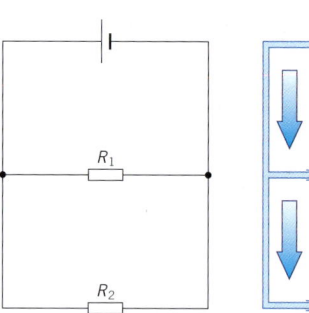 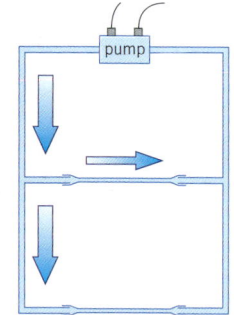

↑ **Figure 2:** Two resistors connected in parallel and the water circuit model for this electric circuit.

Example

A 6 volt battery is placed across a 12 ohm resistor and a 6 ohm resistor connected in parallel. Calculate:

a the current through each resistor

b the total current through the circuit.

a Because they are connected in parallel, each resistor has a p.d. of 6 V across it.

We know that
potential difference = current × resistance,
so for the 12 ohm resistor

6 = current × 12

Dividing each side by 12 gives

current = $\frac{6}{12}$ A = **0.5 A**

And for the 6 ohm resistor

6 = current × 6

which means that

current = $\frac{6}{6}$ A = **1 A**

(Check: The current through the 6 ohm resistor is twice the current through the 12 ohm resistor – does this seem reasonable?)

b The total current through the circuit is the sum of the current through each resistor, so

total current = (0.5 + 1)A = **1.5 A**

Electricity

Cells in series

Cells connected in series behave in a similar way to resistors connected in series. Three cells with potential differences of 1.5 volts, 2.0 volts and 1.8 volts will have a combined potential difference of (1.5 + 2.0 + 1.8) volts = 5.3 volts when connected together in series.

Using electricity – keeping sheep!

As a convenient way of fencing areas, farmers sometimes use **electric fences**. These consist of strands of plastic and metal wound together and running between insulated fence posts. The fence is connected to a power supply arranged so that when an animal (or a person!) touches the fence they receive a short shock as current flows from the fence, through the animal and into the earth. The potential difference between the part of the animal touching the fence and its feet is several thousand volts. Because this voltage is applied for a very short time, it is enough to give the animal an uncomfortable experience – but not enough to harm it.

To test whether the fence is working, some farmers touch it while holding a blade of grass. When they do this, current flows through the grass, then through the farmer into the ground. The grass has a high resistance, so this reduces the current that flows. Nevertheless, this is still not a good idea – the current that flows can still give you a hefty shock!

It is important that the wires of the electric fence do not touch the ground, and that they do not 'short out' on wet grass or other objects. If this happens, a parallel circuit is formed when an animal touches the fence, which reduces the current flowing through the animal so it receives a smaller shock that it may not even notice.

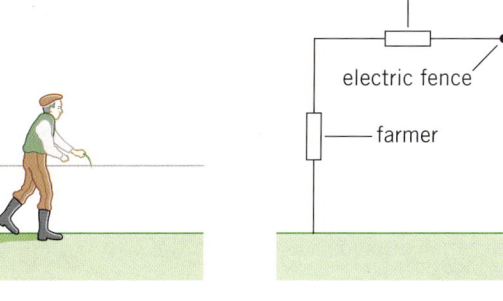

↓ **Figure 3:** A farmer holding a blade of grass completes a series circuit, so current flows from the electric fence through the farmer.

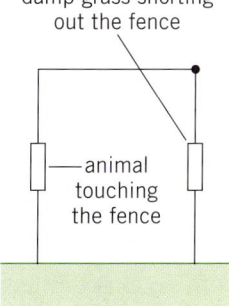

↑ **Figure 4:** An animal touching a fence that is shorted out on some wet grass forms a parallel circuit. A much smaller current flows through the animal as a result.

Questions

1. Four resistors are connected together in series. Their individual resistances are 2 ohms, 5 ohms, 12 ohms and 6 ohms. What is their total resistance?
2. The resistors in question 1 are connected in series with a 5 volt battery. What is the current through each resistor?
3. A 3 volt battery is connected to two resistors in series. One of the resistors has a resistance of 2 ohms, while the resistance of the other is not known. If the current through the circuit is 0.5 amps, calculate the unknown resistance.
4. A battery is connected to two resistors in parallel. One of the resistors has a resistance of 10 ohms, and the other has a resistance of 5 ohms. If the total current though the circuit is 3 amps, then calculate the potential difference across the battery.

Key Ideas

- potential difference = current × resistance
- To find the resistance of resistors in series, add their individual resistances.
- To find the total current through a circuit containing resistors in parallel, add the current through each resistor.

1.4 Current-voltage relationships

Using graphs

Graphs provide a very useful way of exploring the relationship between two variables.

A component like a resistor or a lamp can be connected between terminals A and B in the circuit shown in Figure 1. The circuit can be used to explore the way that the current through the component varies as the potential difference across it changes. The readings on the ammeter and voltmeter are taken for different resistances of the variable resistor.

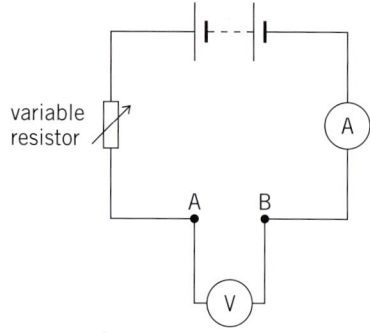

↑ **Figure 1**

The current through a resistor

Figure 2 shows the way that the current through a resistor changes with the potential difference across it. Notice how the current through the resistor increases as the potential difference across it increases – so that doubling the potential difference doubles the current, as long as the temperature of the resistor does not change. The straight line on the graph goes back past the origin, where both potential difference and current become negative. This shows that when we turn the power supply around the current flows the opposite way round the circuit, still doubling when the potential difference doubles. The slope of the graph is a measure of the resistance of the resistor. Since the graph is a straight line its slope is constant, showing that the resistance is constant too.

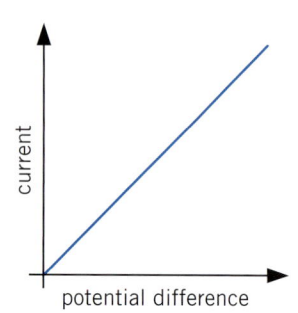

↑ **Figure 2**: A graph of current against potential difference for a resistor.

Filament lamp

A filament lamp is a lamp in which a thin wire filament glows to produce the light. The graph for a filament lamp (Figure 3) is quite different to the graph for the resistor. The graph slopes upwards less and less steeply as the potential difference increases, so doubling the potential difference does not double the current through the lamp.

The behaviour of the lamp is due to the filament. As the current through the filament increases its colour changes from a dull red, through orange and then yellow to brilliant white as its temperature increases. As the filament gets hotter its resistance increases, so the current through the lamp increases less than we would expect. The lamp behaves in exactly the same way when we reverse the flow of current through it.

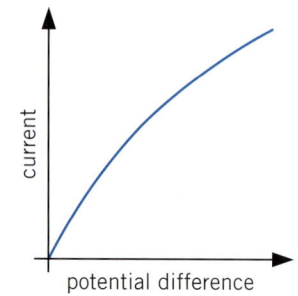

↑ **Figure 3**: A graph of current against potential difference for a filament lamp.

Diode

The graph for a diode is shown in Figure 4. At first the current through the diode increases very slowly as the potential difference increases. The current then increases much more rapidly, and the graph looks like the graph for the resistor. When the potential difference across the diode is reversed, no current flows through it at all.

The diode has a low resistance in one direction, and a very high resistance in the opposite direction. Its equivalent in a water circuit would be a non-return valve, which allows water to flow in one direction but not the other. The circuit symbol for the diode contains an arrow, showing the direction in which the diode will allow a current to pass. Diodes are used when we want to convert the alternating

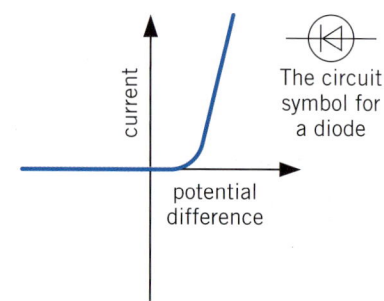

↑ **Figure 4**: A graph of current against potential difference for a diode.

Electricity

current used in the mains into direct current used in electronic circuits. Alternating current flows backwards and forwards, while direct current flows in one direction only – you can find out more about electricity supplies on page 110.

Thermistor

A thermistor is a special kind of resistor. The graph in Figure 5 shows that the thermistor behaves in the opposite way to the filament lamp, and allows more current to flow as the potential difference across it increases. The increased current heats up the thermistor, so the resistance of the thermistor decreases as its temperature increases – the exact opposite of the behaviour of the lamp filament.

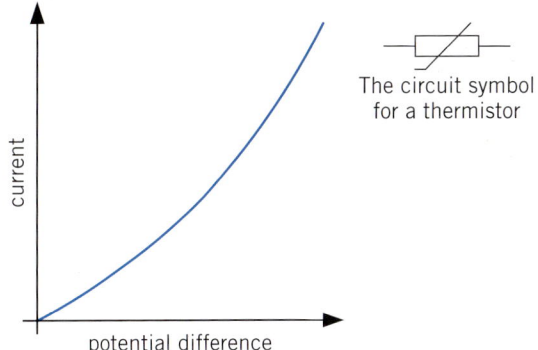

↑ **Figure 5:** A graph of current against potential difference for a thermistor.

Thermistors are used in circuits that measure and control the temperature of systems. One place that a thermistor is used is in the cooling system of a car engine. When a car engine is running and the car is not moving, the engine temperature increases. The engine temperature is measured by a thermistor fixed in the engine. This forms part of a circuit which switches on a cooling fan when the engine temperature rises above a certain value, and switches it off again as the engine cools down.

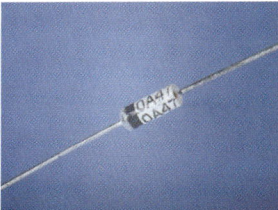

Light-dependent resistor

A light-dependent resistor (LDR) behaves like an ordinary resistor as far as increasing the potential difference across it is concerned. As its name implies, the LDR has another property that makes it useful in circuits – its resistance falls as the light falling on it gets brighter. LDRs can be used in circuits where we want to use light levels to control electrical equipment, switching a light on and off at dusk and dawn for example.

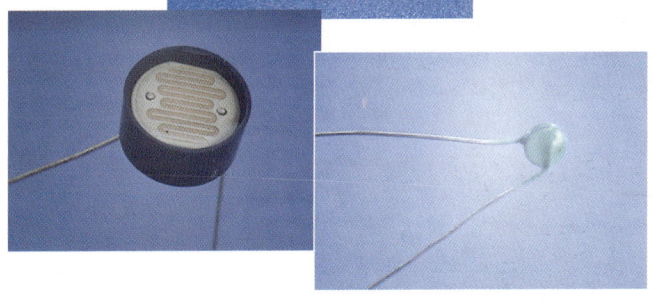

↗ **Figure 6:** Examples of the different kind of resistors described on these pages, clockwise from top left: resistor, filament lamp, diode, thermistor and light-dependent resistor (LDR).

? Questions

1 Copy the table and rearrange the second column so that the resistance of each component is described correctly.

Resistor	Resistance decreases as brightness of light increases.
Filament lamp	Resistance decreases as current increases.
Diode	Resistance constant (provided temperature also constant).
Thermistor	Resistance low when current flows in one direction, very high when it flows in the other.
LDR (light-dependent resistor)	Resistance increases as current increases.

2 'A diode is like a one-way valve in a water circuit'. For the other components in the table in question 1, describe their equivalent components in a water circuit.

Key Ideas

- Current-voltage graphs show how the current through a component varies with the voltage across it.

3 A factory processing films needs an automatic warning system to show if the cover to one of the developing machines has been left off, allowing light to spoil the films inside. Draw a circuit that could be used to light a warning light when this happens.

Electricity

1.5 Energy in circuits

The cell in a circuit is a store of **chemical** energy. When it is connected in a circuit, the cell's chemical energy is transferred to **electrical** energy, which is then transferred to other forms (such as light, kinetic, heat) as electricity flows through the circuit.

The pizza monster

How does energy travel from the cell to the lamp in a circuit? Models are often used to help us to answer questions like this. On these pages we shall look at a model that might be used to help people to understand electrical circuits. As you look at this model, think carefully about it – how well does it represent what goes on in an electric circuit?

Figure 1 shows a factory that produces pizzas. A road runs through the factory so that trucks can take pizzas to a pizza monster who eats them. Once a truck has delivered a pizza to the monster, it returns to the factory, taking back any uneaten pizza to be 'recycled' into new pizzas (the pizza monster does not want to waste anything!)

Pizzas are transferred from the pizza factory to the monster by trucks – one pizza to each truck. The monster takes a bite out of each pizza, so the amount of pizza it eats can be measured by the difference between the size of the pizza as it arrives and the size of the pizza after the monster has finished with it,

↑ **Figure 1:** Another model for electric circuits.

which is measured by the woman in the white coat. We can call this the 'pizza difference', or p.d. for short. The traffic warden measures the rate at which pizzas flow from the factory to the monster by counting the rate at which trucks pass him. If we multiply the pizza difference by the rate at which pizzas flow from the factory to the monster we can calculate the rate at which the monster eats pizzas:

rate of pizza eating = 'pizza difference' × rate at which trucks pass

The pizza factory is like the cell in a circuit, and the pizza monster is like a lamp, or any other resistance. The pizzas represent energy carried from the factory to the monster, and the trucks represent **electric charge**.

The rate at which the monster eats pizzas is equivalent to the rate at which electrical energy is transferred to heat and light energy in the lamp:

rate of energy transfer = potential difference × current
(joules per second, J/s)   (volts, V)   (amperes, A)

Rate of energy transfer is also called **power**. The more powerful a lamp, the more rapidly it can transfer electrical energy to heat and light energy; the more powerful a battery, the more rapidly it can transfer chemical energy to electrical energy. Energy is measured in joules, so both rate of energy transfer and power can be measured in joules per second. Power is such an important thing to measure that it has its own unit – the watt (W): 1 watt = 1 joule of energy transferred each second.

Electricity

More about the pizza monster

The total amount of pizza that the monster eats can be calculated by counting the number of trucks passing and multiplying it by the 'pizza difference':

amount of pizza eaten = 'pizza difference' × number of trucks

Since the amount of pizza eaten is equivalent to energy transferred and the number of trucks is equivalent to the amount of charge, this means that

energy transferred = potential difference × charge
(joules, J)   (volts, V)   (coulomb, C)

This relationship applies to any power supply in a circuit, whether it is a cell, a battery or a power pack connected to the mains. It means that the greater the potential difference across a power supply, the more energy it supplies to a given amount of charge that flows through it.

In the same way, we can calculate the total number of trucks that have passed:

number of trucks = rate at which trucks pass × time

The rate at which trucks pass is equivalent to the rate at which charge passes, which is the size of the electric current, so for the electric circuit this means that

charge   = current   × time
(coulomb, C) (amperes, A) (seconds, s)

This means that when a current of 1 A is flowing, 1 C of charge passes a given point in 1 s.

Science people

The coulomb is named after a French physicist, Charles-Augustin de Coulomb, who lived and worked over 200 years ago, at the time of the French revolution. As well as his work on electrical charge, Coulomb played an important role in developing the metric system of weights and measures that scientists throughout the world use today.

Key Ideas

- power = potential difference × current
- H energy transferred = potential difference × charge
- charge = current × time

Questions

1. Using the pizza monster model, explain why the total current in a parallel circuit is equal to the sum of the current through the individual branches of the circuit.

2. In the pizza monster model, how does the 'pizza difference' across the pizza monster compare to the 'pizza difference' across the pizza factory? What does this tell you about the energy transfers that are happening in the cell of an electric circuit and a resistance connected to it?

3. A model like the one here is intended to help people to understand something. Why do you think some models might make it more difficult for someone to understand something?

4. a The current through a resistor is 0.5 A and the potential difference across it is 6.4 V. At what rate is energy transferred in the resistor?

   b A kettle is marked '220 V, 2.2 kW'. If 1 kW is 1000 W, what current will flow through the kettle when it is plugged in?

   c The voltage across the terminals of a battery is measured as 4.2 V. When a current of 0.2 A flows, what power is the battery producing?

5. a What measuring instrument is the equivalent of the traffic warden in Figure 1?

   b What measuring instrument is the equivalent of the woman in the white coat in Figure 1?

6. At what rate is charge flowing through the battery in question 4 part (c)?

7. A power supply has a voltage of 12 V. How much energy does it transfer when 1.5 C of charge passes?

Electricity

1.6 Electricity from the mains

Direct currents and alternating currents

Although batteries enable things like personal stereos to be carried around with us easily, sometimes it is useful to be able to plug portable equipment into the mains supply. To do this we need to change not only the voltage of the supply, but also the type of current supplied too – the following pages look at why this is.

Cells and batteries supply electric current that flows from the positive terminal to the negative terminal. The size of the current depends on the voltage of the battery and the resistance of the components in the circuit. The direction in which the current flows is always the same. This kind of current is called a **direct current** (shortened to 'd.c.'), so cells and batteries are often referred to as 'd.c. supplies'.

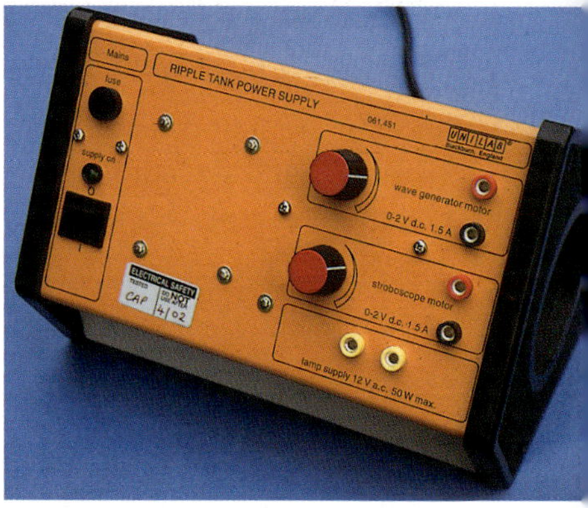

While the red and black terminals of a power supply provide a d.c. current, the yellow terminals supply a different kind of current, known as **alternating current**, or 'a.c.' for short. An alternating current does not flow in the same direction all the time – instead, the current constantly changes direction so that it flows first one way through the circuit and then the other. Electricity from the mains supply is an alternating current.

The **frequency** of an alternating current describes the number of times that the direction of the current changes each second. Frequency is measured in hertz (Hz). Mains electricity has a frequency of 50 Hz, which means that current travels first one way and then the other fifty times each second. The frequency of mains electricity is sometimes referred to as 'fifty cycles per second', which is just another way of saying '50 Hz'.

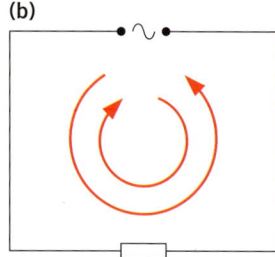

↑ **Figure 1**: This power supply is designed for use in school science laboratories. It supplies a direct current to any circuit connected between the red and black terminals.

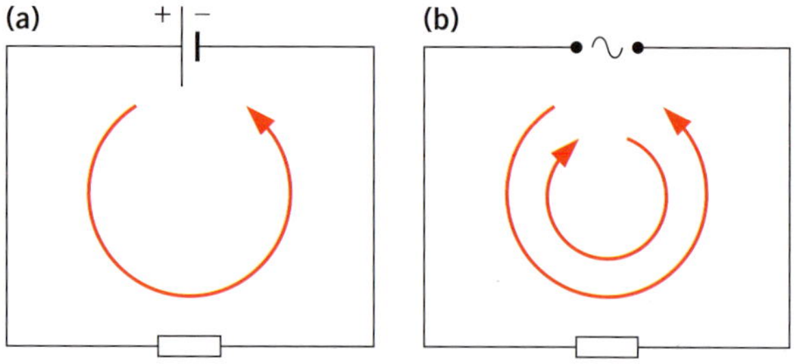

↑ **Figure 2**: (a) Current in a circuit with a d.c. supply flows in a constant direction. (b) In a circuit with an a.c. supply, current flows first one way round the circuit and then the other.

Comparing alternating currents

The meters used for measuring direct currents are designed so that electricity flows in only one direction through them, which is why they must always be connected correctly into a circuit (see Section 1.1). This makes them completely unsuitable for measuring alternating currents. To measure alternating currents we can use specially designed meters, or we can use an **oscilloscope**. An oscilloscope is an instrument which plots a graph of potential difference against time, so connecting it across a resistor in a circuit carrying alternating current shows us how the voltage across the resistor changes with time. Figure 3 shows how an oscilloscope is connected to measure the potential difference across a resistor, and shows some oscilloscope traces.

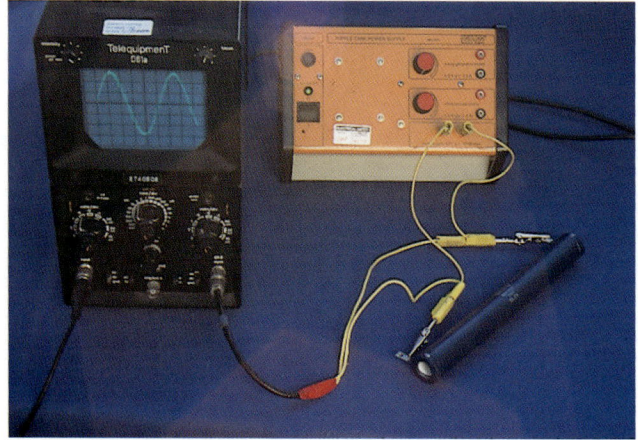

↓ **Figure 3**: Measuring voltages using an oscilloscope.

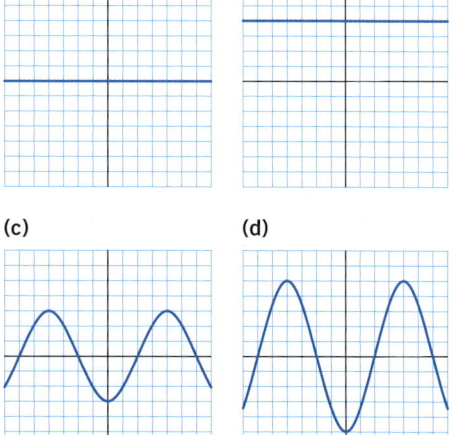

12 Electricity

Before making any measurements, the oscilloscope is carefully adjusted so that the trace lies along the horizontal centre line of the screen (Figure 3(a)).

The trace in Figure 3(b) is a horizontal line, which shows that the voltage is constant – so the circuit is carrying a direct current.

In Figure 3(c) the trace starts above the line and then goes below it, showing how the current in the circuit flows first one way and then the other – it is an alternating current. In Figure 3(d) the trace again shows an alternating current. Notice how the peaks of the trace lie further above and below the centre line on the oscilloscope screen than they do in Figure 3(c). This means that the voltage across the resistor here is greater than the voltage across the resistor in Figure 3(c).

↓ **Figure 4:** Inside an electric plug used to connect appliances to the mains. Removing the top from a plug can be dangerous, and should never be done without adult supervision.

H The voltage of the mains supply

When it is plugged into a socket, the potential difference between the live and neutral pins of a mains plug alternates so that the live terminal is first positive compared to the neutral pin, then negative, then positive again and so on. This makes current flow first one way and then the other through the appliance connected to the plug. The potential difference between the neutral terminal and the earth terminal is very small (a few volts at most), since the earth and neutral wires are usually connected together at some point in the mains supply system. You can find out more about electrical safety in Sections 1.8 and 1.9.

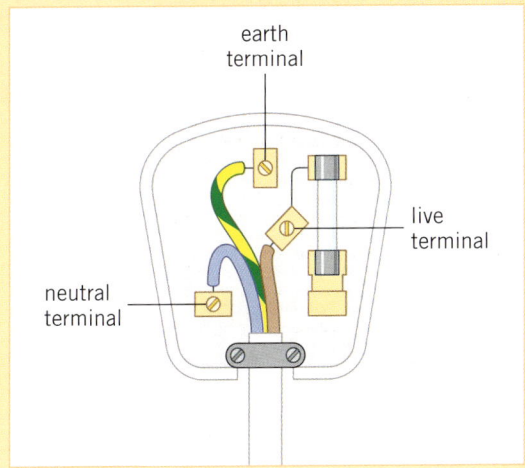

Key Ideas

- Cells and batteries produce direct current (d.c.), which flows in one direction only.
- An alternating current (a.c.) constantly changes direction.
- The frequency of the alternating current is the number of times it changes direction and back again each second.
- Alternating voltages can be compared using an oscilloscope.

Questions

1 A student says: 'The average current through a lamp carrying alternating current is zero – so why does it light?!'

   a Why is the average current zero?

   b Why *does* the lamp light?

2 An oscilloscope was connected across a resistor through which different currents were passed. Use the oscilloscope traces in Figure 5 to describe the voltage across the resistor in each case.

3 The voltage of a supply of alternating current varies between +6 V and −6 V. Sketch a graph to show how the potential difference between the terminals of this supply varies with time.

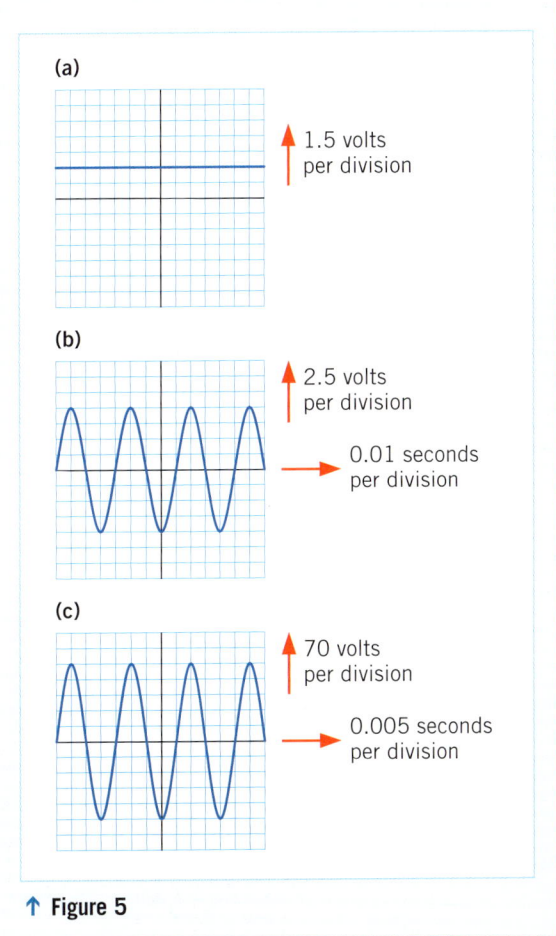

↑ **Figure 5**

Electricity   13

1.7 Energy from electricity

We make good use of electricity in our homes, schools, offices, shops and factories – in fact, in every area of our lives. The reason for this is that electricity is easily transmitted through wires, and it can easily be transferred as heat, light, sound and kinetic energy.

Figure 1 shows a kitchen containing various electrical appliances. Each of these is designed to transfer electrical energy in a particular way – for example, the cooker transfers electrical energy to heat energy (Figure 2).

Figure 1: Electrical energy at work in the kitchen.

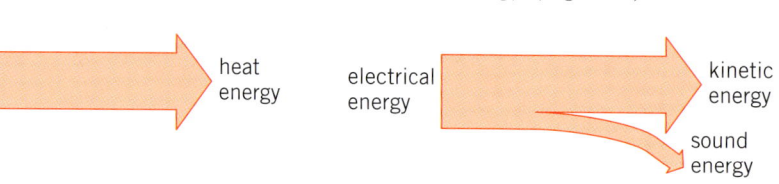

↑ Figure 2   ↑ Figure 3

Figure 3 shows that the food processor transfers electrical energy to kinetic energy and sound energy.

How much energy?

The amount of energy that an appliance transfers depends on how long it is switched on and on the rate at which it transfers electrical energy – its power. Small appliances like radios or hand mixers generally have their power given in watts, while the power of larger appliances may be in kilowatts (kW). (Remember that 1 kW = 1000 W.)

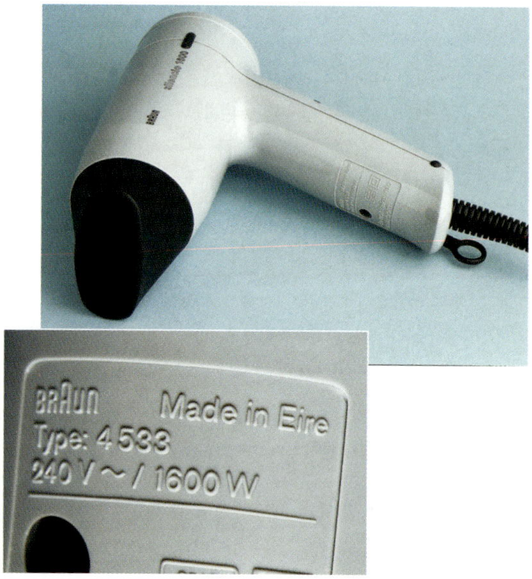

As you would expect, electrical energy is measured in joules. To calculate the amount of energy used by an electrical appliance we use the formula:

energy transferred = power × time
(joules, J)   (watts, W) (seconds, s)

↑ **Figure 4:** The power of a piece of electrical equipment is normally indicated somewhere on it, either on a metal plate or a sticker attached to it, or it may be moulded into the plastic of the casing, as here.

> **Example 1**
>
> Simon uses a food processor for 3 minutes. The power of the processor is 500 W. How much energy is transferred?
>
> We know that
>
>   **energy transferred = power × time**
>
> so we can write
>
>   energy transferred = 500 × 3 × 60 J (Notice that time must be in seconds, so we multiply minutes by 60.)
>
>   = 90 000 J (= 90 kJ)

A joule is a very small amount of energy, so the amount of energy used by (say) a 3 kW electric heater in two hours would involve a very, very large number of joules. To get around this problem, electrical energy is often measured in **kilowatt hours** (kWh), sometimes called **Units** for short. An electrical appliance with a power of 1 kW transfers exactly 1 Unit (= 1 kWh) of electrical energy when it is switched on for 1 hour.

Electricity

Example 2

Pandit switches on a water heater for 3 hours. The power of the heater is 2.5 kW. How much energy is transferred in kWh (Units)?

Once again

   energy transferred = power × time

so we can write

   energy transferred = 2.5 × 3 kWh

(The answer must be in kWh, so we write the power in kW and the time in hours.)

   = **7.5 kWh**

Example 3

Samantha dries some washing in a tumble drier. The tumble drier is switched on for 45 minutes, and transfers 4.5 kWh of energy. What is the power of the tumble drier?

Again we will use the equation

   energy transferred = power × time

so we can write

   4.5 = power × 0.75

(Notice that the time must be in hours. The question gives the time in *minutes* – so we must convert 45 minutes into hours before answering the question.) This means that

$$\text{power} = \frac{4.5}{0.75} \text{ kW}$$

   = **6 kW**

If we know how much 1 kWh of electrical energy costs, we can work out the cost of the electrical energy we have used (see Figure 5):

   total cost of electrical energy = number of Units × cost per Unit

Example 4

Stuart recorded the readings on his electricity meter at the beginning and end of one week. The readings were 27 856 and 28 134. If electrical energy costs 6 p per Unit, what was the cost of the electrical energy used by Stuart's family in this week?

   Total Units used = 28 134 − 27 856
                   = 278

Each unit costs 6 p, so the total cost is

   278 × 6 p = 1668 p = **£16.68**

Key Ideas

- Electrical energy is easily transferred to heat energy, light energy, sound energy and kinetic energy.
- The power of an electrical appliance is measured in watts (W) or kilowatts (kW).
- energy transferred = power × time

↑ **Figure 5:** The meter records the amount of electrical energy used. The meter is read regularly, usually four times each year. The amount of electrical energy used in each period is calculated by subtracting the meter reading at the start of the period from the meter reading at the end of the period.

Questions

1. Draw diagrams to show the energy transfers in the following:

   a a radio **b** a television **c** an oven **d** a vacuum cleaner

2. Calculate the amount of electrical energy used in kWh (Units) for the following meter readings:

   a initial reading 65 127, final reading 65 894

   b initial reading 99 956, final reading 00 312

3. If electrical energy costs 8.4 p per unit, calculate the cost of the electrical energy used in question 2, parts (a) and (b).

4. **a** An electric concrete mixer has a power rating of 5 kW. It is used continuously on a building site for 5 hours. How much energy (in kWh) is transferred in this time?

   b A 3 kW electric fire has used 250 kWh of electricity. How long was it switched on?

   c The electricity bill for running a 500 W light comes to £72.80. If the cost of the electricity supplied to the light is 5.6 p per unit, for how long was it switched on?

Electricity

1.8 Using electricity safely

We tend to take electrical safety for granted. Each time we use anything which is connected to mains electricity, we rely on important safety features built into it. If one of these features goes wrong it can spell danger, since mains electricity can kill.

Making connections – wires, plugs and sockets

When you plug an appliance into a socket, current flows through the cable to the appliance.

Figure 1 shows how a cable is made up:

- Copper cores carry the electric current since copper is a good conductor of electricity.
- Colour-coded plastic covers the copper cores so that the cores can be easily identified. Plastic is a very poor conductor of electricity, so it insulates the three cores from each other.
- An outer layer of plastic holds the three cores together and provides additional insulation to protect anyone touching the cable.

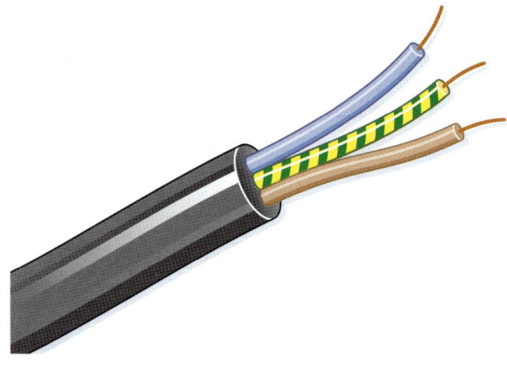

↑ **Figure 1:** Electric cable makes use of the conducting properties of copper and the insulating properties of plastics.

The case of the electric plug is made of plastic or rubber (once again, both good insulators), and there are three pins made of brass (which is a good electrical conductor). The socket contains a shutter which stops anything being poked into the holes and making an electrical connection inside the socket. When the long pin at the top of the plug is pushed into the socket, it opens the shutter allowing the pins to enter the socket and make contact with the wires connected to it.

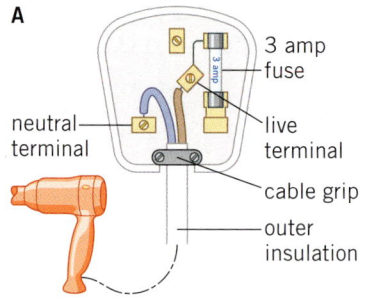
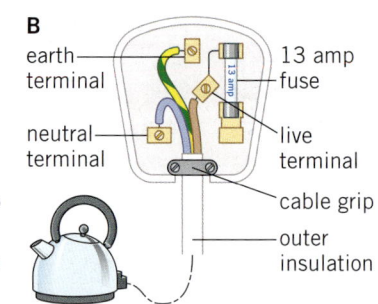

↑ **Figure 2**

Figure 2 shows the inside of two plugs. In both plugs a cable grip holds the cable tightly, so that the cable cannot be pulled out of the plug. Plug A is connected to a hairdryer and has only two wires connected to it:

- the **live** wire on the right, which is covered with brown insulation
- the **neutral** wire on the left, which is covered with blue insulation.

The live and neutral wires carry electric current to and from the hairdryer itself, and are connected to the two short pins of the plug, called the live and neutral pins.

Plug B is connected to an electric kettle, which is made of metal. As well as the live and neutral wires this plug has a third wire, coloured yellow and green. This is the earth wire, connected to the earth pin, which is the long one at the top of the plug. While the live and neutral wires carry current to and from the kettle, the earth wire connects the metal case of the kettle to the earth pin of the plug.

Keeping safe – fuses and earthing

Between the live wire and the pin in each plug there is a **fuse**. This contains a thin wire which heats up as a current flows through it, and melts if the current is too big. This will cause a break in the circuit, stopping any further current flowing. (When this happens we say that the fuse has 'blown'.)

16 Electricity

Without the fuse, a fault in the hairdryer (a short circuit inside it, for example) could make a very large current flow through the cable between the plug and the hairdryer. This would heat the cables up and might cause a fire.

The kettle has a much larger power rating than the hairdryer, and so a much larger current flows through it when it is plugged in. Because of this, the plug connected to the kettle contains a 13 amp fuse rather than a 3 amp fuse, which is suitable for the hairdryer.

Fuses for plugs generally come in sizes of 3 amps, 5 amps and 13 amps. It is important that the fuse should have a value slightly higher than the normal current through the equipment – this means that the current need only rise by a small amount above its usual value before the fuse blows.

The hairdryer's insulating plastic case protects us from the high voltages inside it. However, the kettle could be very dangerous if the live wire inside it became connected to its metal case by accident. With the metal case 'live', a person touching it would have a current flowing through them, which would be enough to kill them, although the current would not be large enough to make the fuse blow.

To ensure that the kettle can be used safely, an earth wire is connected to the metal case. When the kettle is plugged in the earth wire connects to a wire in the house wiring which runs to a metal stake buried in the ground just outside the house. With this arrangement there can be no potential difference between the kettle (connected to earth) and someone touching it (also connected to the earth, since they are standing on it) and so no current will flow through them. If a fault develops and the live wire becomes connected to the metal case a large current will flow through the live and earth wires – this will be large enough to make the fuse blow, protecting anyone using the kettle against electric shock.

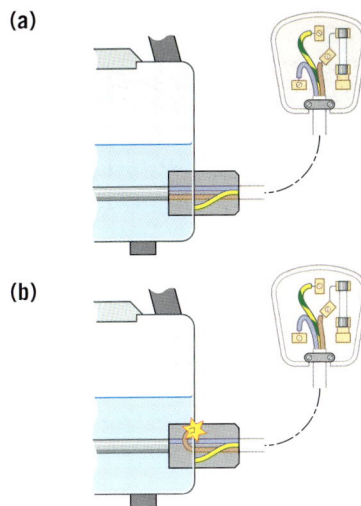

↑ **Figure 3:** A fuse is essential protection if an appliance has a metal case. **(a)** The live wire in the kettle is broken, and touches the case. If there was no earth wire, the case would become 'live', and anyone touching it could receive a fatal shock. With an earth wire connected to the metal case there is a very low resistance path for electricity to flow to earth. **(b)** As soon as the kettle is plugged in and switched on a large current flows and 'blows' the fuse. This means that no more electricity can flow, and so anyone touching the kettle will not get a shock. The blown fuse alerts the person using the kettle that something is wrong.

Questions

1. Why is it important to ensure that the cable grip on a plug is properly tightened around the outer insulation of a cable?

2. Which of the following plugs has been wired up correctly? Explain what, if anything, you think is wrong in each case, and what the danger would be.

   a 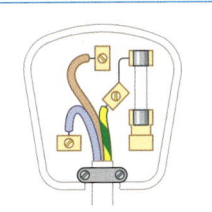 b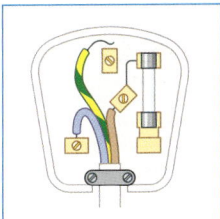

   c 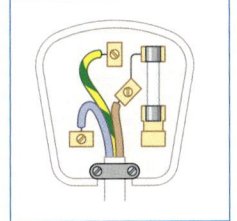 d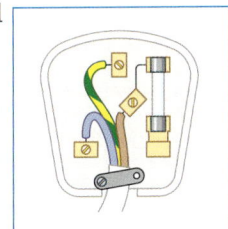

Key Ideas

- Plugs and cables make use of the insulating and conducting properties of different materials.
- A fuse protects appliances and cables from currents greater than those for which they are designed.
- An earth wire protects people from electric shocks when touching the metal case of an appliance.

3. You have a choice of the following fuses to fit in a plug: 3 amp, 5 amp and 13 amp. Which fuse would you use with the following appliances each of which operates at 220 V?

   a 3000 W kettle   b 1000 W hairdryer

   c 1500 W lawnmower   d 60 W light

Electricity 17

1.9 Keeping safe – circuit breakers

Although fuses are effective when large fault currents flow, causing the fuse to blow, they do not work if the fault current is small. Imagine someone mowing the lawn using an electric lawnmower. If they run over the cable and cut it, any fault current that flows is very small – certainly too small to blow the fuse in the plug. With an exposed live wire in the cut end of the cable connected to the plug, there is a real danger that anyone picking up the cable may touch the live wire and receive an electric shock. Remember that the mains current needed to kill someone is very small – only a fraction of an amp – so the fuse will not protect them.

To provide protection against situations where only small fault currents flow, a **circuit breaker** is needed. When equipment is operating normally the current flowing through the live and neutral wires is equal. If a fault occurs, and a current flows between the live wire and earth, the currents through the live and neutral wires will no longer be equal. By constantly monitoring and comparing the currents through the live and neutral wires, a circuit breaker detects when the currents are not equal and cuts off the current in a fraction of a second, so that no-one gets an electric shock.

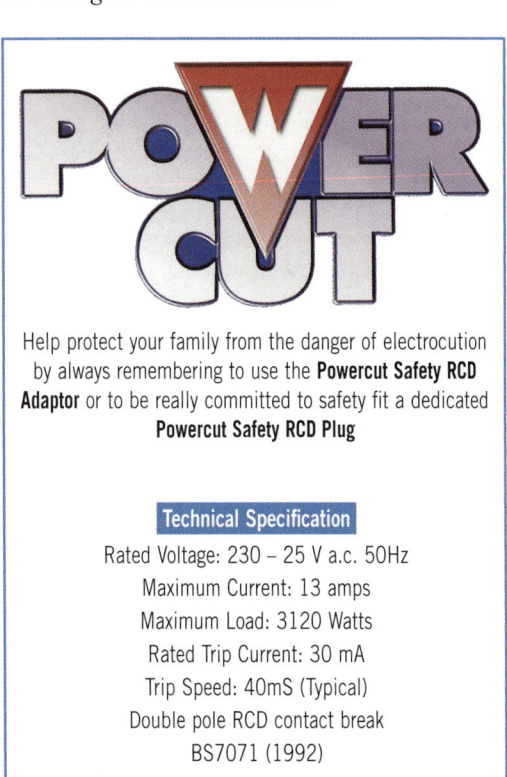

↑ **Figure 1:** Circuit breakers may be permanently fitted in electrical wiring around the home, or portable circuit breakers may be used wherever they are required.

Conductor and insulators

Safe use of electricity is closely linked to our knowledge of the structure of materials. Since an electric current is a flow of charge, there must be something about a conductor that allows charge to flow while an insulator prevents it from doing so.

Metal atoms lose some of their electrons very easily. This means that we can think of the structure of a metal as being something like a grid of metal atoms. Each of these atoms gives up some of its electrons, producing a sort of 'electron soup'. A potential difference across the metal makes the electrons move (see Figure 2) – so an electric current in a metal is simply a flow of electrons.

Insulators like plastics or rubber do not have free electrons. Since there is nothing in these materials to carry charge, no current flows even when a large potential difference is applied to them.

↓ **Figure 2:** A potential difference across the metal makes electrons flow from – to +. Since electric current flows from + to –, the electron flow is in the opposite direction to conventional current.

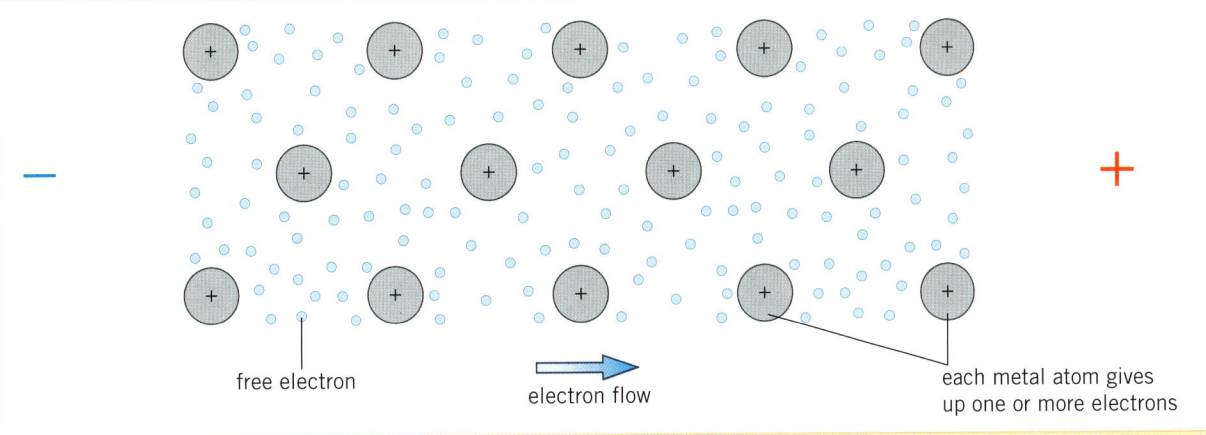

Questions

1. Look at the newspaper report about an accident in the home.

   > Fisherton residents were still in a state of shock last night after the sudden death of popular neighbour Brian Fisher. Mr Fisher (48) was a keen gardener, and had been out cutting the hedge around his immaculate front garden. He was found by his wife when she returned from a shopping trip to nearby Snedborough. Although too upset to talk to our reporter, it is understood that Mrs Fisher found her husband collapsed at the foot of a step ladder that he had been using to reach the top of the hedge. An electric hedge cutter was found nearby, and the cable was wound around Mr Fisher's leg. The cable appears to have been cut. An inquest into the death will be opened tomorrow.

   a Suggest why the accident happened.

   b Suggest ways in which the accident could have been prevented.

   c Design a leaflet to be distributed at garden centres that will bring electrical safety to the attention of people working in the garden.

Key Ideas

- A circuit breaker monitors the current through a circuit and shuts off the current if a fault is detected.
- **H** Electric current in solids is a flow of electrons.

Electricity

1.10 Static electricity

An electric current is a flow of charge from one place to another. But electric charges do not have to move – they can stay in one place. We call these **static electricity**. You have probably come across many examples of static electricity. For example, clothes made of nylon and other artificial fabrics often crackle when you remove them, while a plastic comb rubbed against fabric or combed through your hair will attract hair, dust and small bits of paper.

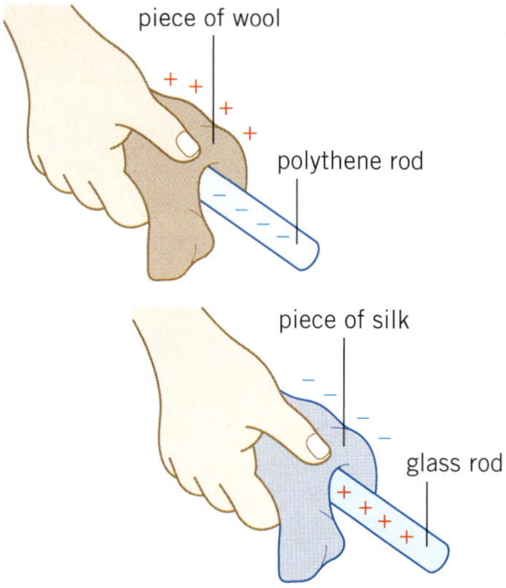

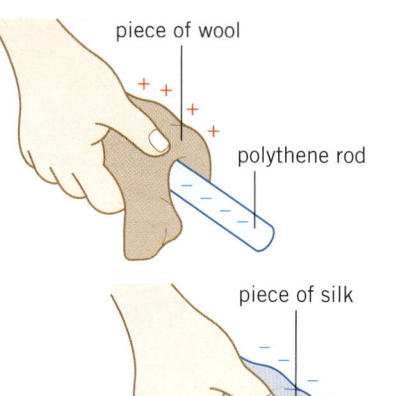

Charging by rubbing

When you rub certain types of insulators together they become charged. Examples of materials that behave like this are polythene rubbed with wool, and glass rubbed with silk (see Figure 1).

Rubbing the glass rod with the silk cloth transfers **negatively** charged electrons from the glass to the cloth. The cloth becomes negatively charged because it gains electrons. The glass becomes **positively** charged because it loses electrons. Polythene and wool behave in the opposite way – rubbing transfers electrons from the cloth to the rod, so the cloth becomes **positively** charged while the rod becomes **negatively** charged. When insulators like these are rubbed together and then separated, **equal** and **opposite** charges are left on the two materials.

Figure 1: Rubbing an insulated rod with a cloth charges both the rod and the cloth.

Attracting and repelling

Objects that have been charged exert a force on uncharged objects – like the comb attracting pieces of paper.

Two objects with **opposite** charges (one positive, the other negative) also exert attractive forces on each other. However, objects with the **same** charge (both positive or both negative) exert repulsive forces on each other, pushing each other apart.

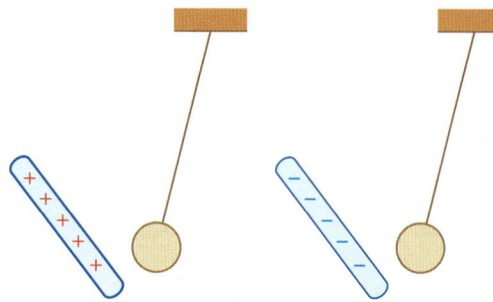

Figure 2: Uncharged objects are attracted to charged objects.

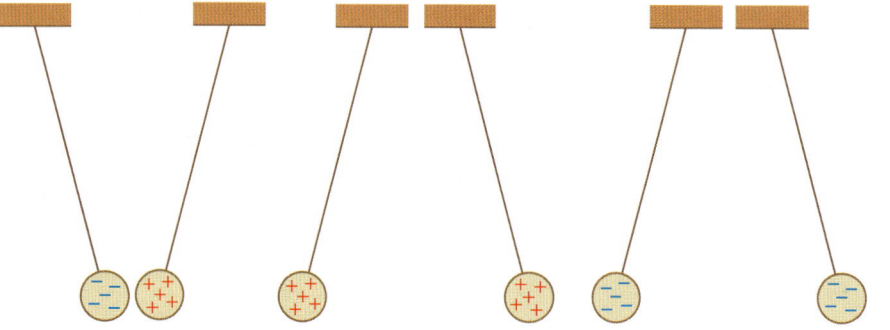

← **Figure 3:** Unlike charges attract, like charges repel.

Losing the charge

Insulators have no free charges that can move to conduct electricity – so any charge given to an insulator will simply stay where it is without moving. However even the best insulator will not stay charged permanently. Charge on an insulator can slowly leak away as traces of moisture and even dust on the surface of the insulator allow tiny amounts of charge to flow.

Electricity

Sometimes we want to make static electricity flow, in order to get rid of the charge on an object. As the amount of charge on an object increases, the potential difference between the object and other things around it increases. Eventually the potential difference may be large enough to cause a spark – which is what happens when a sweater crackles when you remove it. There are many situations where sparks like these may be dangerous, so care must be taken to ensure that large charges cannot build up. The charge on an insulator can be allowed to flow away by connecting the insulator to earth using a conductor.

Refuelling aircraft is just one situation where static electricity could cause big problems. In order to make the time taken for refuelling as short as possible, large amounts of fuel have to be pumped into an aircraft's fuel tanks in a very short time. This means that fuel has to flow very fast through the pipes connecting the tanker to the aircraft. Both aviation fuel and the flexible pipe it flows through are insulators – so charge can build up and may cause a spark …

To ensure that no spark occurs while an aircraft is being refuelled, a conducting wire called a **bonding cable** is connected between the aircraft and the tanker, so that any charge transferred as the fuel rushes through the flexible pipe is neutralised safely.

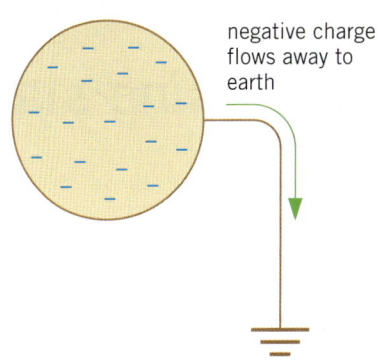

↑ **Figure 4:** Because the conductor contains charges that can move, it allows charge to flow through it to discharge the insulator without a spark occurring.

→ **Figure 5:** The bonding cable allows charge to flow between the aircraft and the tanker, so static electricity cannot cause a spark.

Science people

In a highly risky experiment in 1752, the American scientist Benjamin Franklin flew a kite during a thunderstorm to test his hypothesis that lightning was electricity. Electricity was conducted down the damp string of the kite to a key at the bottom end of the string. When Franklin put a finger near the key he felt a tingling sensation, and a spark jumped from the key to his finger. As a result of this experiment Franklin concluded that lightning is a huge electrical spark jumping from the clouds to Earth. He suggested that tall buildings might be protected from lightning strikes by fixing a pointed metal rod to the top of the building – the lightning conductor.

Not all experimenters were as lucky as Franklin when experimenting during thunderstorms. In 1753 the Russian, Georg Richmann, was killed by lightning as he attempted to perform an experiment using a metal rod during a thunderstorm.

Key Ideas

- When insulating materials are rubbed against each other they become electrically charged.
- There are two types of charge – positive and negative.
- Charged objects may attract uncharged objects.
- Like charges repel – unlike charges attract.
- Electrostatic charges may be dangerous in some situations, when they must be discharged safely to earth.

Questions

1. If you rub a balloon on your clothing, it will then 'stick' to a wall or ceiling. Why?
2. 'If two insulators attract, one or both of them may be charged. If two insulators repel each other, both must be charged.' Explain this statement.
3. Explain why you may get a shock when you touch a metal object after walking across a carpet.
4. Electronic circuits may be damaged by high voltages. Why do computer repair technicians wear wrist straps that connect them to earth?

Electricity

1.11 Using static electricity

Another name for static electricity is **electrostatic charge** – this means exactly the same, but sounds much more impressive! Electrostatic charges are used in many important ways.

The photocopier/laser printer

The document to be copied is placed face down on the glass top of the photocopier (Figure 1), where very bright light is shone onto it. Light reflected from the document passes through a series of lenses and mirrors until an image of it is focused on a rotating drum. This drum is made from a special material. This material is an electrical insulator that becomes an electrical conductor when light falls on it. Before the copy starts to be made, the entire surface of the drum is charged with static electricity.

The white areas of the document being copied reflect large amounts of light. This light falls on the surface of the drum. The light makes the material in these areas conduct electricity, so the static charge is conducted away. Dark areas of the document reflect very little light onto the drum's surface. The material in these areas remains insulating, and so the static charge stays on the surface of the drum here.

Fine black powder (called **toner**) is attracted to the areas of the drum that are charged. As the drum rotates, the toner is transferred to a sheet of paper, copying the original document exactly. Before moving out of the machine the paper passes through a heater, which makes the toner stick firmly to the paper.

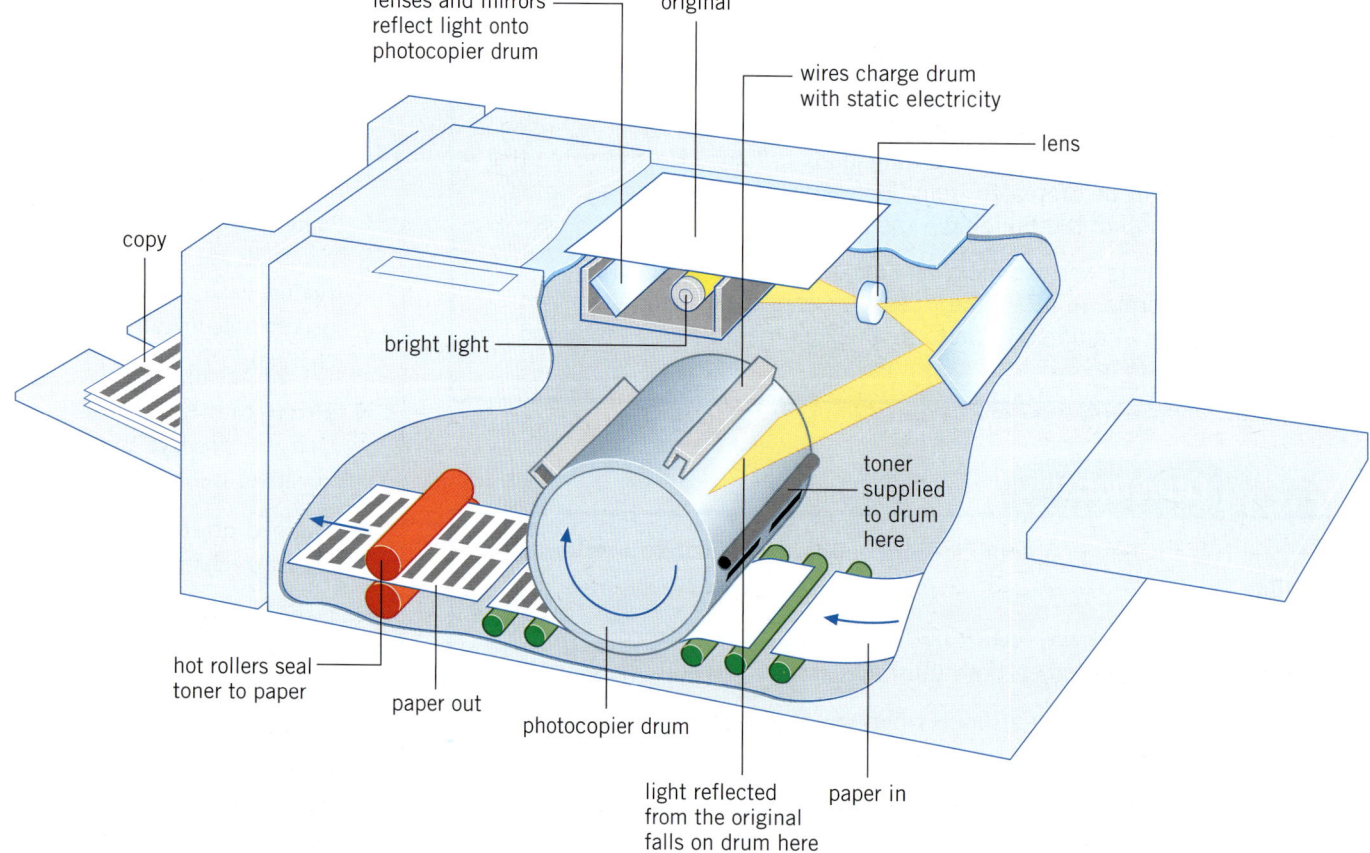

↓ **Figure 1:** The internal workings of a photocopier.

Electricity

A laser printer works in a very similar way, except that electronic circuits control a beam of laser light that shines on the drum to make the surface conduct electricity. Where the beam does not shine, the drum remains charged and so toner sticks to these areas and is transferred to the paper as the drum rotates. A heater makes the toner stick to the paper before it passes out of the printer.

The inkjet printer

An inkjet printer produces text and pictures on paper in monochrome (black and shades of grey) or colour. It does this by spraying tiny droplets of ink onto the paper.

The printer sprays tiny droplets of ink onto the surface of the paper through a very fine nozzle. As the droplets pass through the nozzle they become electrically charged. The droplets pass between metal plates (Figure 2). A voltage can be applied so that one plate is negative and the other is positive. Charged droplets of ink are attracted to the plate with the opposite charge, and repelled by the plate with the same charge – so the direction in which the drop travels can be controlled. The charge on the droplets or the plates can be controlled very precisely, so that the place where the ink droplet lands on the paper can be targeted exactly.

The printer contains an arrangement of gears and pulleys that move the print nozzles across the paper as it travels through the printer. In this way an image consisting of many millions of tiny dots of ink is built up.

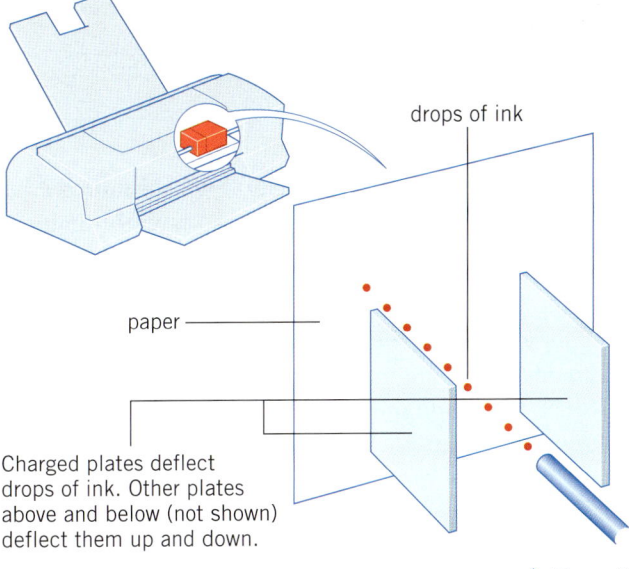

Charged plates deflect drops of ink. Other plates above and below (not shown) deflect them up and down.

↑ **Figure 2**

← **Figure 3:** The print from an inkjet printer is made up of millions of tiny dots, formed where drops of ink hit the paper.

Questions

1. A copy that has just come out of a photocopier may be quite hot – why?
2. Would it matter whether the charge on the photocopier drum was positive or negative? Explain your answer.
3. You might see a sign inside a photocopier warning about high voltages. What would a high voltage be used to do inside the photocopier?
4. How do inkjet printers charge the drops of ink that come out of the nozzles of the printer?

Key Ideas

- Photocopiers, laser printers and inkjet printers use electrostatic charge to produce text and images on paper.

Electricity 23

1.12 Electrolysis

So far we have seen that electricity flows through conductors when electrons move. But electricity can also flow through liquids.

If you dissolve some ordinary common salt in water and then connect up a circuit like to one shown in Figure 1, you will find that the lamp lights. This shows that current is flowing between the two wires (called **electrodes**) dipping into the solution. We already know that current is conducted through metal wires by electrons moving through them. A solution of salt in water does not contain electrons that can move to conduct electricity – so it must be something else that is carrying the current.

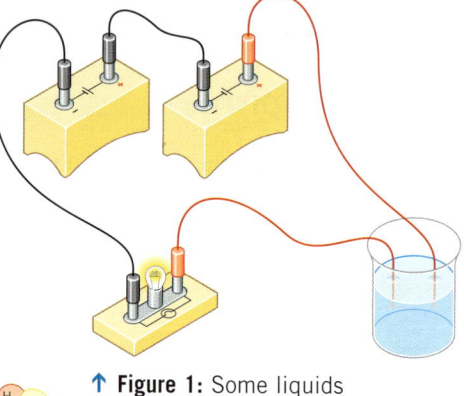

↑ **Figure 1:** Some liquids conduct electricity.

Common salt is made up of electrically charged particles called **ions**. It contains two types of ions – positively charged sodium ions (Na^+) and negatively charged chloride ions (Cl^-). In solid salt these ions are held tightly together as the positive and negative charges attract each other. But when salt dissolves in water the ions break apart and become free to move anywhere in the solution.

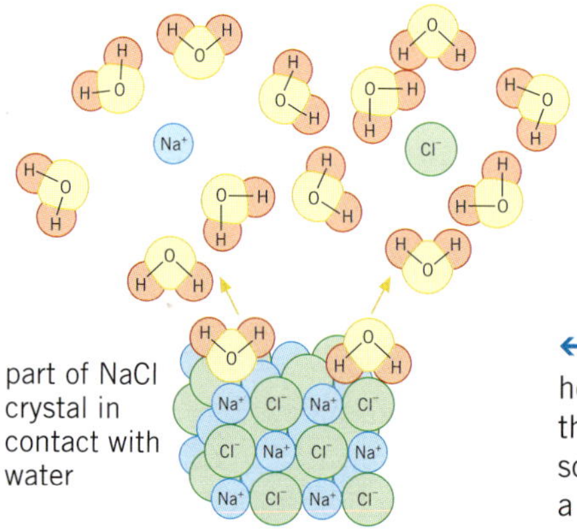

← **Figure 2:** Although they are held tightly together in solid salt, the ions can move freely when the solid is dissolved in water to make a solution.

When two electrodes connected to an electric circuit are dipped into a salt solution, positive sodium ions are attracted to the negative electrode and negative chloride ions are attracted to the positive electrode. The moving ions conduct electricity through the solution, allowing current to flow round the whole circuit. Chemical changes take place at the electrodes – in a solution of sodium chloride, chlorine gas is produced at the positive electrode, while hydrogen gas is given off at the negative electrode.

As well as breaking ions apart by dissolving them in water, we can also break them apart by heating – turning a solid into a liquid. In a solid the ions are held tightly together in a rigid structure, but in a liquid the ions can move freely, carrying a current in just the same way as they do in solution. When molten sodium chloride conducts electricity chlorine is formed at the positive electrode, and sodium metal is formed at the negative electrode.

Splitting up substances using electricity is called **electrolysis**.

→ **Figure 4:** Jewellery can be covered with a thin layer of silver by dipping it into a solution containing silver ions, which are positively charged. The jewellery is given a negative charge by connecting it into an electric circuit. Silver ions are attracted to the jewellery, forming a thin layer of metal over the surface.

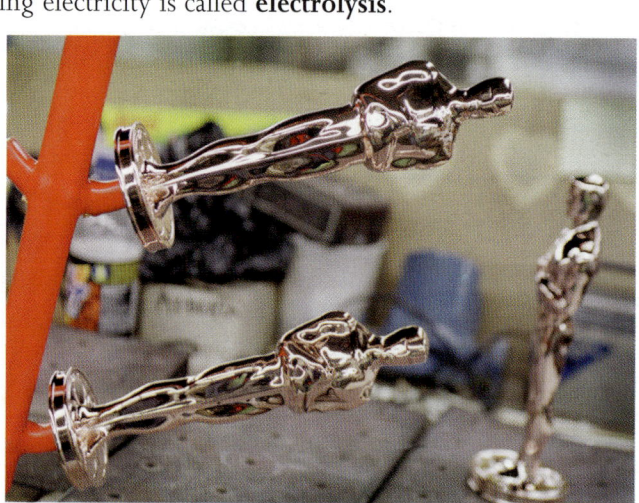

positive ions

→

move towards the negative electrode

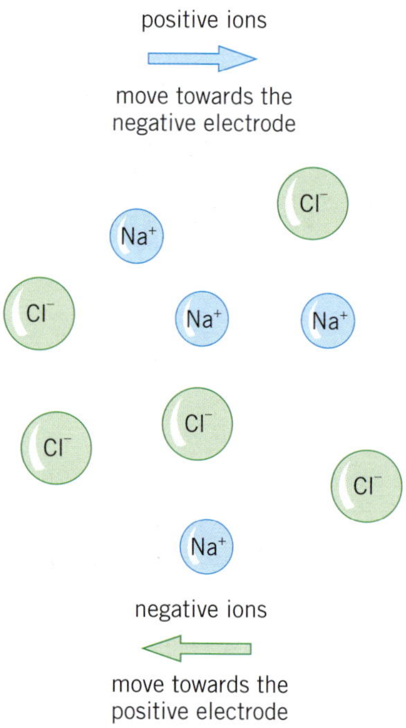

↑ **Figure 3:** Moving ions carry the current through a solution.

negative ions

←

move towards the positive electrode

24 Electricity

H The amount of substance produced by electrolysis

Think about a conducting liquid with a negative electrode and a positive electrode dipping into it. Positive ions are attracted to the negative electrode. Here electrons can be transferred to the positive ions from the negative electrode, producing neutral atoms. At the positive electrode the opposite process takes place – electrons are removed from the negative ions, also producing neutral atoms.

The amount of substance that is formed when a current is passed through a liquid depends on the number of electrons transferred – the more electrons transferred the greater the number of neutral atoms produced from charged ions. The number of electrons transferred will depend on two things – the size of the current flowing, and the time for which the current flows. This means that the mass of substance produced is proportional to the current and the time for which the current flows.

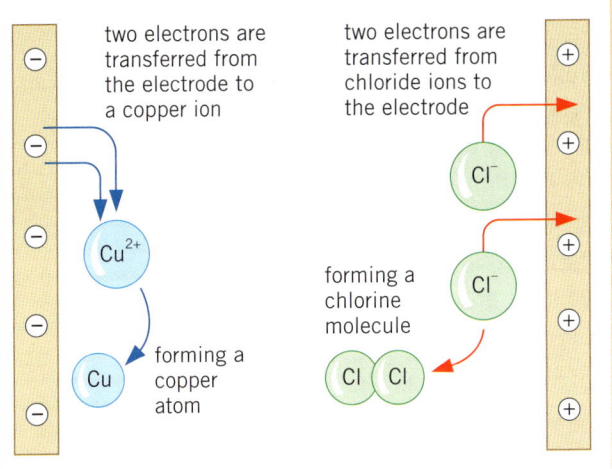

↑ **Figure 5:** In electrolysis, neutral atoms are produced from positive and negative ions by transferring electrons between ions and electrodes.

Science people

Electrolysis was investigated by Michael Faraday more than 150 years ago, when he set out the relationship between the amount of substance produced in electrolysis, current and time.

Questions

1. Why do molten salt and a solution of salt in water conduct electricity, when solid salt does not?
2. Explain how a thin layer of silver can be coated onto a piece of metal using electrolysis.
3. **H** A jewellery manufacturer wishes to increase the thickness of gold plated onto the jewellery they produce using electrolysis. Suggest **two** ways in which they could do this.
4. Car bodies can be protected from corrosion by plating them with zinc during manufacture – a process called **galvanising**. One way of doing this is to dip the car body into a solution containing zinc ions and to pass electricity through the solution.
   a. Should the car body be made positive or negative in order to plate it with zinc?
   b. If the current through the zinc solution is doubled, how will this affect the amount of zinc deposited on the metal?
   c. If the time that the current flows through the car body is halved, how will this affect the amount of zinc deposited on the metal?
   d. A car manufacturer wishes to speed up the rate at which car bodies are coated with zinc. How can this be done while keeping the thickness of zinc plating the same?

Key Ideas

- When some chemical compounds containing ions are melted or dissolved in water, they conduct electricity.
- Charged ions in the liquid are attracted to electrodes with the opposite charge.
- Simpler substances are produced at the electrodes.
- The amount of substance produced during electrolysis increases with the current passing and the time for which the current flows.

Electricity   25

1.13 End of chapter questions

1 This circuit shows three identical lamps which are controlled by the three switches S_1, S_2 and S_3.

   The switches in the diagram are all open.

   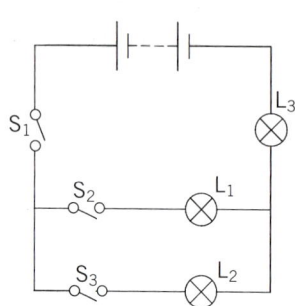

   a Complete the following table to show which lamps are on.

Switches closed	Lamps on
S_1 and S_2	
S_2 and S_3	
S_1 and S_3	

   (3 marks)

   b Which switches need to be closed to light all three lamps? (1 mark)

   (Total 4 marks)
   AQA specimen question

2 a Copy and complete the table showing the power rating and current used by a number of different domestic appliances.

Appliance	Power rating (watts)	Operating current (amperes)
vacuum cleaner	1200	
dishwasher	2880	
electric shower		25
hairdryer	960	
food mixer		1
lamp	60	

   (6 marks)

   b Which appliance will cost most to run for one hour? Explain your answer clearly. (2 marks)

   (Total 8 marks)

3 a The diagram shows a 13 amp plug.

   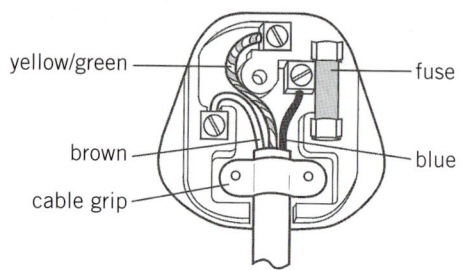

   i What is wrong with the way this plug has been wired? (1 mark)

   ii Why do plugs have a fuse? (1 mark)

   b The diagram shows an immersion heater which can be used to boil water in a mug.

   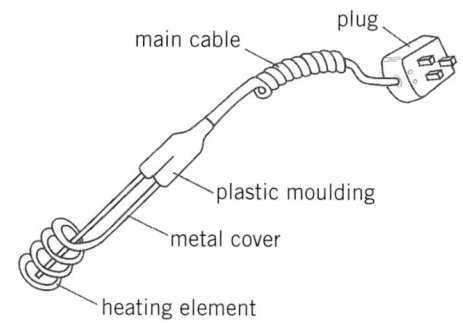

   Which part of the immersion heater should be connected to the earth pin of the plug?

   (1 mark)

   (Total 3 marks)
   AQA specimen question

26 Electricity

4 The diagram shows a fan heater.

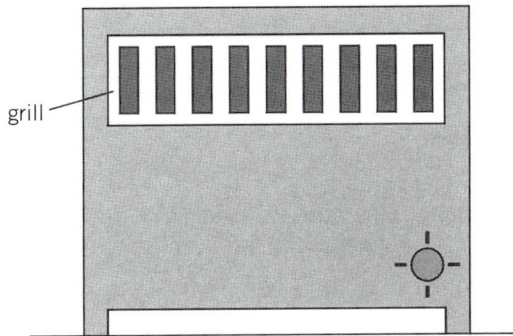

a The power of the fan heater is 2.75 kW.
   Calculate how many kilowatt hours (kWh) of energy are transferred when the fan heater is used for 6 hours. (2 marks)

b How much will it cost to use the fan heater for 6 hours if one Unit of electricity costs 7p? (2 marks)

(Total 4 marks)
AQA specimen question

5 A student investigated how the current flowing through component X changes with the voltage across it.

The diagram shows the circuit used.

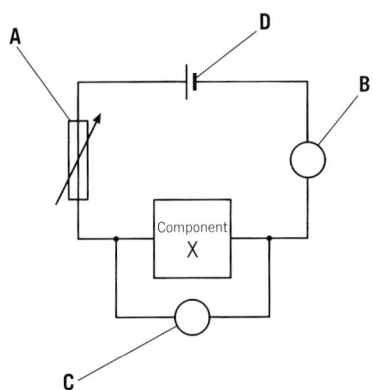

a Use words or phrases from the list to label parts A, B, C and D.

**ammeter   cell   switch   variable resistor
voltmeter** (4 marks)

b The table shows the results obtained for component X.

Voltage (V)	−0.4	−0.2	0.0	0.2	0.4	0.5	0.6	0.8	1.0
Current (mA)	0	0	0	0	1	4	10	30	50

i Draw a graph of current against voltage. (3 marks)

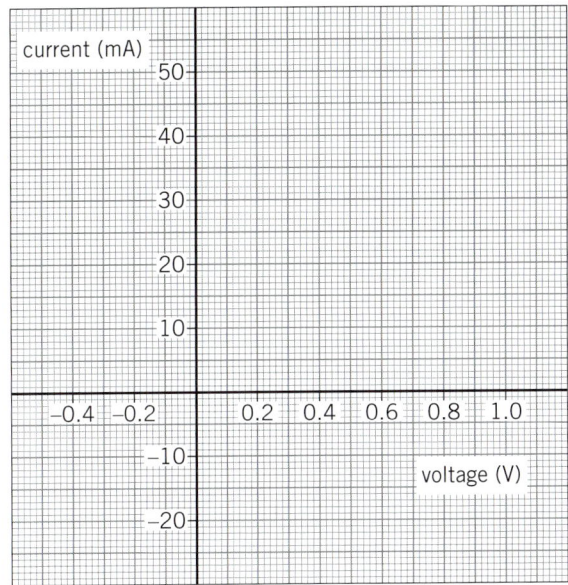

ii Name component X. (1 mark)

(Total 8 marks)
AQA specimen question

6 The diagram shows a a device called an **electrostatic precipitator**. This is used to remove dust particles from waste gases passing up the chimneys of power stations. The smoke and dust particles travel up the chimney past a fine wire mesh and become positively charged.

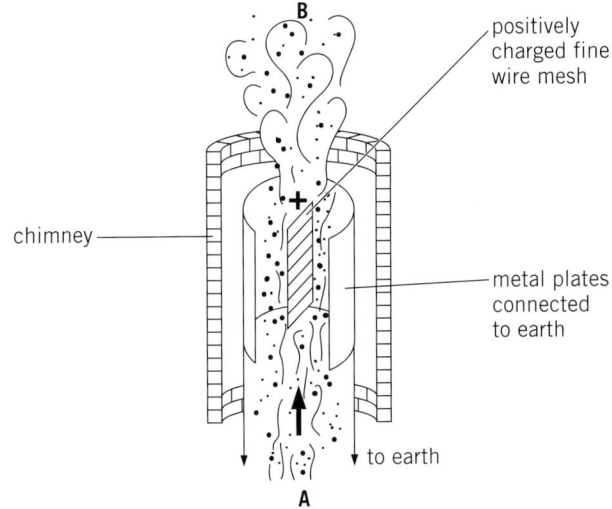

a What happens to the charge on the dust particles as they travel up the chimney past the wire mesh? (1 mark)

b What effect does this have on the movement of the dust particles? (2 marks)

c Compare the composition of the waste gases at A to those at B. (1 mark)

d Periodically the metal plates in the precipitator are struck sharply with a mallet. Explain why this is done. (1 mark)

(Total 5 marks)

Electricity 27

2.1 Distance, speed and time

We can work out the speed of something if we know the distance it has travelled and the time it has taken.

$$\text{speed (metres/second, m/s)} = \frac{\text{distance travelled (metres, m)}}{\text{time taken (seconds, s)}}$$

In science, speed is usually measured in metres per second, which can be shortened to m/s. Car drivers (in the UK at least) are more used to measuring speed in miles per hour, which is calculated by dividing distance in miles by time taken in hours.

Calculations like this always tell us the **average speed** – a car travelling 70 miles in two hours is unlikely to have travelled at exactly 35 miles per hour, for example.

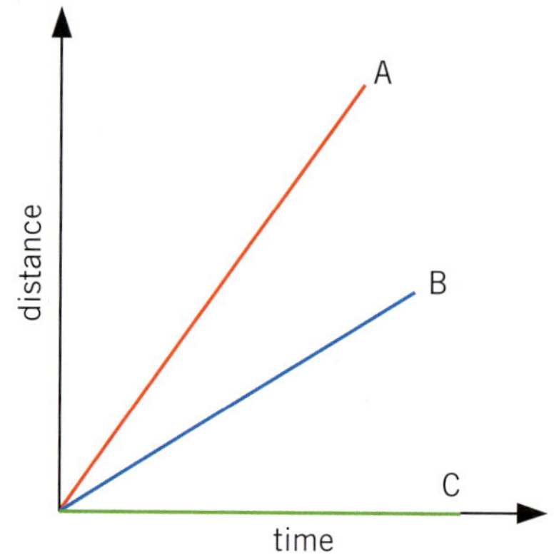

Distance, speed and time – using graphs

We can use a graph to represent the distance that an object travels. A **distance-time graph** shows how far something has moved in a particular time. The graph in Figure 1 shows the distance travelled by three cyclists.

Notice how the lines on the graph are straight. This tells us that the cyclists all travel with steady speeds, which do not change. Cyclist A travels furthest, while cyclist C travels no distance at all, and cyclist B is in between these two. The slope of an object's distance-time graph represents its speed, the rate at which its distance from its starting point is changing – the greater the slope, the greater the speed. A horizontal line represents a speed of zero – in other words, something that is stationary.

↑ **Figure 1:** A distance-time graph is an important way of measuring and representing the speed of something.

Changing motion – speeding up, slowing down and changing direction

As well as slowing down and speeding up, objects do not usually travel in just one direction, as you will quickly realise if you think about your journey to and from school. While the **speed** of an object simply describes the rate at which it is travelling, we describe an object's velocity as both its speed and the direction it is travelling in. We might say:

'the speed of the runner was 8 m/s'

or 'the velocity of the aeroplane is 180 m/s due North'.

Velocity-time graphs are used to represent the movement of objects, just like distance-time graphs. Figure 2 shows a velocity-time graph for a cyclist travelling away from a set of traffic lights.

Just as with the distance-time graph, the slope of the velocity-time graph is important. The slope of an object's velocity-time graph represents the rate at which its velocity is changing – its **acceleration**. A horizontal velocity-time graph represents motion with zero acceleration – in other words, constant velocity.

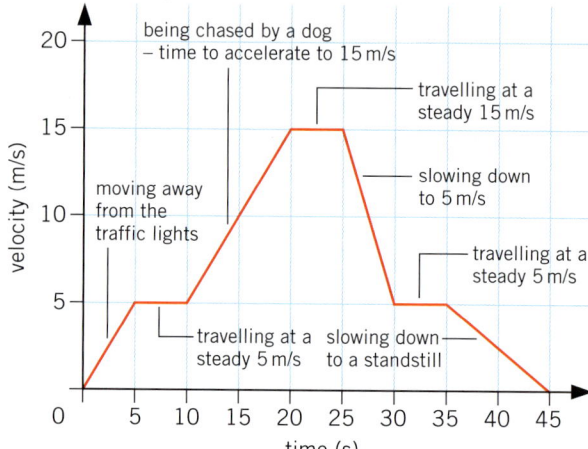

↑ **Figure 2:** A velocity-time graph provides us with a 'picture' of the way something is moving.

Calculating acceleration

We can calculate the acceleration of an object if we know its change in velocity and the time taken for the change:

$$\text{acceleration (metres/second}^2\text{, m/s}^2\text{)} = \frac{\text{change in velocity (m/s)}}{\text{time taken for change (s)}}$$

Example

A formula 1 racing car can brake from a speed of 80 m/s to rest in 2 s. What is the car's acceleration?

Once again, we know that $\text{acceleration} = \dfrac{\text{change in velocity}}{\text{time taken for change}}$

so we can write

$\text{Acceleration} = \dfrac{(0 - 80)\, \text{m/s}}{2\, \text{s}} = -40\, \text{m/s}^2$

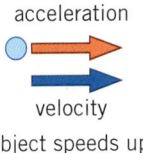
acceleration
velocity
object speeds up

acceleration   velocity
object slows down

↑ **Figure 3:** When acceleration and velocity are in the same direction, the object speeds up. When they are in opposite directions, the object slows down.

Notice that the way velocity is calculated means that a **decrease** in velocity means that the acceleration is **negative**, because the acceleration is in the opposite direction to the velocity (Figure 3).

H More about velocity–time graphs

The slope or **gradient** of a velocity–time graph represents acceleration, as we have just seen. The area under the graph tells us something too. To find the area under the graph we must multiply a velocity (measured along the y-axis) by a time (measured along the x-axis. Since velocity × time = distance, the area under an object's velocity–time graph represents the distance it has travelled. Figure 4 shows this.

The total area under the graph is the area under the red line plus the area under the blue line:

area under red line = 2 m/s × 40 s   = 80 m
area under blue line = ½ × 2.0 m/s × 10 s = 10 m
total area   = 80 m + 10 m   = 90 m

The total distance travelled is 90 m.

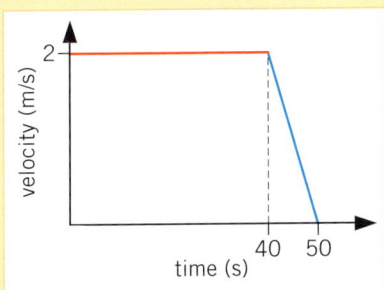
↑ **Figure 4**

🔑 Key Ideas

- For any object the distance travelled, time taken and average speed are related:

  $\text{average speed} = \dfrac{\text{distance travelled}}{\text{time taken}}$

- The steeper the slope of a distance–time graph, the greater the speed it represents.

- An object's velocity is its speed in a given direction.

- The steeper the slope of a velocity–time graph, the greater the acceleration it represents.

- The acceleration of an object can be found from the relationship:

  $\text{acceleration} = \dfrac{\text{change in velocity}}{\text{time taken for change}}$

- **H** The area under a velocity–time graph represents the distance travelled.

? Questions

1. Which of the following is *not* a unit of speed?

   a metres per second **b** miles/hour **c** cm/kg
   d km per year **e** mm/minute

2. Calculate the speed of these objects:

   a A car which travels 100 m in 5 s
   b A golf ball which moves a distance of 20 m in 2 s.

3. How far does a girl running at a speed of 3 m/s travel in 6 s?

4. Sketch a graph of a person who cycles 200 m in 20 s, then stops for 5 s, then cycles a further 100 m in 30 s.

5. **H** As accurately as you can, describe the movement of the car that produced the velocity–time graph shown in Figure 5.

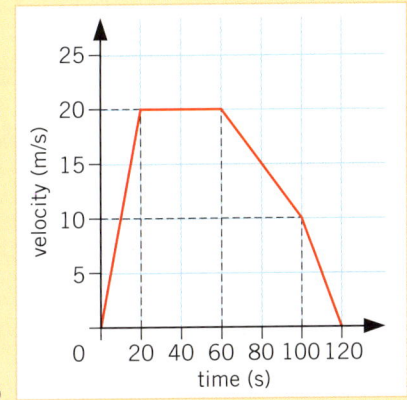
→ **Figure 5**

Forces and motion   29

2.2 Changing motion

Getting going

To get something moving we know that we have to give it a push or a pull. In scientific language we call a push or a pull a **force**, which we measure in **newtons**.

Balanced and unbalanced forces

If you balance a book on the palm of your hand, you have to push upwards on the book to prevent it falling – you provide a **reaction force**. To keep the book perfectly still, the reaction force of your hand acting upwards on the book must exactly equal the weight of the book acting downwards on your hand. The same thing is true for you standing on the floor of a room – except that the upward force is provided by the floor pushing on the soles of your feet. (Unlike your arm, the floor doesn't have muscles to push upwards – instead, the reaction force is caused by the slight downward movement of the floor as you stand on it.)

Isaac Newton was the first person to explain what happens when one object exerts a force on another object. He did this in his third law of motion, which in modern language states:

> whenever two objects exert forces on each other, the forces are equal in size and opposite in direction.

When forces cancel each other out, we say that they are **balanced**.

Now imagine what will happen if the person holding the book takes their hand away. The book no longer has an upward force acting on it, although its weight still acts downwards on it – we say that there is an **unbalanced** force acting on it. Because of this unbalanced force the book starts to fall – we are all familiar with what happens when we drop something!

Whenever an unbalanced force occurs, it affects the way an object is moving. If it is stationary, the object will start to move in the direction of the unbalanced force. If it is moving in the same direction as the unbalanced force, the object will speed up. And, if it is moving in the opposite direction to the unbalanced force it will slow down.

↑ **Figure 1:** A push to get it moving ... and a pull to stop it again.

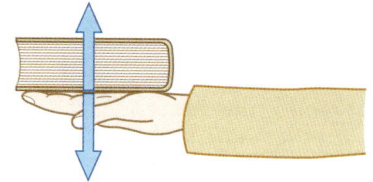

↑ **Figure 2:** The upward force of the hand on the book exactly balances the downward force of the book's weight and the book remains stationary. We represent the size of a force by the length of the arrow – in this case, both forces are represented by arrows of the same length.

↓ **Figure 3:** The effect of an unbalanced force – in which direction is it acting?

↑ **Figure 4: (a)** As a car moves, it experiences frictional forces that tend to slow it down. Here, these forces are smaller than the thrust provided by the engine. Because the forces do not cancel each other out, an unbalanced force is produced in the direction in which the car is travelling, so it speeds up.
(b) Here the frictional forces on the car are larger than the thrust provided by the engine. The unbalanced force acts backwards, and so the car slows down.

Forces and motion

The size of the unbalanced force

To change an object's speed (in other words, to make it accelerate) requires an unbalanced force, as we have seen. Look at the picture of the race with three cars (Figure 5).

Imagine the three cars line up at the traffic lights. If the car with the smallest engine has four people in it, the one with the middle-sized engine has two people in it and the one with the largest engine has only the driver in it, which car will accelerate most rapidly?

It seems fairly obvious that the car with the largest engine will accelerate more rapidly, as the engine can exert a larger force on the car than the engine in either of the other two cars. The smallest engine also has to accelerate more people – so it looks as if this car will accelerate more slowly away from the start than the others!

As this example suggests, the greater the size of the unbalanced force on an object, the greater its acceleration. And the bigger the mass of an object, the larger the unbalanced force that is needed to give it a particular acceleration.

↑ **Figure 5:** The three cars have the same mass but different engines. Which car will have the greatest acceleration?

Key Ideas

- Balanced forces do not affect an object's motion.
- Unbalanced forces affect an object's motion. Depending upon the direction of the unbalanced force, it may cause the object to speed up, slow down or change direction.

Questions

1. Using the idea of forces, explain exactly what you have to do to move a supermarket trolley full of shopping. Your answer should include the words: push, force, unbalanced, accelerate.

2. Copy Figure 6 and add arrows to show the forces acting on a wheelbarrow being pushed at a steady speed along a piece of flat, level ground.

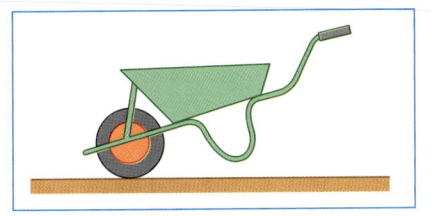

← Figure 6

3. Describe what happens in the following situations:
   a. A ball at rest on the ground experiences an unbalanced force acting in a horizontal direction.
   b. A falling leaf experiences an unbalanced force acting in a horizontal direction.
   c. A car travelling in a straight line along a road experiences an unbalanced force acting in the direction in which it is travelling.

4. Figure 7 shows a cyclist travelling along a flat road.

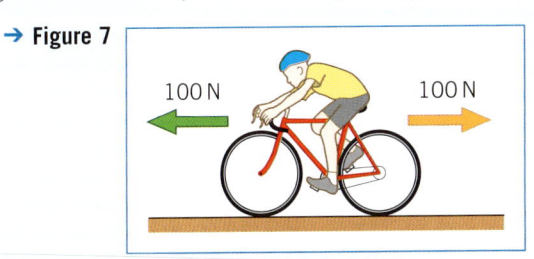

   → Figure 7

   a. Calculate the total force acting on the cyclist in a horizontal direction and describe the motion of the cycle and cyclist.
   b. The wind speed increases, and the drag force increases to 150 N, while the forwards force on the cyclist does not change. Calculate the total force acting on the cyclist in a horizontal direction and describe the motion of the cycle and cyclist now.
   c. The drag force continues at 150 N, while the cyclist now pedals harder so that the forward force acting increases by 50 N. Calculate the total force acting on the cyclist in a horizontal direction and describe the motion of the cycle and cyclist now.

Forces and motion

2.3 The link between force, mass and acceleration H

You can investigate how force, mass and acceleration are related using apparatus found in many school physics laboratories.

One way of doing this is to use a 'ticker-tape timer', which produces dots on a piece of paper tape. The tape can then be cut up to produce a velocity-time graph (Figure 1).

Another way of producing velocity-time graphs is to use special equipment that can be connected to a computer. The computer measures the speed of the object at different points, and plots it on a graph that can be displayed on a monitor and printed out.

Investigations to explore the relationship between force, mass and acceleration usually involve measuring the acceleration of a trolley. With two other variables (force and mass) to vary, one of these variables must be kept constant while the other is changed. Figure 3 shows some graphs plotted in such an investigation.

You should be able to use the graphs in Figure 3 to show that:

- doubling the resultant force acting on an object doubles its acceleration (while mass is kept constant), and tripling the resultant force triples its acceleration
- doubling the mass of an object halves its acceleration (while resultant force is kept constant), and tripling its mass reduces its acceleration to one third.

In other words:

- acceleration is proportional to force
- acceleration is proportional to $\frac{1}{\text{mass}}$

We can combine these results to produce an important relationship which is sometimes known as Newton's second law of motion:

$$\text{force} = \text{mass} \times \text{acceleration}$$
(newtons, N) (kilogram, kg) (metres per second^2)

The newton (N) is the unbalanced force needed to give a mass of one kilogram an acceleration of one metre per second^2.

Figure 2: Equipment like this makes the job of measuring velocities and plotting velocity-time graphs relatively simple.

Trolley travels along bench. Paper tape attached to trolley is pulled through the ticker-tape timer, which puts 50 dots each second onto the tape.

The distance between two dots shows the distance travelled in $\frac{1}{50}$ s.

To make a velocity-time graph from the tape, it must be cut up into strips that are ten gaps long. Each strip then shows the distance travelled in $\frac{10}{50}$ s = $\frac{1}{5}$ s.

To produce a velocity-time graph, the strips are then stuck side by side in the order in which they were produced.

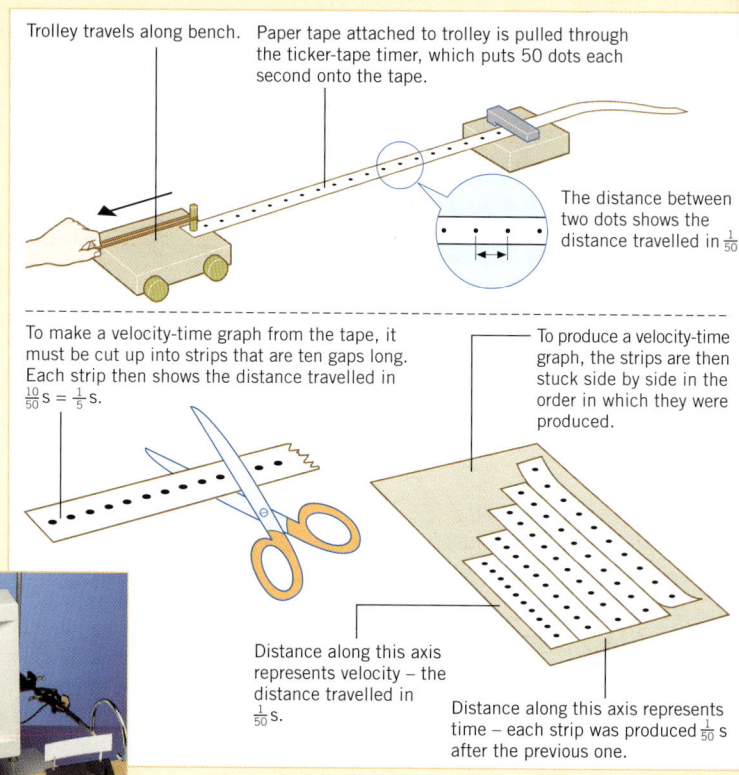

Distance along this axis represents velocity – the distance travelled in $\frac{1}{50}$ s.

Distance along this axis represents time – each strip was produced $\frac{1}{50}$ s after the previous one.

Figure 1

Figure 3: (a) In this investigation the mass of the trolley was kept constant while the resultant force on it was varied. **(b)** In this investigation the resultant force on the trolley was kept constant while the mass of the trolley was varied by placing metal blocks on it.

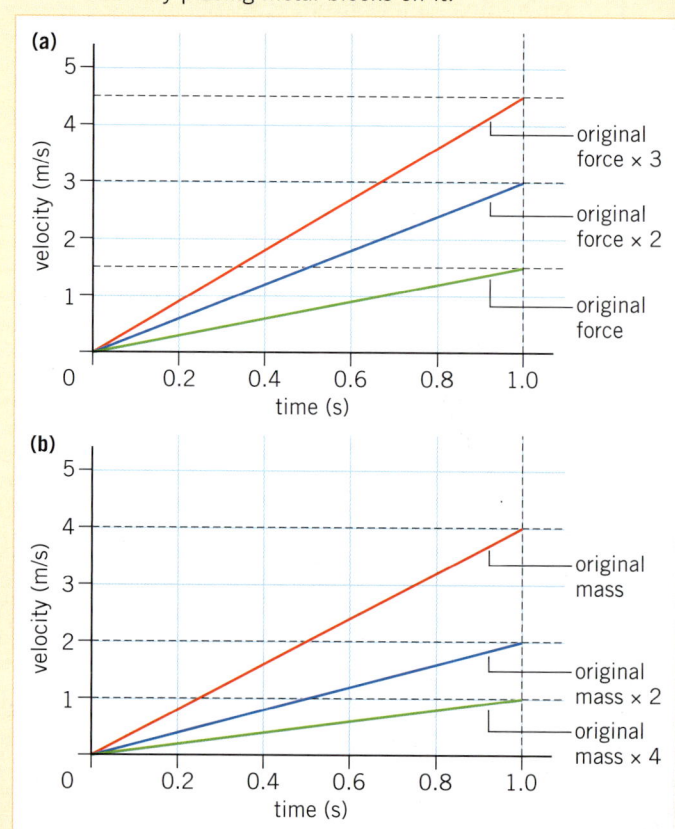

32 Forces and motion

Example

A fish escaping from a predator has an unbalanced force of 15 N acting on it in a forward direction. If the mass of the fish is 3 kg, what is its acceleration?

We know that

force = mass × acceleration

so we can write

15 N = 3 kg × acceleration

We can divide each side of this equation by 3 kg, which gives

$$\text{acceleration} = \frac{15}{3} \text{ m/s}^2$$
$$= 5 \text{ m/s}^2$$

Key Ideas

- Investigations in which a mass is accelerated with a force show that:
  * acceleration is proportional to force
  * acceleration is proportional to 1/mass
- These results can be combined to produce a law which is sometimes called Newton's second law of motion:
  force = mass × acceleration
- One newton will accelerate a mass of one kilogram at a rate of one metre per second^2.

Questions

1. A bird with a mass of 0.2 kg accelerates at a rate of 5 m/s^2. What unbalanced force must be acting on the bird to cause this acceleration?

2. A cyclist and bicycle have a mass of 90 kg. What unbalanced force is needed to accelerate them at a rate of 3 m/s^2?

3. A car accelerates at a rate of 5 m/s^2. Its engine exerts an unbalanced force of 6000 N on it – what is the car's mass?

4. At take-off a space rocket's engines exert a force of 2 500 000 N. The mass of the rocket at take off is 50 000 kg.

   a What is the rocket's acceleration just as it leaves the ground?

   b The rocket's acceleration increases as it rises. Suggest a possible reason for this.

5. Use the data in the table below to answer the following questions.

   a Which car:
      i has the greatest mass
      ii has the greatest fuel consumption
      iii has the highest top speed
      iv accelerates most slowly from 0–60 mph?

   b Plot bar charts of power output, 0–60 mph, and maximum speed data for each car. Put the names of each car on the x-axis.

   c Compare the shapes of the charts from part (b). Is there a link between these three ways of measuring performance of a car? What advice would you give to someone buying a car?

Manufacturer	Model	Mass (kg)	Maximum speed (mph)	0–60 mph (seconds)	Fuel consumption (mpg)	Engine size (cc)	Power output (bhp)
Audi	2.8SE	1450	143	8.1	30.0	2771	193
BMW	318tds	1340	113	13.0	46.8	1665	90
Citroen	Xantia 2.0iSX	1238	122	9.6	33.2	1998	135
Ford	Mondeo 24V Ghia X	1377	131	8.4	30.0	2544	167
Isuzu	Trooper 3.2 V6 LWB	1880	106	11.4	19.3	3165	174
Lada	Samara 1.1 3dr	900	85	16.7	37.5	1099	53
Mazda	MX5 1.8i S	990	116	9.9	32.0	1839	130
Nissan	Micra 1.3 GX 3dr	810	104	10.6	46.3	1275	75
Porsche	Targa	1370	168	5.2	25.2	3600	285
Rover	216 Sli 5dr	1040	113	8.9	40.8	1589	109

Forces and motion

2.4 Frictional forces

When an object is moving, frictional forces tend to slow it down again. These frictional forces are caused by solid surfaces in contact with one another – for example, the metal surfaces in the axle of a bicycle wheel – and by the resistance of the air as the object moves through it. (An object such as a fish moving through water experiences frictional forces due to the water.) Frictional forces always act in the opposite direction to the direction in which the object is moving.

← **Figure 1:** Even smooth surfaces are really very rough, as this highly magnified photograph of a polished metal surface shows. Oil pushes rough surfaces apart, reducing the frictional forces between them.

Using frictional forces

Brakes make use of frictional forces. As the brakes of a car or bicycle are applied, a large frictional force is exerted on the wheels. This force is in the opposite direction to the direction that the car or bicycle is moving in, and makes it slow down. As this happens the brake pads get hot and also get rubbed away – this means that they must be checked regularly, so that they can be replaced before they get dangerously worn.

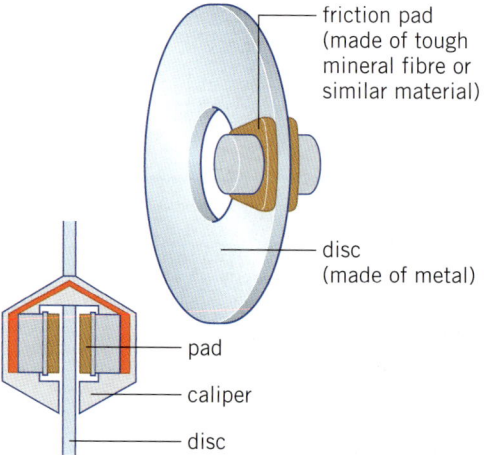

As a vehicle travels faster, it needs a larger braking force to stop it in a certain time. If the same braking force is used, a vehicle will take longer to stop when it is travelling fast than when it is travelling more slowly – and it will travel further in the time that the brakes are applied, too. To make a vehicle stop as quickly as possible the brakes must be kept in good condition to ensure that the frictional force they exert is as large as possible.

The tyres and road surface are important too. There must be a large grip or frictional force between the tyre and the road if the vehicle is to stop quickly, otherwise the vehicle may skid if the braking force is large. The frictional force between the tyre and the road can be made large if the road surface is rough, dry and doesn't have oil or grease on it. Tyres have grooves or 'tread' cut in them to increase the frictional force even further if the road surface is wet – the grooves help to push water out of the way of the tyre, keeping it in contact with the road.

← **Figure 2:** Car brakes use friction caused by solid surfaces rubbing together.

↓ **Figure 3:** The tyres on the left-hand side of this photograph are called 'slicks' – they are used in dry weather only. Slicks have no tread, so more of the tyre is in contact with the road surface for a better grip.

Stopping distance

The distance a vehicle travels between the driver seeing an obstacle in the road ahead and the vehicle coming to rest is called the **stopping distance**. The stopping distance of a vehicle is made up of two parts (Figure 4).

→ Figure 4

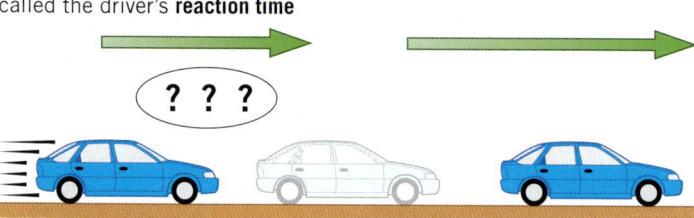

thinking distance – the distance travelled by the vehicle in the time between the driver seeing something that means the brakes must be applied, and actually applying the brakes. This time is called the driver's **reaction time**

braking distance – the distance the vehicle travels while the brakes are applied

34 Forces and motion

The overall stopping distance is the sum of the 'thinking distance' and the 'braking distance'. Stopping distance increases if:

- the vehicle's speed before applying the brakes is greater
- the road is wet or icy
- the driver is tired or under the influence of drink or drugs
- the vehicle's brakes or tyres have been poorly maintained.

Science people

Jonathan Wortley

Physics plays a vital part in making cars and other road vehicles safer, both for those travelling in them and for other road users on foot or on two wheels. At the Motor Industry Research Association's laboratories, Jonathan Wortley is involved in carrying out tests on new vehicle designs on behalf of car manufacturers. A whole range of tests can be carried out on vehicles to see how they are likely to perform in a road accident, including tests using a 'HyGe sled', a special piece of equipment that can simulate crashes at different speeds. Jonathan works closely with vehicle manufacturers to see how changing different aspects of a vehicle's design affect the way in which the driver and passengers are protected in a crash. Sometimes this involves new ways of preventing passengers colliding with the inside of the car during an accident, while other changes to vehicle designs may make it less likely that a pedestrian is injured if they are struck by a car as they cross the road.

Jonathan's work at MIRA relies on a good knowledge of physics. Having always had an interest in applying physics while he was studying the subject at school, Jonathan went to Bristol University where he took a degree in Mechanical Engineering before he joined MIRA. His job gives him the opportunity to use physics to make our roads safer, to the benefit of all road users.

Figure 5: Jonathan Wortley

Key Ideas

- Frictional forces tend to make a moving object slow down.
- The braking distance of a vehicle increases as its speed increases.
- The stopping distance of a vehicle is made up of two parts:
  - thinking distance
  - braking distance.

Questions

1 Draw up a table like this one and write down some places where friction is useful, and somewhere it has to be overcome.

Places where friction is useful	Places where friction must be overcome
bicycle brakes	in a car engine

2 When a jet airliner lands, you can often see a cloud of smoke coming from the tyres as they first touch the runway. Why does this happen?

3 Explain how the following affect the 'thinking distance' and the 'braking distance' (Figure 6) of a car as it comes to rest:

   a decreasing the speed of the car before the brakes are applied

   b the driver is drunk

   c the car's brakes are worn

   d the road surface is slippery.

↓ **Figure 6:** Thinking and braking distances.

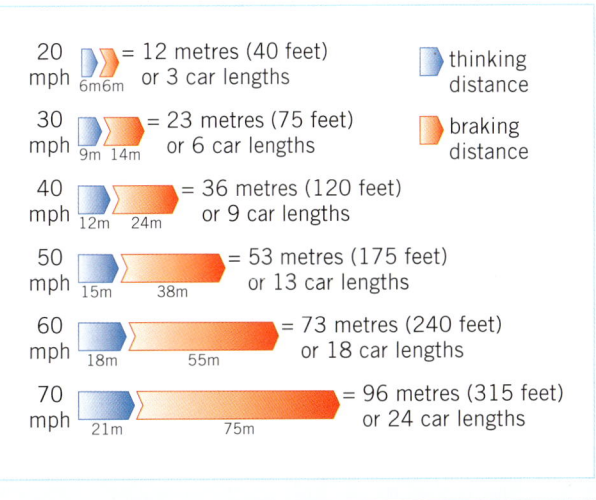

20 mph 6m 6m = 12 metres (40 feet) or 3 car lengths

30 mph 9m 14m = 23 metres (75 feet) or 6 car lengths

40 mph 12m 24m = 36 metres (120 feet) or 9 car lengths

50 mph 15m 38m = 53 metres (175 feet) or 13 car lengths

60 mph 18m 55m = 73 metres (240 feet) or 18 car lengths

70 mph 21m 75m = 96 metres (315 feet) or 24 car lengths

▮ thinking distance
▮ braking distance

Forces and motion

2.5 Falling freely

Mass and weight

No matter where it is, an object always has the same mass, which we measure in kilograms (kg). If it is in a gravitational field an object will have a weight that can be found from the relationship:

weight = mass × gravitational field strength
(newtons, N) (kilograms, kg) (newtons/kilogram, N/kg)

At the surface of the Earth, the gravitational field strength is about 10 N/kg, so if you have a mass of 40 kg, your weight will be 400 N. Remember that weight is a force, and the direction of this force when you are in the Earth's gravitational field is always towards the centre of the Earth.

Drag forces

As an object moves through a gas or a liquid (a **fluid** – something that flows), it experiences a frictional force in the opposite direction to the direction in which it is moving. This frictional force is sometimes called a **drag force**. The size of this force increases as the speed of the object increases – which is why racing cyclists like the one in Figure 1 take so much care to reduce their air resistance, making the drag forces acting on them as small as possible.

↑ **Figure 1:** To travel really fast means that you need to make drag forces as small as possible. How is this cyclist attempting to reduce the drag forces?

Free fall

The fact that the drag force on an object travelling through air increases with the speed of the object has an important effect on the movement of an object as it falls towards the surface of the Earth. To understand what this is, look at Figure 2 which shows a parachutist falling from a balloon.

As the parachutist jumps out of the balloon (A), her vertical velocity is zero at first, so the drag force acting on her is zero. She therefore has an unbalanced force (her weight) acting downwards on her, and she accelerates downwards.

A little later the parachutist is falling through the air (B). Her air resistance acts in the opposite direction to her weight, so the unbalanced force on her is smaller than it was at A, and so she is accelerating more slowly.

Eventually the parachutist reaches a point where her velocity has increased to the stage where her air resistance exactly balances her weight (C). Now there is no unbalanced force acting on her, so she is not accelerating. The velocity at which this happens is called the **terminal velocity.** Terminal velocity for a person without a parachute is about 56 m/s.

When the parachute opens (D), the air resistance increases greatly. Now there is an unbalanced force acting upwards – and the parachutist slows down.

Finally the parachutist reaches a new terminal velocity (E). This new terminal velocity is much smaller than the previous terminal velocity – about 10 m/s.

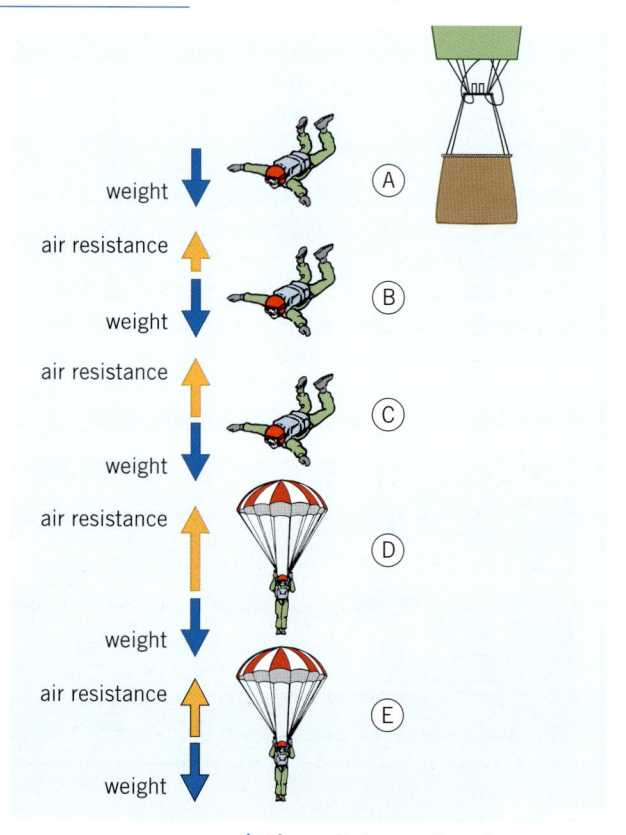

↑ **Figure 2:** Free fall and terminal velocity.

Forces and motion

Questions

1 Complete the table, to show details about the mass and weight of a spacecraft. (The Earth's gravitational field strength is about six times that of the Moon.)

	At Earth's surface	At Moon's surface	In deep space
mass	5000 kg		
weight			

2 A newly discovered planet has gravitational field strength of 25 N/kg. What will be the weight of an astronaut with a mass of 85 kg on this planet?

3 Explain why a shark has a long, pointed shape, while a jellyfish is shaped like a parachute.

4 The Space Shuttle uses a parachute called a 'drag chute' to slow it down when it lands at the end of a mission. Why do you think this method of braking is not used in jet airliners?

5 Drag racing cars accelerate quickly to high speeds on a short track called a 'drag strip'. They use a parachute to slow down at the end of a race. Copy the graph showing the velocity of a drag racer during a race, and add the labels below at the correct point on the graph. Complete the final label in your own words.

   a The drag racer slows down using its brakes alone.

   b The drag racer accelerates quickly to its maximum speed.

   c The parachute starts to slow the drag racer down.

   d The rate at which the drag racer slows down here is decreasing because …

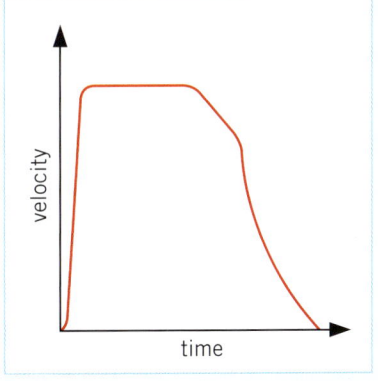

↑ Figure 3

6 An example of an 'extreme sport' is **free diving**. In this sport, competitors dive to great depths below the surface of the sea, carrying no air other than that in their lungs. In one type of free diving competition competitors descend while holding onto a heavy weight or 'sledge', which they then drop at the bottom of the dive before they come back up to the surface. The diver starts the dive from rest at the surface of the water.

   a Describe the motion of a diver as they descend from rest while holding onto the 'sledge'.

   b Why does the diver let go of the 'sledge' at the bottom of the dive?

   c The record for dives using a 'sledge' is deeper than the record for dives done without one. Why?

   d Apart from using a 'sledge', how else could divers ensure that they reach the greatest possible depth?

Key Ideas

- No matter where it is, an object always has the same mass.
- Frictional forces may be caused by solid surfaces rubbing together, or by the resistance of a fluid (a gas or a liquid) as something moves through it.
- An object falling freely through the atmosphere will eventually reach a terminal velocity.

Forces and motion

2.6 End of chapter questions

1 The diagram shows four distance-time graphs.

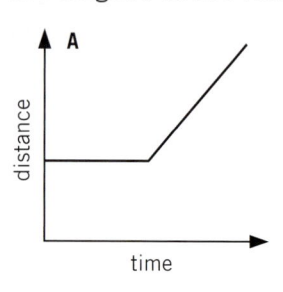

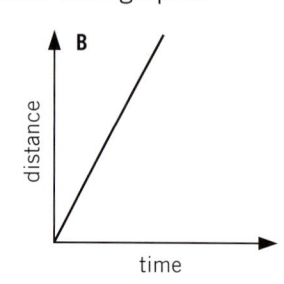

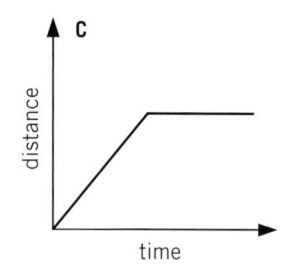

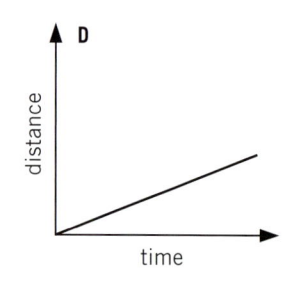

   a Which graph shows an object which moves at a steady speed to start with and then stops?

   b Which graph shows an object which is moving at a steady speed faster than all the others?

   c Which graph shows an object which is moving at a steady speed slower than all the others?

   d Which graph shows an object which is stationary to begin with and then moves away at a steady speed?

2 A sky-diver jumps from a plane.

   The sky-diver is shown in the diagram.

   a Arrows **X** and **Y** show two forces acting on the sky-diver as he falls.

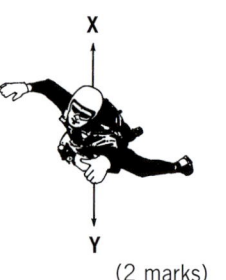

   i Name the forces **X** and **Y**. (2 marks)

   ii Explain why force **X** acts in an upward direction. (1 mark)

   iii At first forces **X** and **Y** are unbalanced. Which of the forces will be bigger? (1 mark)

   iv How does this unbalanced force affect the sky-diver? (2 marks)

   AQA specimen question

   b After some time the sky-diver pulls the rip cord and the parachute opens.

   The sky-diver and parachute are shown in this diagram.

   After a while forces **X** and **Y** are balanced.

   Write down the answers which correctly describe the situation.

   i Force **X** has

   increased/stayed the same/decreased.

   ii Force **Y** has

   increased/stayed the same/decreased.

   iii The speed of the sky-diver will

   increase/stay the same/decrease.
   (3 marks)

   (Total 9 marks)

3 The diagrams in this figure show someone riding a bicycle. The mass of the bicycle and rider is 45 kg.

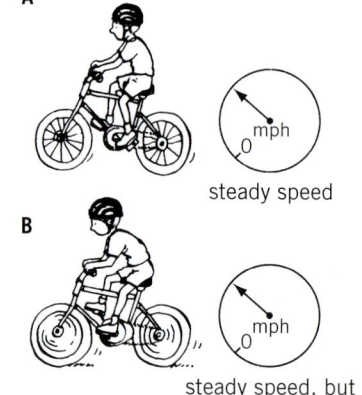

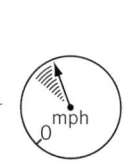

   A steady speed
   B steady speed, but into a headwind
   C accelerating
   D braking hard

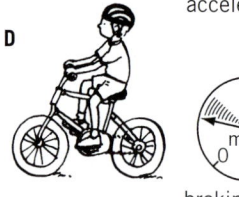

   a Copy each diagram and add arrows to show the horizontal forces acting, like this →.

   Use the **length** of each arrow to represent the **size** of the force. (4 marks)

   b The acceleration in diagram C is 3 m/s^2. Calculate the resultant force acting. (2 marks)

   c The acceleration in diagram D is −4 m/s^2. Calculate the resultant force acting. (2 marks)

   (Total 8 marks)

Forces and motion

4 A van is being driven along a road.

  a The van has a fault and leaks one drop of oil every second.

  The diagram below shows the oil drops left on the road as the van moves from W to Z.

  W   X   Y   Z

  •   •   •   •   ••••••   •   •   •   •

  Describe the motion of the van as it moves from:

  W to X

  X to Y

  Y to Z   (3 marks)

  b The van was travelling at 30 m/s. It slowed to a stop in 20 seconds. Calculate the van's deceleration. Write the equation you are going to use, show clearly how you get to your answer and give the unit.   (4 marks)

  (Total 7 marks)
  AQA specimen question

5 A sky diver jumps from an aeroplane. The graph shows how her vertical velocity varies with time.

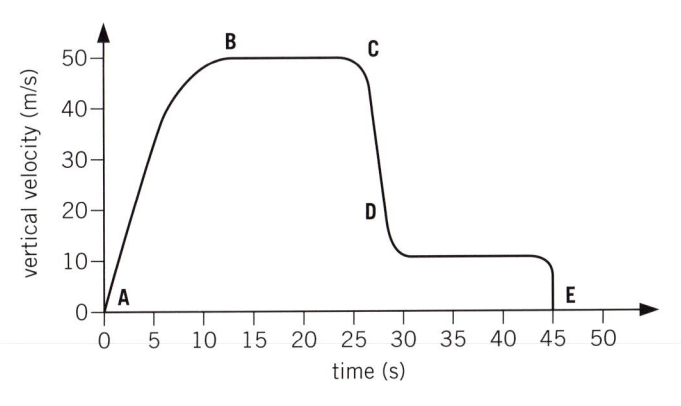

  a What is the skydiver's vertical acceleration between points B and C?   (1 mark)

  b Use your answer to (a) to work out the total resultant force acting on the skydiver between points B and C.   (1 mark)

  c Explain carefully what happens to the skydiver's motion between points C and D. Give reasons for your answer.   (2 marks)

  d The vertical acceleration of the skydiver at point A is 10 m/s². If her mass is 50 kg, what is the resultant force acting on her at this point?

  e At the same instant as the first skydiver leaves the aircraft, another skydiver also jumps out of the same aircraft. He has the same mass as the first skydiver, but uses a parachute with a larger area. Copy the graph and add a line to it to show the vertical velocity of this skydiver as he falls.

6 A student carries out an experiment with a steel ball bearing and a tube of thick oil.

  The diagram shows the apparatus used.

  The student releases the ball bearing and it falls through the oil.

  The forces X and Y act on the ball bearing as it falls through the oil.

  This is shown on the diagram.

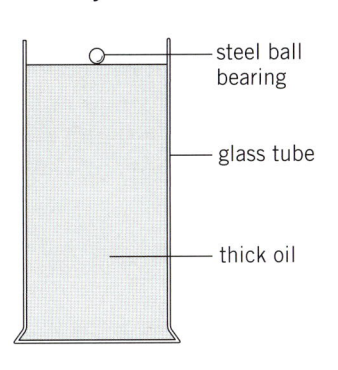

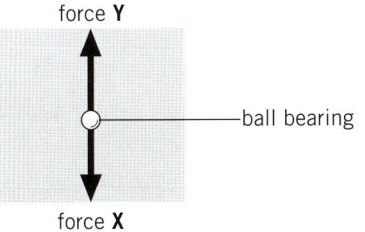

  The graph shows how the speed of the ball bearing changes as it falls through the oil.

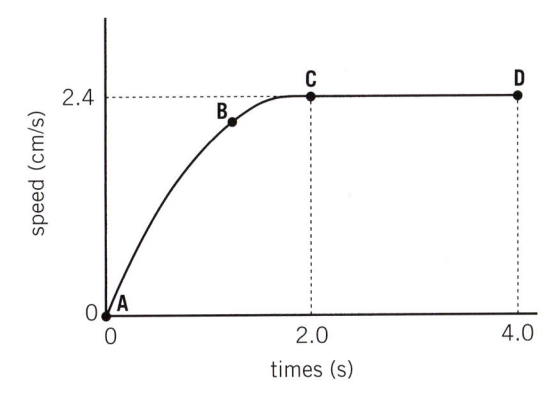

  a **i** What is happening to the speed of the ball bearing between points A and B?   (1 mark)

  Explain, in terms of forces X and Y, why this happens.   (1 mark)

  ii What is happening to the speed of the ball bearing between points C and D?   (1 mark)

  Explain, in terms of forces X and Y, why this happens.   (3 marks)

  b Use the graph to help you to calculate the distance travelled by the ball bearing between points C and D.   (2 marks)

  (Total 8 marks)
  AQA specimen question

Forces and motion

3.1 The behaviour of waves (1)

Studying waves

How can we explain the behaviour of waves on the surface of the sea, the behaviour of light as it travels through space or the behaviour of sound as it is reflected from a hard surface to produce an echo? To do this we need a way to study waves in the laboratory. By understanding the behaviour of waves using simple laboratory models, we can then extend our ideas to situations outside the laboratory.

We can study waves by using ropes or springs, or using water waves travelling across the surface of water in a specially designed tank called a **ripple tank**.

You can make waves travel along a spring in two ways. If you fix one end of the spring and move the other end from side to side (Figure 2) each part of the spring moves from side to side a little after the part of the spring before it. The wave travelling along the spring is called a **transverse** wave, because the wave consists of a series of disturbances made **across** the direction in which the wave itself is moving. (The word 'transverse' means 'across'.) Water waves travelling across the surface of water are also transverse waves. You can see this if you look at a boat on the sea – the waves move along the surface of the water, while the boat bobs up and down.

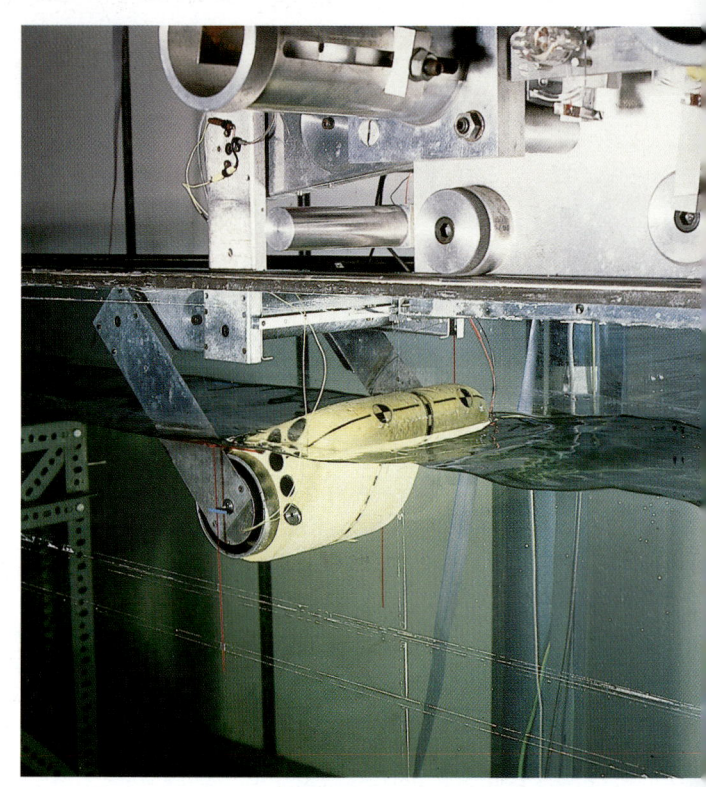

Figure 1: Laboratory models are a very important way for us to understand the behaviour of waves. Here, 'Salter's Duck', a wave energy device, is undergoing tests in a wave tank at Edinburgh University.

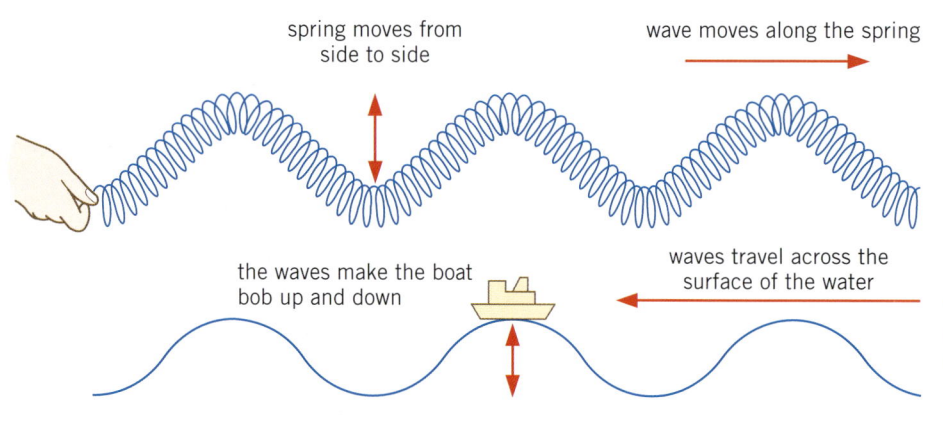

Figure 2: A transverse wave has vibrations that move to and fro **across** the direction in which the wave is travelling.

If you now hold one end of the spring and move your hand backwards and forwards rather than side to side (Figure 3), a different kind of wave travels along the spring. This time each part of the spring moves backwards and forwards, so that the wave consists of a disturbance in which the spring is compressed followed by another disturbance in which that is stretched out. Sound is a longitudinal wave – and so are **shock waves**, the waves that travel through something when it is struck or hit.

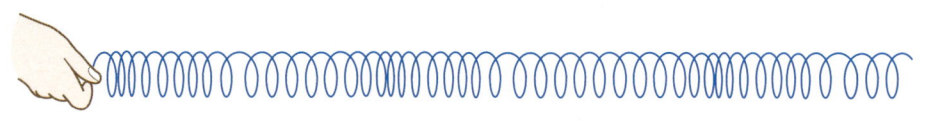

Figure 3: A longitudinal wave has vibrations that move to and fro in the same direction in which the wave is travelling.

Waves

Drawing waves

A transverse wave can be drawn as in Figure 4, just as if you were drawing a wave on the surface of the sea.

Longitudinal waves are more difficult to draw. They can be represented by **wavefronts** (Figure 5(a)). You can imagine each wavefront as a line joining the compressions of a longitudinal wave. Wavefronts can represent transverse waves too. In this case each wavefront is a line joining the crests of a wave as you look down on it (Figure 5(b)).

↑ Figure 4

(a) A longitudinal wave spreads out from a point. The wavefronts pass through the compressions of the wave.

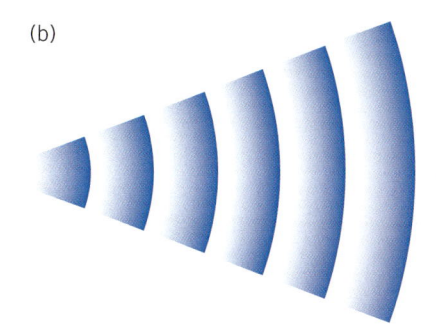

(b) A transverse wave spreads out from a point. The wavefronts pass through the crests of the waves.

↑ Figure 5

Describing waves

Sometimes we need to be able to measure waves. For example, if we want to describe some waves on the sea we would probably want to be able to say how big they are, their speed, and how far apart their crests are. Because we need to be able to make measurements like this for lots of waves, physicists describe waves using four words: **wavelength, frequency, amplitude and wave speed.**

The **wavelength** of a wave tells us the distance between one point on a disturbance and a similar point on the next disturbance. The number of waves that pass a point each second is the **frequency** of the wave, which is measured in hertz (Hz) – so if a wave has a frequency of 20 Hz, it means that 20 waves are passing each second. The maximum disturbance of a wave is called its **amplitude**.

The speed of waves is related to their frequency and wavelength:

wave speed = frequency × wavelength
(metres/second, m/s) (hertz, Hz) (metres, m)

↑ Figure 6

Key Ideas

- There are two types of wave. In **transverse** waves the disturbance is across the direction in which the wave travels. In **longitudinal** waves the disturbance is along the direction in which the wave travels.
- The amplitude of a wave is its maximum disturbance.
- For any wave, wave speed = frequency × wavelength

Example

A wave travels across a pond at a speed of 1.5 m/s. The distance from one crest of the wave to the next is 0.75 m. What is the wave's frequency?

The wavelength of the wave is 0.75 m and its speed is 1.5 m/s. We know that

wave speed = frequency × wavelength

so we can write

1.5 = frequency × 0.75

Dividing each side of this relationship by 0.75 gives

frequency = $\frac{1.5}{0.75}$ Hz

= 2 Hz

The wave's frequency is 2 Hz.

Questions

1. Copy and complete the following table containing information about some water waves and sound waves.

Wavelength (metres)	200		10	0.5		0.1
Frequency (Hz)	0.1	110		3000	4	
Wave speed (m/s)		330	2		5	5000

Waves

3.2 The behaviour of waves (2)

Hearing an echo can be a really strange experience, especially when there is a gap of several seconds between the original sound and the echo itself. Just as an echo is produced when sound is reflected from a hard surface, light is also reflected from surfaces, which is how we see objects that do not produce light themselves.

When a ray of light is reflected from a flat, shiny surface like a plane mirror (the word 'plane' is simply another way of saying 'flat'), the way it is reflected obeys a very simple rule, as Figure 2 shows. A ray of light which meets the mirror at a right angle is called a **normal** ray. Rays that meet the mirror at 90° are always reflected back along the same path.

Light and sound can also be refracted, which means that they change direction when they travel from one substance into another, except when they meet the line between the two substances at right angles. When a ray meets the boundary between two substances along a normal, the ray carries on without a change in direction.

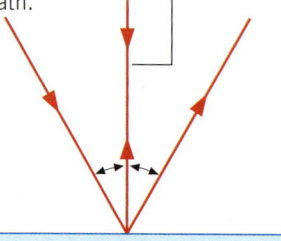

Figure 1: An echo is produced when sound bounces back from a hard surface, like the rocky sides of a mountain.

A **normal** ray is one which meets the mirror at right-angles. A normal ray is always reflected from the mirror back along the same path.

← **Figure 2:** The light ray is reflected from the mirror at the same angle as it arrives.

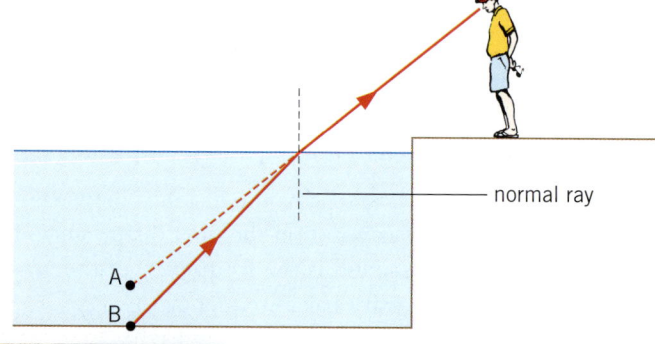

Figure 3: Because it knows that light travels in straight lines, your brain is fooled into thinking that the ray of light coming from the bottom of the swimming pool comes from A instead of B. This is why the pool seems shallower than it really is.

A ripple tank is a useful way to investigate the behaviour of waves (Figure 4).

The vibrating dipper at the top of the picture sends ripples across the surface of the water. A strong beam of light shone through the water can be used to project an image of the ripples on a screen underneath the ripple tank.

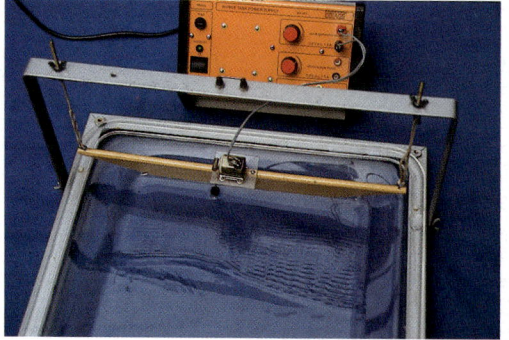

← **Figure 4:** A ripple tank.

Reflection

A straight barrier, like a metal or plastic block, placed in a ripple tank shows that water waves can be reflected. Water waves follow the same rule for reflection as light – the angle of incidence equals the angle of reflection (Figure 5).

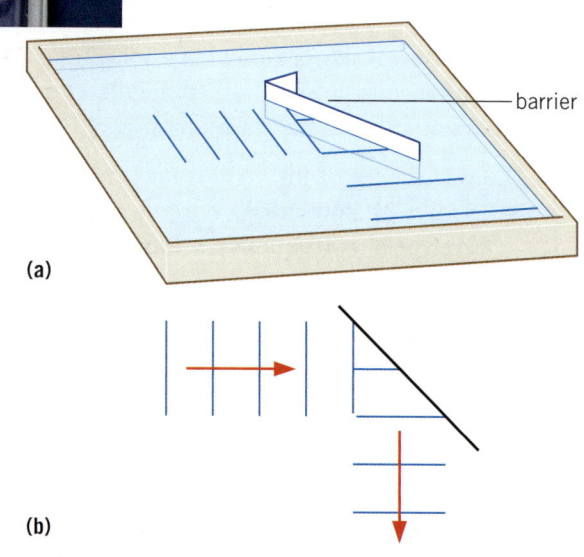

→ **Figure 5:** Reflecting water waves in a ripple tank. As waves hit the barrier they are reflected from it.

Waves

Refraction

The depth of water in which they are travelling affects the speed of water waves – the shallower the water, the slower the waves travel. When the depth of water in a ripple tank is reduced, for example by placing a flat piece of plastic on the bottom of the tank, water waves are refracted.

The reason why refraction happens is all to do with the change of speed. Imagine some cyclists cycling in a row (Figure 7). If they cycle at an angle from a concrete surface onto muddy grass, they will slow down in turn as they meet the grass. This means that the cyclists at one end of the line will slow down before the cyclists at the other end – so the line of cyclists will change direction – and the more they are slowed down, the more the line will bend. Of course, if the line of cyclists meets the edge of the concrete at right angles, they will all cycle onto the mud at the same time. This means that they all change speed at the same time – so there is no change of direction! Waves behave in just the same way – which is why waves travelling along the normal do not get bent.

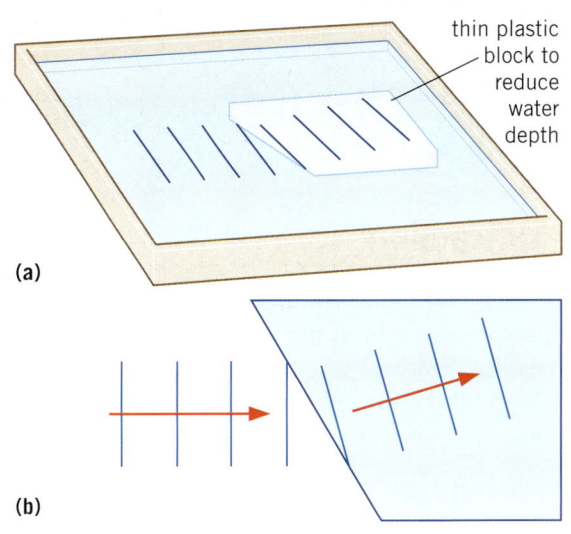

Figure 6: Refraction of water waves in a ripple tank. Because they slow down as they travel over the plastic, the waves change direction, unless they are travelling along the normal.

On a hot day the dark road absorbs energy and heats up the air above it.

The temperature of the air decreases as it rises.

Light travels faster in the hot air just above the surface of the road.

A ray of light from the sky gets refracted so that someone standing on the road sees it as if it is coming from the surface of the road.

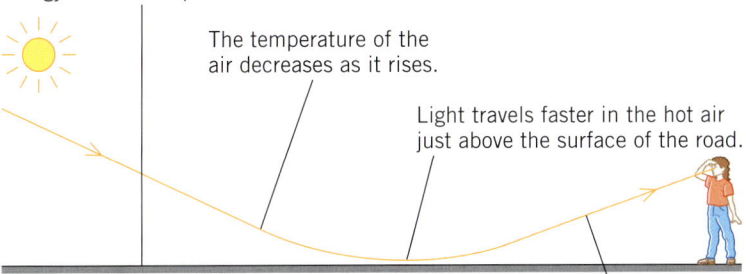

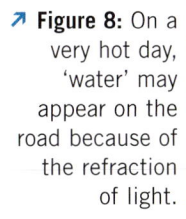

Figure 7: A row of cyclists may not seem much like a wave – but both will change direction due to a change in speed.

Figure 8: On a very hot day, 'water' may appear on the road because of the refraction of light.

Questions

1. A ray of light hits a mirror at an angle of 30°. At what angle is it reflected?
2. A person shouts at a cliff and hears an echo exactly 3 seconds later. If the speed of sound is 340 m/s, how far is the person from the cliff?
3. As waves on the sea get closer to the shore, their speed decreases as the water gets shallower. Explain why waves on the sea meet the shore at right angles, or nearly so.

Key Ideas

- When a light ray is reflected from a plane surface, the angle at which it leaves is the same as the angle at which it arrives.
- Waves may be reflected and refracted.
- Reflection happens when a wave bounces off a solid object.
- Refraction happens when a wave changes speed.

Waves

3.3 The behaviour of waves (3)

Diffraction

When waves pass through a narrow gap, they tend to spread out from the edges. This behaviour is called **diffraction**, and happens most when the size of the gap is about the same as the wavelength of the wave passing through it.

Diffraction plays an important role in the reception of certain types of radio waves. These waves are diffracted by objects like hills and large buildings, which make it possible for someone to hear a radio programme even though the radio transmitter is hidden by obstacles.

(a)

Waves as energy carriers

The waves that pound the seashore have travelled many miles. Waves on the surface of the sea are produced many miles out, where strong winds whip up the surface and disturb it from a flat surface. The kinetic energy of the wind is carried across the sea by the waves. Although the waves travel across the sea, because water waves are transverse waves the sea only moves up and down. This illustrates an important point that is true about all waves – waves transfer energy from one place to another without any matter being transferred.

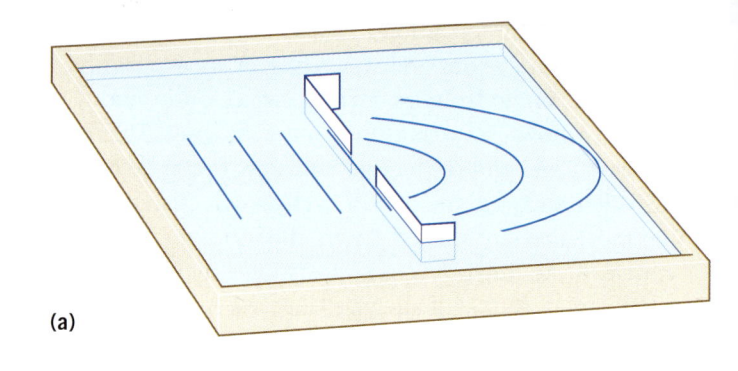

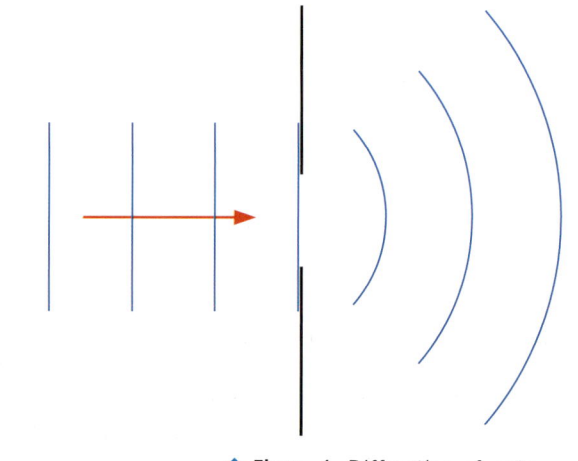

(b)

↑ **Figure 1:** Diffraction of water waves. Diffraction also happens as waves move past an obstacle.

← **Figure 2:** These waves have transferred energy over a distance of many tens or even hundreds of miles.

44   Waves

Ideas and Evidence

Light – is it a particle, is it a wave … ?

It took many years for our current ideas about light to be developed. In ancient times, some people believed that objects could be seen only when they were touched by light rays given off by the eyes, while others thought that visibility was due to the light rays given off by objects meeting other light rays given off by the eyes.

↑ **Figure 3:** Ancient ideas about light were far from our current ideas, which developed over many years.

By the end of the 17th century, there were two competing theories about light. The great physicist Sir Isaac Newton argued that light consisted of a stream of tiny particles. He argued that if light was a wave, then we should expect the edges of the shadows of objects formed on a sunny day to have 'fuzzy' edges, rather than the sharp edges that we actually see. In opposition to Newton, the Dutch physicist Christiaan Huygens believed that the behaviour of light was best explained in terms of waves, an idea that was supported by other prominent scientists of the time, including Robert Hooke and Robert Boyle. Hooke and Boyle also showed that light behaving as a wave provided a very convincing explanation for the colours that are produced when a thin film of oil floats on the surface of water.

At the time, no one realised that only very tiny objects are able to diffract light, and Newton's arguments carried the day. For the next 100 years or so it was accepted that light behaved as a particle. However, work carried out by Thomas Young published in 1802 made it impossible to continue to think of light as anything other than a wave, and ideas slowly began to change. The final confirmation of light as a wave came some fifty years later, when the French physicist Léon Foucault showed that the speed of light in water is slower than its speed in air.

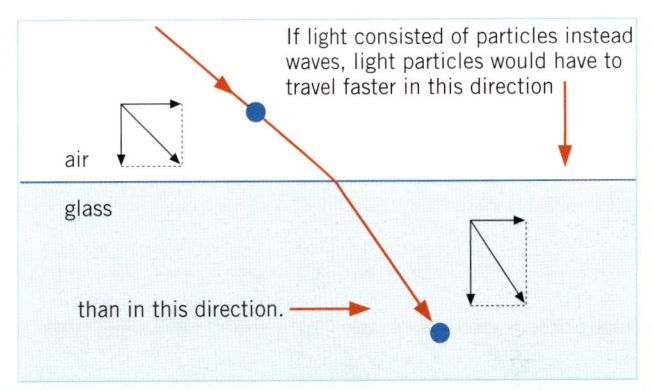

↑ **Figure 4:** Refraction of light in the particle model requires light to travel faster in water or glass than it does in air. In addition, this change of speed must occur in one direction only. Foucault was able to show that light does not behave like this – providing conclusive support for the wave model.

Intriguingly, the final part of the story comes back to Newton. In the early part of the 20th century Albert Einstein was studying the way in which light shone on a metal surface can knock electrons out of it. He found that the behaviour of light under these circumstances can only be understood if it is thought of as a particle rather than a wave! Physicists now think of light as behaving sometimes like a wave, and sometimes like a particle – behaviour that is called **wave-particle duality**. For most of the time (which is all of the time as far as GCSE Physics is concerned!) light behaves like a wave – but there are times when we have to think of it as a particle.

Questions

1. 'Long wave' radio waves have a wavelength of about 1 km. Why can you still receive Long Wave radio broadcasts even when there is a hill between you and the transmitter?

2. A simple 'crystal radio' receiver enables radio broadcasts to be heard using earphones, even though it contains no battery. Where does the energy come from that produces the sound waves from the earphones?

3. Although Newton's ideas about light were wrong, it took many years before people chose not to accept them. Suggest some possible reasons for this.

Key Ideas

- Diffraction happens when a wave travels through a gap or past an object that is about the same size as its wavelength.

- Waves transfer energy from a source to other places without transferring any matter.

Waves 45

3.4 Light waves

Like water waves, light can be reflected and refracted – and diffracted too – evidence that it is also a wave.

Light waves are transverse waves that can travel through a vacuum. They are refracted when they travel from one substance into another (for example from air into glass) because they travel at different speeds in different substances.

Figure 1 shows how a ray of light travelling from air into glass bends towards the normal, unless the ray is travelling along the normal. The same thing happens when light travels from air into water, because light travels more slowly in both glass and water than it does in air. Light travelling from water or glass into air speeds up, so a ray of light leaving glass or water bends away from the normal. Figure 2 shows what happens to the light leaving a lamp below the surface of a swimming pool. When light (or any other wave) is reflected like this we call it **total internal reflection.**

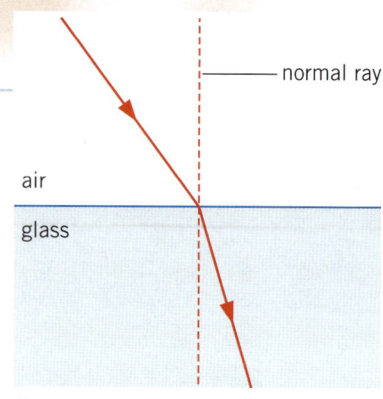

Figure 1: Light travels more slowly in glass than it does in air. The refraction that this change of speeds causes means that the direction of a ray of light changes as it travels from air into glass.

(a) This ray splits. A little bit of light is reflected back into the water, while most is refracted and leaves the pool. angle < critical angle

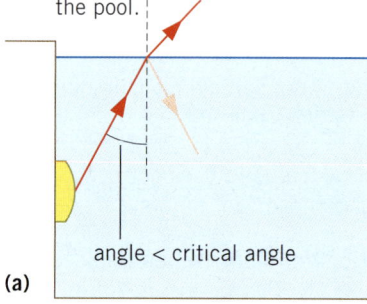

(b) This ray also splits. Quite a bit of the light is reflected back into the water, while the rest is refracted and leaves the pool, travelling along the surface of the water. angle = critical angle

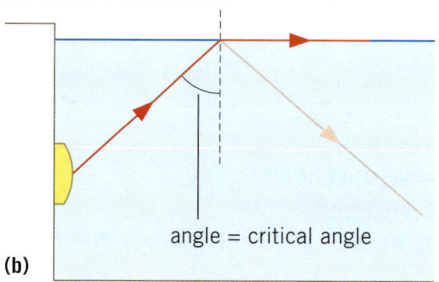

(c) Here the angle at which the ray meets the surface is even larger, so none of the light can leave the pool. All of the light is reflected back into the water – **total internal reflection**. angle > critical angle

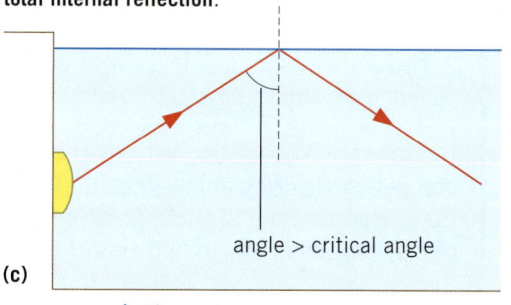

Figure 2: Three rays of light leaving a lamp below the surface of a swimming pool illustrate how total internal reflection happens.

The angle at which the ray leaving the denser medium travels along the surface (Figure 2(b)) is called the **critical angle**. The critical angle varies according to the material – different materials have different critical angles:

Material	Critical angle
water	49°
glass	41°
diamond	24°

Optical instruments like binoculars, cameras and periscopes use glass prisms in which light is reflected by means of total internal reflection. Using prisms in these instruments has big advantages over using ordinary mirrors, which can lead to a faint second image appearing near the main image, which could be very distracting for the person using the instrument. This faint second image happens as a small amount of the light is reflected from the glass surface of the mirror while most of the light travels through the glass and is reflected from the shiny surface behind the glass. This problem can be prevented by putting the shiny surface on the **front** of the glass, rather than the back, but the shiny surface is then very easily damaged. Prisms avoid this difficulty.

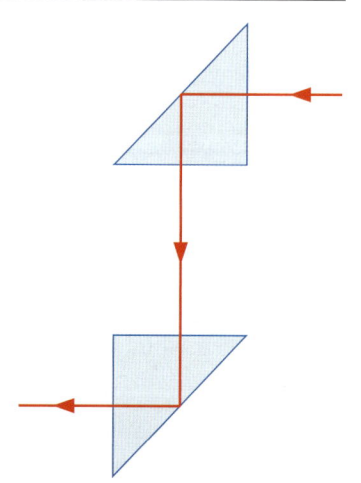

Figure 3: Two prisms arranged like this can be used as a periscope.

Figure 4: It is the low value for the critical angle of diamond that gives diamonds their special sparkle.

Waves

Total internal reflection can also be used to make light travel along very thin fibres made of glass – these fibres are called **optical fibres**. Optical fibres are used in equipment like **endoscopes**, which doctors can use to see inside a patient's body without actually cutting them open. They are also used in telephone and other communication systems (see page 52).

Finally, light is also diffracted, although its very small wavelength (less than one thousandth of a millimetre) means that very small gaps or objects are needed before diffraction can be seen. Radio waves have wavelengths of many metres and may be diffracted by hills and buildings.

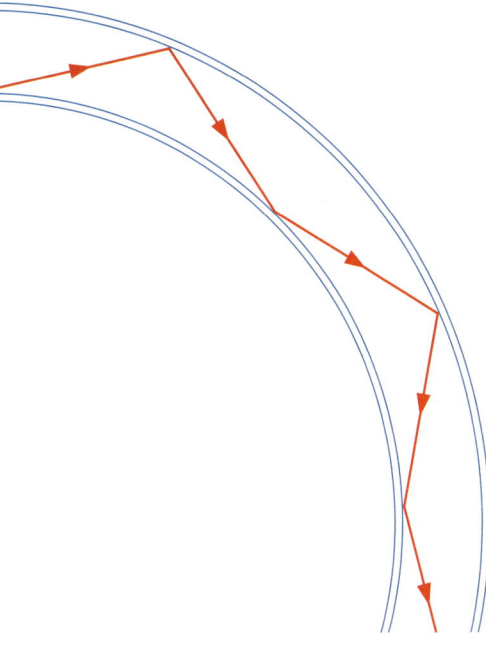

← **Figure 5:** As light travels along an optical fibre it is totally internally reflected each time it hits the wall of the fibre. In this way, the light stays inside the fibre, which is sometimes called a **light pipe**. The fibre must be thin enough to keep the angle that the light meets the glass above the critical angle. The fibre must not bend too sharply either – this might damage it, and could lead to the angle that the light meets the glass being less than the critical angle.

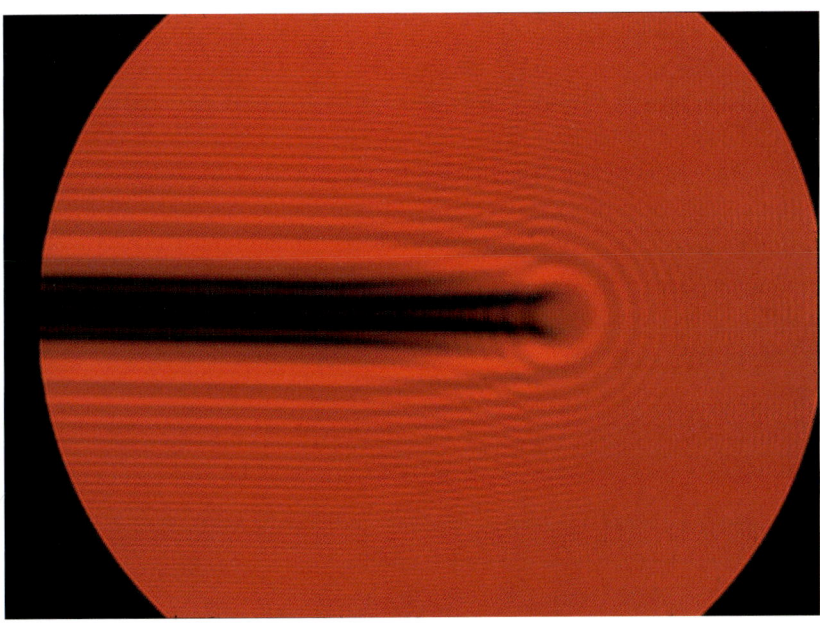

→ **Figure 6:** Light is diffracted by the point of a pin.

Questions

1. A refraction trick – put a cup or mug on a table, and put a coin in the bottom of it. Now ask a friend to look at the coin and then move slowly away from the cup until the coin has just disappeared. Now fill the cup with water – and your friend will be able to see the coin! Explain how this trick works, using clear, labelled diagrams.

2. Sound travels faster in water than in air. A swimmer on the bottom of a still, perfectly quiet swimming pool cannot hear her coach shouting to her – why not?

Key Ideas

- Light waves are transverse waves that can travel through a vacuum.
- Like other waves, light may be reflected, refracted and diffracted.
- When light travels from glass or water into air, it may undergo **total internal reflection**.
- Light can be made to travel down an optical fibre, undergoing total internal reflection each time it meets the wall of the fibre.
- Optical fibres are used in telecommunication and in medical instruments for seeing inside a patient's body.

Waves

3.5 The electromagnetic spectrum

A rainbow is produced when white light is split by diffraction into light of different colours as it passes through raindrops. In the science laboratory a prism will do the job of a raindrop, and we can observe what happens as the light is diffracted. The colours that are produced are called a spectrum. The colours in the **spectrum** are usually said to be red, orange, yellow, green, blue, indigo, and violet – how many can you see?

The colours split up because different colours of light travel at different speeds in water and glass. This means that they are refracted by different amounts, so they bend through different angles – red least and violet most.

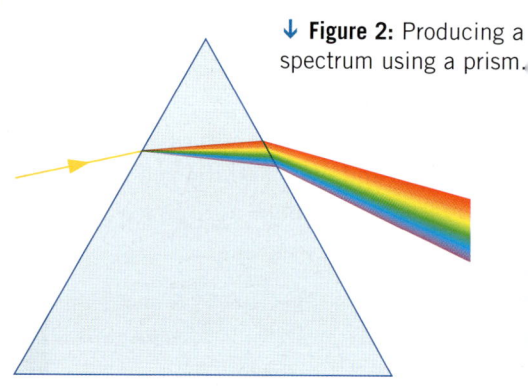

The spectrum of different colours of light belongs to a family of waves which we can see, and which we call **visible light**. But visible light itself is just part of a much larger family of waves called the **electromagnetic spectrum**, made up of many different types of electromagnetic waves.

All electromagnetic waves travel through a vacuum at the same speed at about 300 000 kilometres per second – the speed of light. However, they all have different wavelengths and frequencies which affect how they behave. Despite their differences, all electromagnetic waves carry energy, which can raise the temperature of anything that absorbs them, and they can all create an alternating current with the same frequency as the electromagnetic wave itself. (This is how a radio aerial picks up radio waves.) Like light, all electromagnetic waves can be reflected, refracted and diffracted.

The electromagnetic spectrum goes far beyond the end of the visible spectrum, as Figure 3 shows.

↑ **Figure 1:** The beauty of a rainbow – all done by waves!

↓ **Figure 2:** Producing a spectrum using a prism.

↓ **Figure 3:** The effects and uses of different types of electromagnetic radiation depend on their properties.

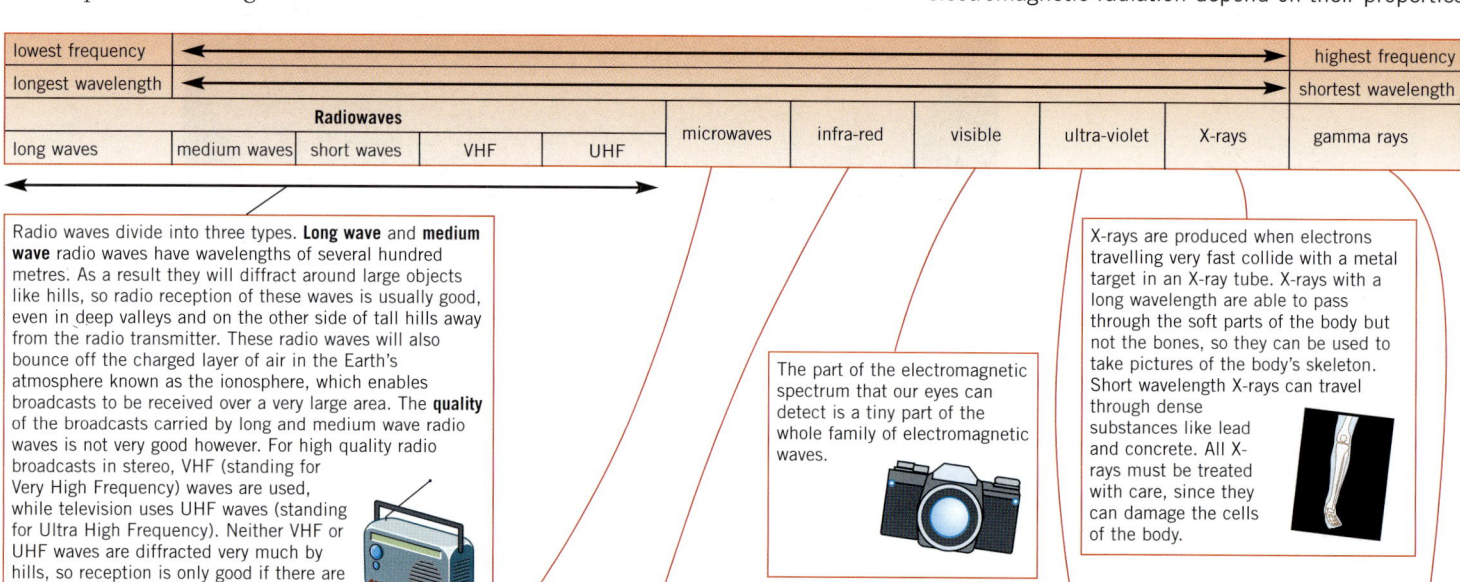

lowest frequency											highest frequency
longest wavelength											shortest wavelength
	Radiowaves					microwaves	infra-red	visible	ultra-violet	X-rays	gamma rays
long waves	medium waves	short waves	VHF	UHF							

Radio waves divide into three types. **Long wave** and **medium wave** radio waves have wavelengths of several hundred metres. As a result they will diffract around large objects like hills, so radio reception of these waves is usually good, even in deep valleys and on the other side of tall hills away from the radio transmitter. These radio waves will also bounce off the charged layer of air in the Earth's atmosphere known as the ionosphere, which enables broadcasts to be received over a very large area. The **quality** of the broadcasts carried by long and medium wave radio waves is not very good however. For high quality radio broadcasts in stereo, VHF (standing for Very High Frequency) waves are used, while television uses UHF waves (standing for Ultra High Frequency). Neither VHF or UHF waves are diffracted very much by hills, so reception is only good if there are not many large obstacles between the transmitter and receiver.

Microwaves pass easily through the Earth's atmosphere, and are used for carrying telephone calls and other signals between the ground and satellites in orbit round the Earth, and between large cities. Some wavelengths of microwave radiation are strongly absorbed by water. They are used in microwave cookers to heat and cook food.

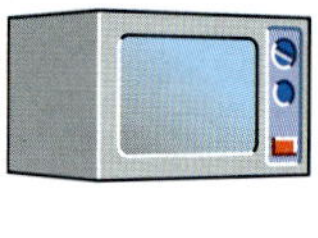

Hot objects all radiate infra-red waves. Infra-red waves are used in cookers, grills and toasters, and in the remote controls that we use to change TV channels and start our video recorders working.

The part of the electromagnetic spectrum that our eyes can detect is a tiny part of the whole family of electromagnetic waves.

Ultraviolet radiation cannot be seen, although there is a great deal of it in sunlight. Special tubes in sun beds produce ultraviolet waves, to produce a chemical in the skin that turns it brown. Some chemicals absorb ultraviolet light and emit the energy again as visible light – this is called **fluorescence**. These chemicals are used to mark property in a way that cannot be seen without using ultraviolet light, so that it can be identified if it is lost or stolen. They are also used in washing powders to make white clothes look especially clean.

X-rays are produced when electrons travelling very fast collide with a metal target in an X-ray tube. X-rays with a long wavelength are able to pass through the soft parts of the body but not the bones, so they can be used to take pictures of the body's skeleton. Short wavelength X-rays can travel through dense substances like lead and concrete. All X-rays must be treated with care, since they can damage the cells of the body.

Gamma rays have the shortest wavelength of all the electromagnetic waves. They are produced by changes in the nuclei of radioactive atoms. Gamma rays can seriously damage the cells of living things. This property can be used to kill harmful organisms in food and on instruments used in hospital operating theatres, and to kill cancer cells.

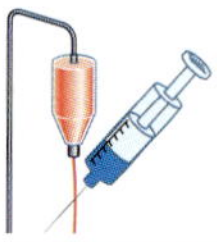

Waves

Science people

While some people were busy investigating the properties of electromagnetic waves at the end of the 19th century, others were busy trying to put the waves to practical use. One such person was the Italian, Guglielmo Marconi.

Marconi first became interested in using radio waves to send messages, and by 1895 had managed to send radio signals over a distance of a few kilometres. Four years later he sent signals across the English Channel, and in 1901 successfully communicated across the Atlantic, sending a signal from Poldhu, in Cornwall to St John's, in Newfoundland, Canada.

The British and Italian navies were soon using Marconi's system. By 1907 a transatlantic wireless telegraph service was set up for public use. Marconi was awarded the 1909 Nobel Prize for Physics for his pioneering work in transmitting radio waves.

↑ **Figure 4:** Marconi used a kite to lift the transmitting aerial about 100 metres above the ground.

Key Ideas

- Electromagnetic radiation has a wide range of wavelengths. The wavelength of the radiation has a direct effect on its properties, and on the way it is useful.
- When electromagnetic radiation is absorbed by an object, it may increase the object's temperature, and it may produce an alternating current in the object which has the same frequency as the radiation itself.

Questions

1 Copy and complete the table.

Type of radiation	Radio waves		Visible light		X-rays
Approximate wavelength				10^{-7} to 10^{-8} metres	
Uses		Carry telephone calls between ground and satellites			

2 Marconi used a kite to lift the aerial of his radio transmitter as high above the ground as possible. Suggest a reason why he did this.

3 Figure 5 shows a transmitter broadcasting a radio signal. Copy and complete the diagram to show how the signal reaches the distant radio receiver.

→ **Figure 5**

Waves

3.6 The effect of electromagnetic waves on cells

Microwaves

Microwaves are strongly absorbed by water and other molecules in cells. This heats the cell, which may be killed or damaged by the rise in temperature. (Powerful radio waves can have the same effect – one good reason why climbing up the mast of a radio transmitter is not a good idea.) Microwaves can travel several centimetres into the body, damaging cells below the surface of the skin.
Mobile phones use microwave radiation to transmit and receive the signal. Although the strength of this signal is very small, some scientists have expressed concerns about the safety of using mobile telephones heavily over long periods. Other scientists think that there is no need to worry and point out that the intensity of the radiation is well below current safety limits.

Infra-red waves

The body senses infra-red waves as heat. Cells below the skin are unlikely to be damaged by infra-red waves, as they are absorbed by the skin.

Ultraviolet waves

penetrate the skin, and are absorbed by some of the chemicals inside cells. Dark pigment within skin cells helps to protect cells from damage by ultraviolet waves.

X-rays and gamma rays

can both pass through the body, although some of their energy is absorbed by cells.

Cell damage

High doses of ultraviolet waves, X-rays and gamma rays can all kill cells. Doctors kill cancer cells by using gamma rays, but all of these **ionising radiations** can kill normal cells too in high enough doses. Lower doses may also cause normal cells to turn into cancer cells, when they grow and divide uncontrollably within the body.

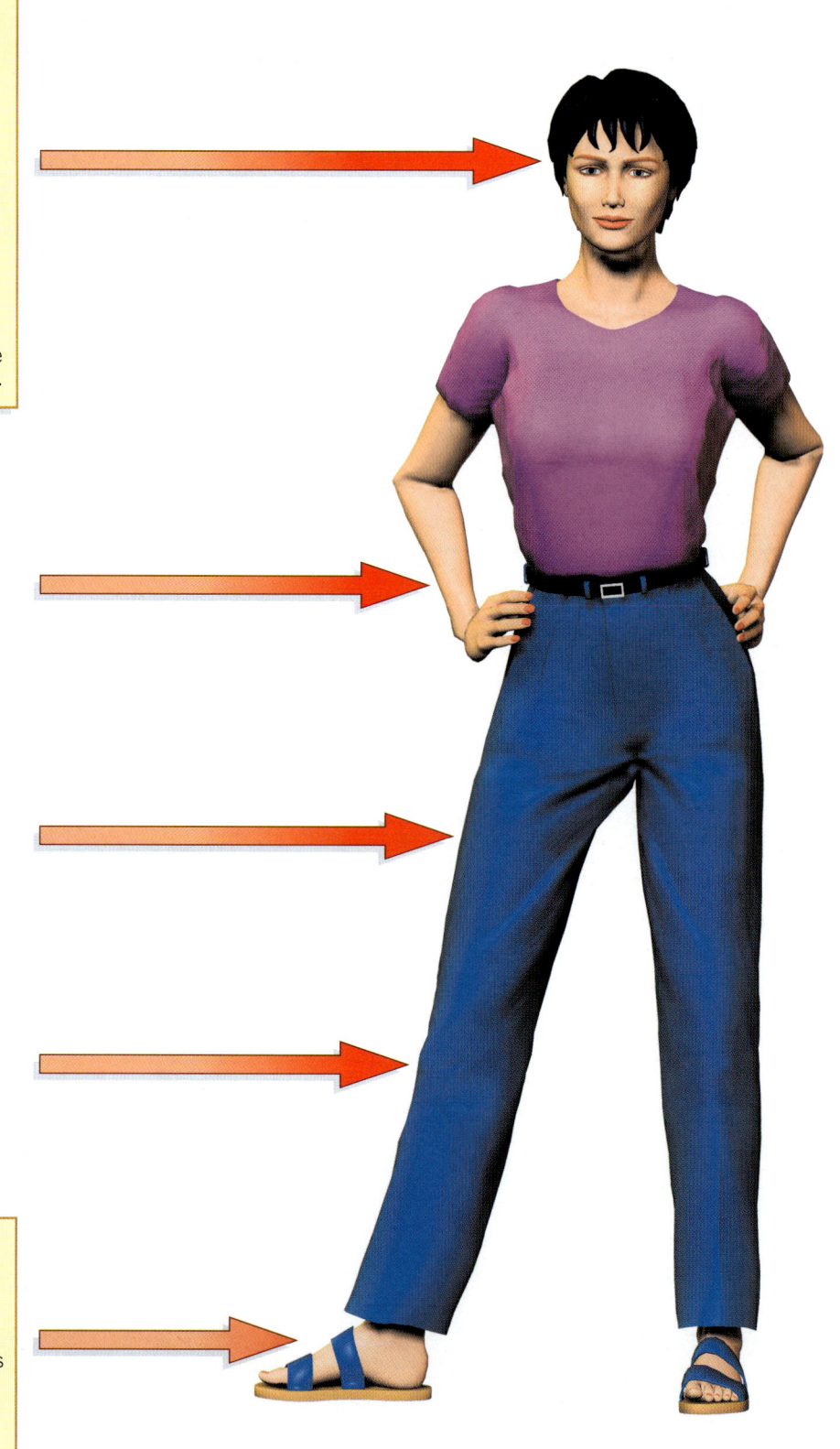

↑**Figure 1:** All electromagnetic waves have an effect on cells, even radio waves.

Ideas and Evidence

Mobile phones

Not just a way of keeping in touch, but a vital fashion accessory – that's how many people feel about the mobile phone that goes with them wherever they are. But some people are concerned about the effect that mobile phones may have on our health. Although no evidence has been found to show that mobile phones can cause damage to health, it is very difficult to prove that there is no risk at all.

Concern about mobile phones comes from the fact that the phones use electromagnetic radiation with a frequency around 1 GHz (10^9 Hz), just below the microwave region of the electromagnetic spectrum. Radio signals are transmitted from the phone to the nearest base station and incoming signals are sent from the base station to the phone at a slightly different frequency. Once the signal from the telephone reaches a base station it is fed into the main telephone network, and then is carried by cables.

Like all waves, electromagnetic waves carry energy. If the energy carried by the electromagnetic waves transmitted from a mobile phone is absorbed by the person using it, there is a possibility that it may harm them. However, scientists are unable to say whether this is very likely or not, although some think that children may be particularly at risk. Because children and adolescents are still growing, their heads are smaller and their skulls are thinner. Both of these factors may make them more vulnerable to microwave radiation.

↑**Figure 2:** The signal from a mobile phone is transmitted to the nearest base station using electromagnetic waves.

Questions

1 Look at Figure 3. Make a list of all the different kinds of electromagnetic waves that the people are exposed to, and describe how they can limit their exposure.

Key Ideas

- Different types of electromagnetic radiation affect living cells in different ways, and may damage or even kill them.

2 Scientists are most concerned about the dangers of young people using mobile phones excessively. Design a poster aimed at young people, setting out the arguments for being cautious about the amount they use mobile phones. As well as seeking to get your message across, you should include information about the effects of electromagnetic waves in your poster in order to explain the possible dangers as clearly as you can.

← Figure 3

Waves

3.7 EM waves and communications

During the 19th century, it became possible to send messages over long distances by converting the information into electrical signals. At first words were sent by coding letters using a series of dots and dashes (short and long electrical pulses), a system known as **Morse code**, after its inventor, Samuel Morse. Later it became possible to send these signals using electromagnetic waves to carry them.

A great deal of information transmitted along wires or using electromagnetic waves is sent as an **analogue** signal, which means that the signal 'looks like' the information that produced it (Figure 1).

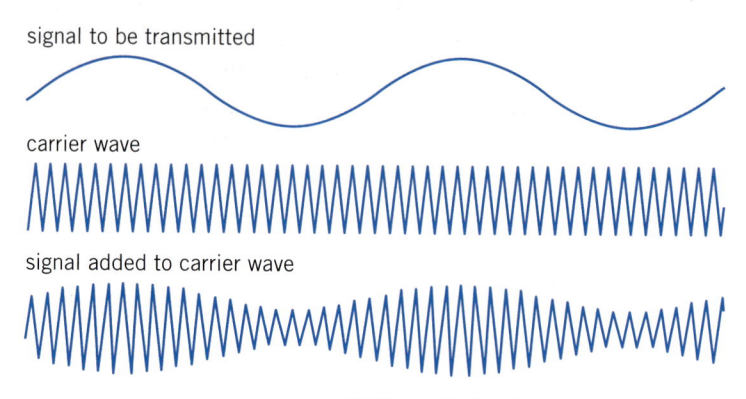

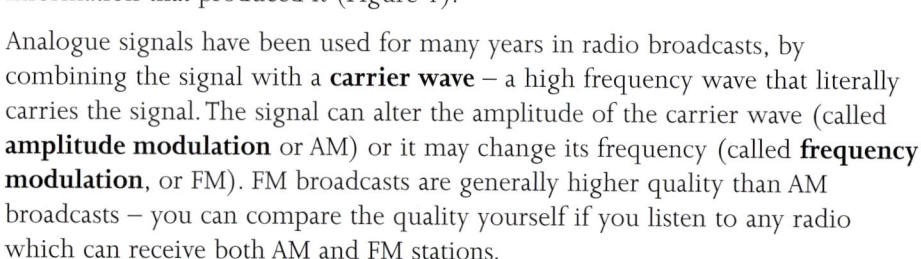

Analogue signals have been used for many years in radio broadcasts, by combining the signal with a **carrier wave** – a high frequency wave that literally carries the signal. The signal can alter the amplitude of the carrier wave (called **amplitude modulation** or AM) or it may change its frequency (called **frequency modulation**, or FM). FM broadcasts are generally higher quality than AM broadcasts – you can compare the quality yourself if you listen to any radio which can receive both AM and FM stations.

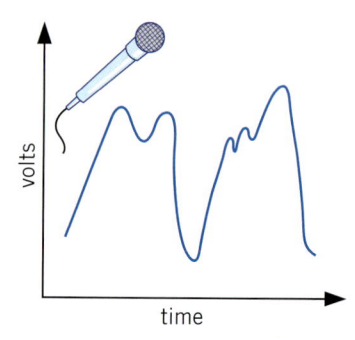

Another way of sending signals is to chop them up and code them as a series of pulses, rather like the original Morse code. These pulses may consist of flashes of light or infra-red waves sent along optical fibres, or they may be made up of electrical signals carried through a wire – or they could be a radio wave travelling through the atmosphere. Figure 3 shows a signal like this, which is called a **digital** signal. Notice how the signal has only two possible values – **On** or **Off** – compared to the analogue signal, which can have any value between an upper and a lower limit.

Digital signals have two big advantages over analogue signals. First, the signals are of much higher quality, because noise and interference picked up by the signal does not change the information that it carries. Second, a particular cable, optical fibre or carrier wave is able to carry more information if it is transmitted as a digital signal than if it is transmitted as an analogue signal. In this way a simple copper cable can carry many hundreds of telephone calls at the same time.

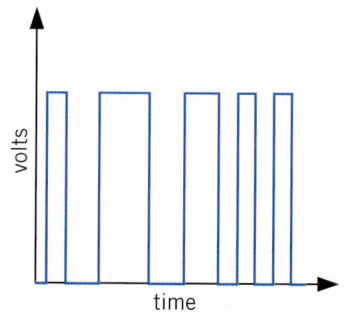

Figure 1: An electromagnetic wave used to carry a signal is known as a carrier wave.

Figure 2: The output from a microphone can be plotted on a graph like this, showing how the voltage first increases, then decreases and then increases again.

Figure 3: A digital signal consists of a series of pulses, much like Morse code.

H As a signal travels it becomes weaker. It also picks up noise, which distorts it and tends to 'cover up' the wanted part of the signal. You can hear this effect if you listen to an AM broadcast from a distant radio station – the signal is very faint, and it is often difficult to hear it due to hisses, pops, crackles and other noises introduced as the radio wave travels through the Earth's atmosphere. To be able to be heard, the signal must be amplified. Unfortunately, this also amplifies the noise. If an analogue signal has to travel a long distance (through a cable under the Atlantic Ocean between the UK and America, for example) it may need to be amplified several times. Figure 4 shows this happening.

Waves

Figure 4: Amplifying an analogue signal several times means that the noise is amplified too – and eventually the wanted part of the signal almost disappears.

Now compare the situation with a digital signal. This consists of a series of pulses, where there is either a signal at a given instant or there is not. As it travels, the strength of the signal decreases and it also picks up noise. However, it is still possible to detect whether there is a pulse at a given instant or not, so the original signal can very easily be produced again. (This is called **regenerating** the signal.)

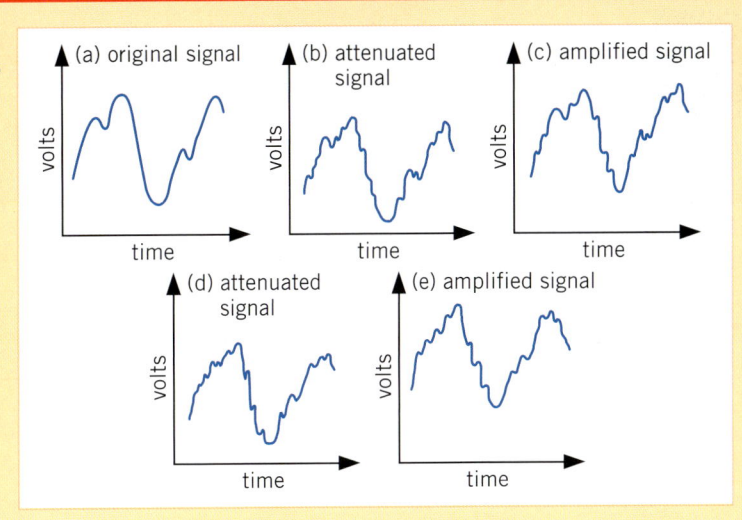

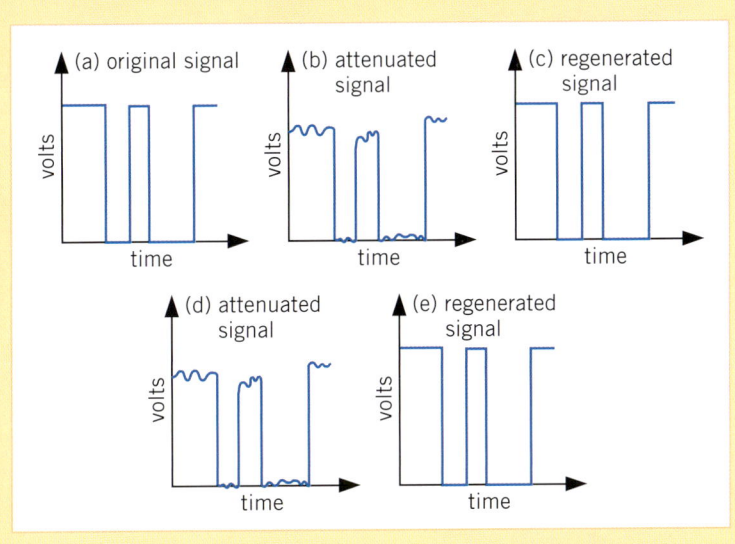

Figure 5: The high quality of a digital signal is due to the fact that the original signal is always reproduced without the noise.

You can very easily simulate the way that the quality of an analogue signal is reduced as it is amplified over and over again. First record a few seconds of speech onto a cassette tape using an ordinary cassette recorder. Now copy the speech on this tape onto another tape and repeat the process a few more times. When you listen to the copies you have made, you will hear how the quality of the signal decreases each time it is re-recorded. As each new copy is made the noise is amplified as much as the signal, and if you do this enough times, you will find that the speech you first recorded almost disappears! Sound engineers talk about the 'signal-to-noise ratio' of a signal, which is a measure of its quality – the lower the signal-to-noise ratio, the lower the quality of the signal.

Ideas and Evidence

Modern communication technology enables us to communicate easily and quickly with people on the other side of the world in a way that only fifty years ago would have been thought impossible. This has changed the way we live and work in many ways, including the way that scientists are able to share expert knowledge with one another.

For example, a surgeon in one country can help with an operation being carried out by someone in another country. Pictures of the patient, taken by cameras both outside and inside the body, are sent from the operating theatre to the watching surgeon. This surgeon is able to talk to the people performing the operation and advise them what to do, making highly specialised knowledge available where and when it is most needed.

Key Ideas

- Electromagnetic waves may be used to transmit information from one place to another.
- Information may be transmitted as **analogue** or **digital** signals. Digital signals have the advantage that they are higher quality and more information can be carried in a given time.

Questions

1 Apart from the hazard of falling, it can be very dangerous to climb the mast of a radio transmitter while it is broadcasting radio waves. Explain why.

2 Why will the recording demonstration described above not work if you use a digital tape recorder?

Waves

3.8 Sound waves

Sound is an example of a longitudinal wave. Unlike light, sound cannot travel through a vacuum. Just like light however, sound can be reflected and refracted, can undergo total internal reflection, and can be diffracted too.

Objects produce sound when they are vibrating. The faster an object vibrates, the higher the pitch of the sound that is produced, while the larger the amplitude of the vibrations, the louder the sound.

Electronic circuits provide us with an easy way to produce sounds of different loudness and pitch. For example, the loudspeaker in a radio is driven by an electronic circuit which amplifies the electrical signals picked up by the aerial. The electronic circuit produces electrical signals that make the loudspeaker cone move in and out, making a longitudinal sound wave travel through the air (Figure 2).

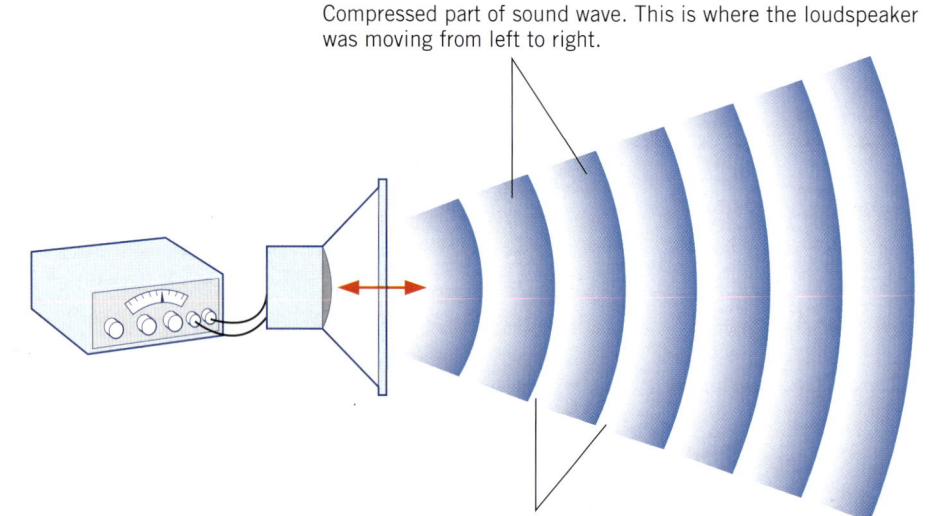

↑ **Figure 1:** In foggy weather this lighthouse emits very loud sounds with a very low pitch from its foghorn. Low-pitched sounds are not absorbed very well by fog, so they travel a long way.

Compressed part of sound wave. This is where the loudspeaker was moving from left to right.

Stretched part part of sound wave. This is where the loudspeaker was moving from right to left.

← **Figure 2:** An electronic circuit can be used to drive a loudspeaker, producing a sound wave.

Electronic circuits can also be used to detect and measure sound waves. A simple way of doing this is to connect a microphone to an instrument called an **oscilloscope**. This produces a trace of the wave on a screen, so that its amplitude and frequency can be measured. (See page 12.)

If the frequency of a sound wave lies between about 20 Hz and 20 000 Hz, it may be detected by the human ear – although the range of frequencies that we can detect changes with age, so that children can hear sounds with higher frequencies that older people (like your teacher!) cannot hear. Sounds with a frequency above 20 000 Hz cannot be heard by humans at all, and are called **ultrasound**, or **ultrasonic waves**.

Ultrasonic waves are produced from the electrical oscillations made by electronic circuits, but instead of a loudspeaker turning the electrical signals into longitudinal waves, special crystals are used. Ultrasonic waves can be used to clean sensitive and delicate parts of equipment. The parts to be cleaned are placed in a bath of liquid, and ultrasonic waves are then passed through it. The waves literally shake the dirt off the equipment, cleaning it without the need to take it apart. The shaking effect of ultrasonic waves can also be used to make two liquids mix when they would not normally do so, producing something called an emulsion. This is how homogenised milk (milk in which the cream and milk do not separate) is made.

Waves

Ultrasound can also be used to clean dirty objects that would otherwise be difficult to clean, perhaps because they are delicate or have an intricate shape that would make them 'fiddly' to clean any other way. Ultrasonic waves can be used to help chemicals mix together, for example when DNA is taken from a sample of human tissue. Perhaps the most well known use of ultrasound is in pre-natal scanning, producing an image of a baby as it develops in its mother's womb, to check that there are no problems.

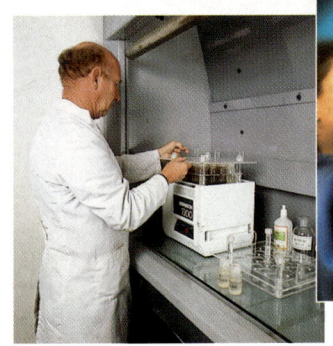

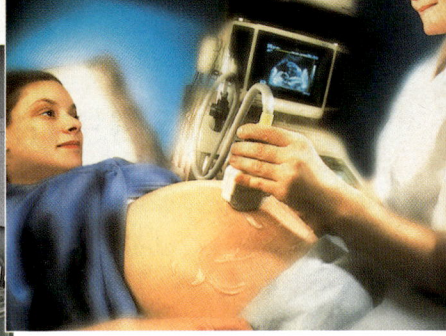

Figure 3: Two very different uses of ultrasound.

H

Using ultrasonic waves to 'see' makes use of the echoes produced whenever the waves pass from one medium into another – for example from air into water, or from fatty tissue to muscle inside the body. By measuring the time taken for these echoes to return from where they happen to a detector, the distance that the echo has travelled can be measured (Figure 4).

The probe produces and detects ultrasonic waves. It is placed on the skin of the mother's stomach, with a little jelly to help the ultrasonic waves travel from the probe into the skin. Electronic circuits measure the time taken for ultrasonic waves to return after bouncing off either side of the baby's head. More complex electronic circuits can be used to build up a picture of the baby, like that in Figure 5.

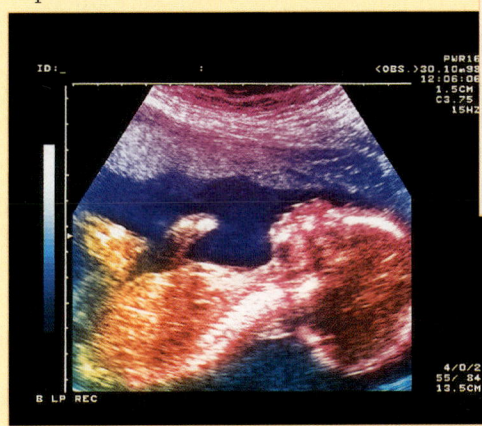

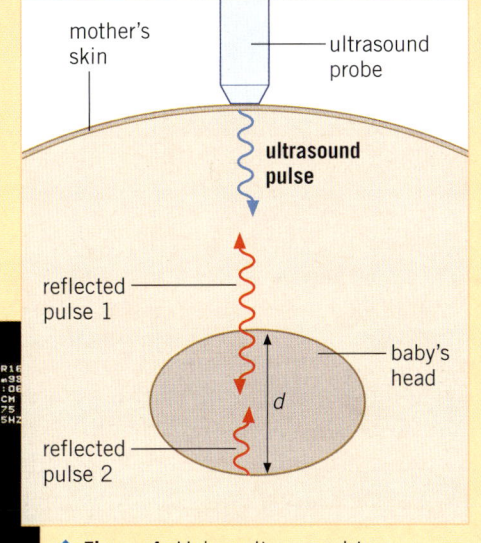

Figure 4: Using ultrasound to measure the diameter of an unborn baby's head.

Figure 5: This ultrasound scan of a baby clearly shows the baby's head (on the right of the picture) and spine.

Questions

1. Why can sound not travel through a vacuum?
2. In an ultrasound scan of an unborn baby's head, two ultrasound echoes are detected, 0.008 seconds apart. The speed of sound through human tissue is about 1500 m/s.
   a. Explain how the diameter of the baby's head can be calculated from this information.
   b. Calculate the diameter of the baby's head.
3. A fishing trawler uses pulses of sound to locate shoals of fish. Sound travels through water at a speed of 1500 m/s.
   a. A pulse of sound is produced by the trawler. It travels down to the seabed and back again in 0.4 s. How deep is the sea at this point?
   b. A little later the trawler is above a shoal of fish. A pulse of sound is produced by the trawler, and two echoes are heard, one after 0.1 s, the other after 0.3 s. What does this tell the skipper of the trawler?

Key Ideas

- Sounds are produced when objects vibrate – the larger the amplitude of the vibration, the louder the sound, while the faster the vibration, the higher the pitch of the sound.
- Electronic systems can be used to produce and to detect ultrasonic waves.
- Ultrasonic waves are reflected when they travel from one medium into another. The reflections can be timed, and used to build up a picture of the inside of an object.

Waves 55

3.9 Seismic waves

The deepest mines go down to about 3500 m, while geologists have drilled down to more than 12 000 m in Russia. Although these figures seem large, they are tiny compared with the diameter of the Earth, which is about 12 800 km – more than one thousand times the deepest hole drilled! Yet scientists lay claim to large amounts of knowledge about the structure of the inside of the Earth – knowledge that has come about thanks to the behaviour of waves.

Earthquakes occurring around the Earth release large amounts of energy. This energy travels through the body of the Earth as seismic waves. These waves can be detected using sensitive instruments called seismometers, which are sensitive to tiny vibrations. The structure of the Earth affects the way in which seismic waves travel through the Earth. By observing how seismic waves travel, scientists have built up a detailed picture of the inside of the Earth.

The Earth is made up of layers that formed many millions of years ago, early in the history of our planet. Heavy matter sank to the centre of the Earth while lighter material floated on top, producing a structure consisting of a dense **core**, surrounded by the mantle, outside which is a thin layer called the **crust** or **lithosphere**.

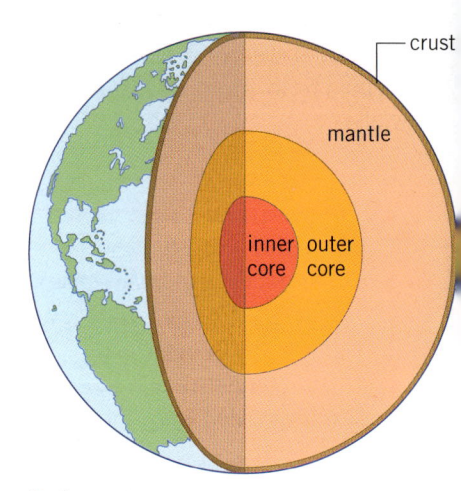

↑ **Figure 1:** The structure of the Earth.

At one time scientists believed that features like mountain ranges on the surface of the Earth were the result of the crust shrinking as the Earth cooled down after it was formed, rather like the skin on the surface of a bowl of custard shrinks and wrinkles as the custard cools down. However, scientists now have a better explanation for the formation of features on the Earth's surface, as we shall see in on page 58.

Core	Mantle	Crust (or lithosphere)
⊙ radius of about 3500 km ⊙ made of nickel and iron ⊙ inner core is solid, outer core is liquid	⊙ extends to about 3000 km below Earth's surface ⊙ rather like a thick, syrupy liquid – behaves like a solid, but is able to flow	⊙ about 100 km deep

By making careful measurements, physicists have been able to measure the mass of the Earth, and to calculate its density. The density of the Earth as a whole is much greater than the density of the rocks found in the crust. This suggests that the centre of the Earth must be made from a different material to the crust, and that this material must have a much greater density than the material which makes up the crust.

H The seismic waves that travel through the Earth are of two types, called P (for **primary**) and S (for **secondary**) waves.

P waves	S waves
⊙ P waves are longitudinal waves, with vibrations backwards and forwards along the direction in which the wave is travelling, just like sound waves. ⊙ P waves travel through liquids as well as solids.	⊙ S waves are transverse waves, with vibrations across the direction in which the wave is travelling, just like light waves. ⊙ S waves travel only through solids.

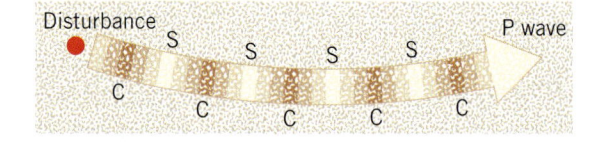

↑ **Figure 2:** In P waves the rocks are compressed (C) and stretched (S).

↑ **Figure 3:** In S waves the rocks move up and down.

P waves travel more quickly than S waves. The speed of both types of waves increases with distance below the surface of the Earth. This suggests that the particles in matter far below the surface are packed more closely together, making it easier for one particle to pass vibrations on to its neighbour. This fits with the idea that the core of the Earth is made of denser material than the crust.

Figure 4 shows how the velocity of P and S waves varies with depth below the surface of the Earth.

As seismic waves travel through the body of the Earth, changes in their velocities cause refraction, a property of waves we met on page 43. This refraction may be gradual, or it may be sharp. These changes can be interpreted and understood in terms of changes in density in and between different layers inside the Earth.

Figure 5 shows the refraction of P and S waves as they pass through the body of the Earth. Notice that S waves do not travel through the outer core, which is liquid. As the distance below the Earth's surface increases, the density of each layer increases and the waves are gradually refracted. However, the sharp refraction at the boundary between layers can only be explained in terms of different materials with two adjoining layers, producing large changes in density.

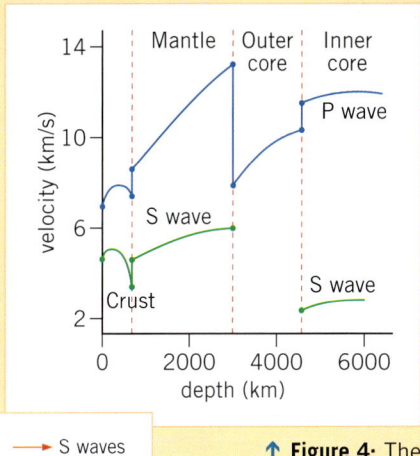

Figure 4: The velocities of P and S waves through the body of the Earth.

Figure 5: The refraction of seismic waves travelling through the Earth.

Key Ideas

- Our knowledge of the structure of the Earth comes mainly from studying how seismic waves travel through it.
- The Earth consists of a thin crust surrounding the mantle, which is able to flow like a liquid. Inside the mantle is a very dense core, containing nickel and iron.
- There are two types of seismic waves – P waves, which are longitudinal, and which can travel through liquids, and S waves, which are transverse, and which cannot travel through liquids.
- The speeds of these waves vary as they travel through the body of the Earth, causing them to be refracted.

Questions

1. Explain why scientists think that the Earth's core is much denser than its crust.
2. On the opposite side of the Earth to an earthquake there is a shadow zone – a region where seismic waves are not detected (Figure 6). Use your knowledge of the behaviour of waves to explain why this is.

Figure 6

Waves

3.10 Moving plates beneath our feet

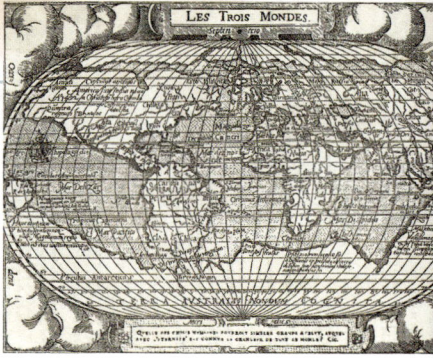

Even quite a quick look at the western coastline of Africa and the eastern coastline of South America shows that these edges of the two continents have a remarkably similar shape. Computer analysis of the two coastlines shows just how closely they fit together, confirming the similarity of shape which people have commented on for hundreds of years (Figure 1).

Just as remarkable is the similarity of the fossils and rock structures that we find when we look in Africa and South America. Fossil remains of the fresh-water reptile Mesosaurus and those of a plant called Glossopteris (Figure 2) are found in both continents. And the layers of rock in the two continents are arranged in the same sequence, with layers of sandstone lying above seams of coal.

Strange as it may seem, scientists believe that the explanation for the similarity in the shapes of the continents and of the rocks and fossils found there is because the two continents were once joined together as one land mass. Figure 3 shows the vast 'super-continent' of Pangaea which is believed to have existed up until about 250 million years ago. Slowly Pangaea split in two, forming the northern continent of Laurasia and the southern continent of Gondwanaland about 100 million years ago. The land masses continued to move apart until about 50 million years ago they began to closely resemble the map of the world we know today.

Figure 1: As long ago as 1620, an English philosopher called Francis Bacon drew attention to the similar shapes of the west coast of Africa and the east coast of South America.

Figure 2: Glossopteris was a tree-like plant growing about 230 million years ago. It had tongue-shaped leaves, and grew to a height of about 4m.

Figure 3: The break up of Pangaea into Laurasia and Gondwanaland led eventually to the formation of the land masses we recognise today. Notice how, 100 million years ago, India is still moving rapidly northwards to take up the position it occupies today. The collision between India and the continent of Asia produced the mountain range we call the Himalayas.

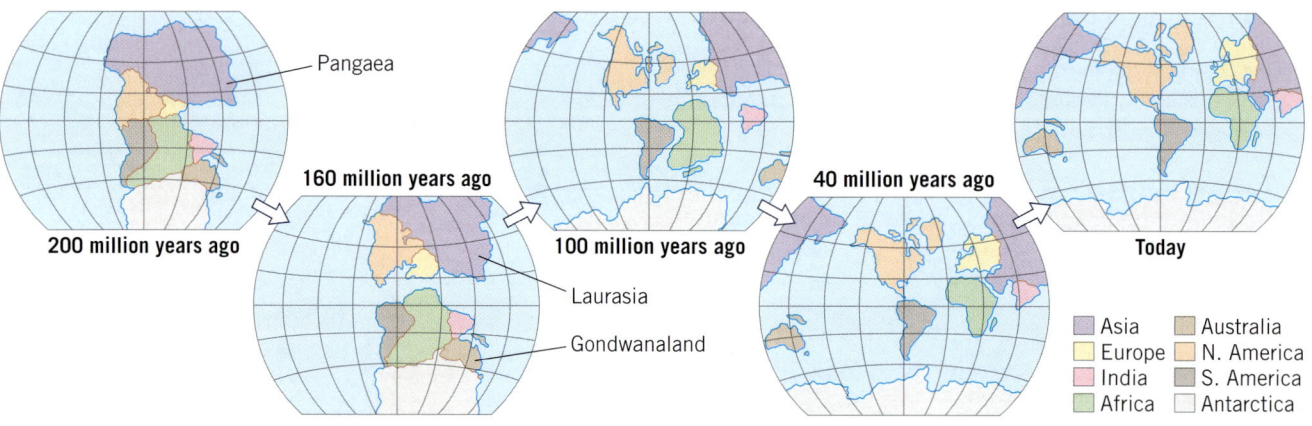

- Pangaea
- 200 million years ago
- 160 million years ago
- Laurasia
- Gondwanaland
- 100 million years ago
- 40 million years ago
- Today

Asia, Australia, Europe, N. America, India, S. America, Africa, Antarctica

Of course the rate at which the continents moved and split up was very tiny – only a few centimetres each year. They moved because the Earth's crust is cracked into a number of large pieces called **tectonic plates**. Deep within the Earth, radioactive decay produces vast amounts of energy, heating molten minerals. These minerals expand, become less dense and rise towards the surface, being replaced by cooler material. It is these **convection currents** that pushed the tectonic plates over the surface of the Earth.

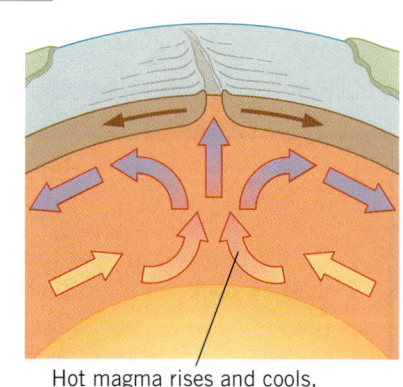

Figure 4: Radioactive decay deep within the Earth provides the energy that drives the tectonic plates over the Earth's surface.

Hot magma rises and cools, pushing the plates apart

Waves

The processes that split up Pangaea and drove the continents apart continue today, pushing Europe and the Americas apart. Where the boundaries of the plates meet, huge forces are exerted, making the plates buckle and deform and causing earthquakes and volcanoes.

→ **Figure 5:** The distribution of volcanoes around the world largely follows the boundaries of the tectonic plates.

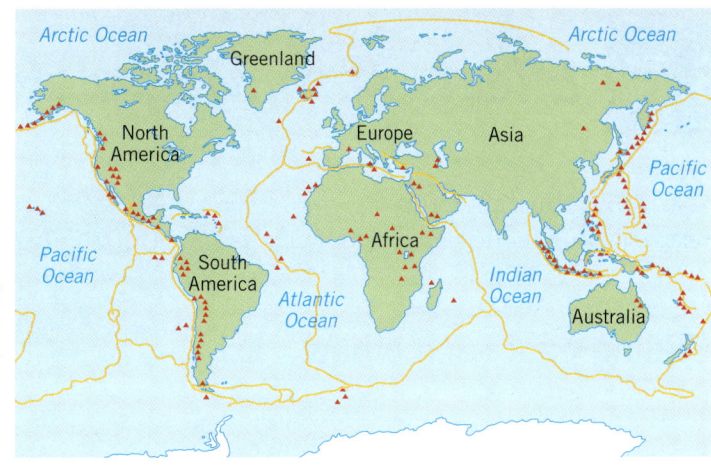

Ideas and Evidence

Wegener's revolutionary theory

The idea that huge land masses once existed as the ancestors of the continents we know today was put forward in the late 19th century by the geologist Edward Suess. However, rather than a process of continental drift, Suess thought that a huge southern continent had sunk, leaving a vanished land bridge between Africa and South America.

The idea of continental drift was put first forward by Alfred Wegener, a meteorologist, in 1915. Wegener suggested that our current arrangement of continents is the result of the break up of one large land mass due to the movement of plates across the surface of the Earth. He presented a wide variety of evidence for this theory, including fossil and geological data, as well as the observation that longitude measurements suggested that Greenland had moved one mile further away from Europe in 100 years. Despite all his evidence, Wegener was unable to suggest how the continents were pushed across the surface of the Earth.

Wegener's ideas were not welcomed by many of his fellow scientists – as one of them put it: 'If we are to believe Wegener's hypothesis, we must forget everything that has been learned in the last 70 years and start again.' His case was not helped by the fact that he did not have a **mechanism** to account for how the continents moved. It also did not escape the notice of many of Wegener's opponents that he was not a geologist.

Wegener died during an expedition to Greenland in 1930, and his theory lay largely forgotten for the next 30 years. However some scientists, such as Alexander du Toit, kept Wegener's ideas alive and they were re-examined in the 1960s. New work on seafloor spreading and the pattern of magnetic 'stripes' on either side of ocean ridges led to the need to find new explanations and Wegener's work was used as the basis for a new theory called plate tectonics. This theory became widely accepted by scientists relatively quickly once it was realised how it could explain both recent and historical observations. By the late 1960s, Western scientists were almost unanimous in their support of plate tectonics.

Questions

1. Imagine that you are a scientist who has just heard Wegener talking about his ideas for the first time. Write a letter to another scientist explaining what Wegener has said and describing how you feel about his ideas.

2. Figure 6 shows convection currents beneath the surface of three plates on the surface of the Earth. Describe what is happening at points A and B on the surface, and what you might see at these points.

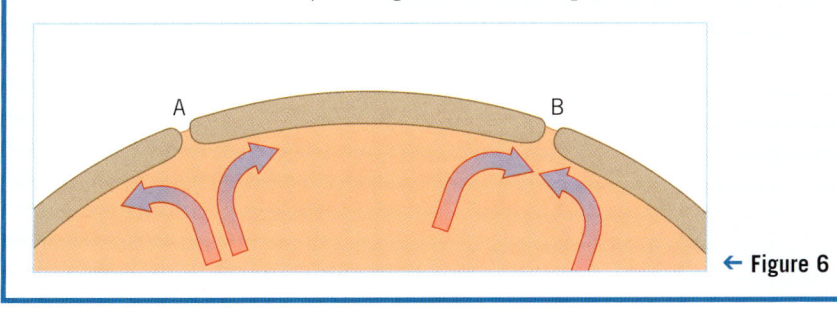

← Figure 6

Key Ideas

- The Earth's crust is cracked into a number of pieces (tectonic plates) that are constantly moving.

- Evidence for the existence of tectonic plates comes from the similarity in rocks and fossils in different continents, and from the pattern of earthquakes and volcanoes that exists along the edges of the plates.

Waves

3.11 Effects of moving plates H

Where two plates meet, they may move relative to one another in three different ways.

Sliding past each other

When two plates move past each other in opposite directions there is no problem as long as the two rock masses continue to move smoothly, usually at a rate of a few centimetres each year. If the rocks get stuck and stop moving, huge forces may build up. Eventually the rocks may move several metres in a fraction of a second, producing an earthquake.

Moving towards each other

When two plates move towards each other, one plate may be forced down under another, a process called **subduction**. Some of the material in a thin, oceanic plate, which is forced under a thicker continental plate, will melt producing molten rock or magma. The huge pressure beneath the plates may force some of this magma up through fissures (cracks) in the continental crust producing volcanoes. This process is happening on the west coast of South America, beneath the range of mountains called the Andes.

As an oceanic plate is forced under a continental plate it compresses the edge of the continental plate and causes faults in the rock. You can imagine how this happens if you think about the folds and ridges that form if you push the edge of a rug with your foot. As well as melting the oceanic plate, the energy produced as the two plates push past each other melts the rocks in the continental plate, producing metamorphic rocks – rocks that have been changed by heat. (Marble is an example of a metamorphic rock, formed when calcite melts and then cools.)

↑ **Figure 1:** The San Andreas fault in California is an example of two plates sliding past each other. Sudden sliding of the plates past one another produced an earthquake in Los Angeles in 1994 that killed 57 people and destroyed thousands of homes and other buildings.

↑ **Figure 2:** Subduction, when one plate is forced down under another, may cause earthquakes and volcanoes.

Moving away from each other

When two plates move away from one another this causes a different kind of fault in which new material is deposited as magma fills the gap between the plates. This is happening in the middle of the Atlantic Ocean, where the new material is being pushed up above the surface of the spreading seabed, forming the **mid-Atlantic ridge**. The magma rising to the surface at this point is rich in iron, which is of course magnetic. As the iron is deposited, it becomes magnetised by the Earth's magnetic field. The pattern of magnetisation of the material on either side of the ridge shows 'stripes' parallel to the ridge. When this observation was coupled with the knowledge that the Earth's magnetic field has reversed its direction at least 170 times in the last 100 million years, this provided important evidence for the theory of plate tectonics.

↓ **Figure 3:** The pattern of stripes formed as magnetic material spreads out from the ridge and acts as a record of the Earth's magnetic field.

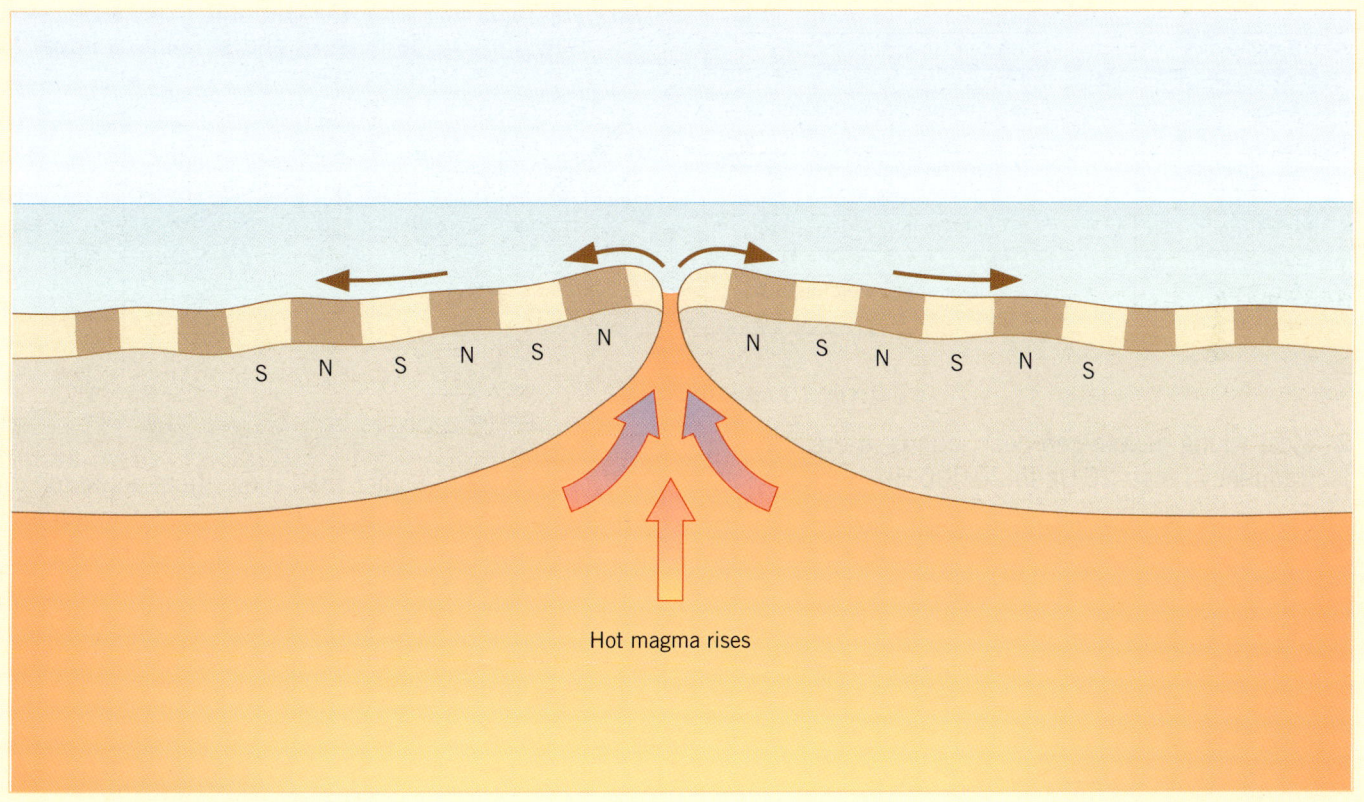

Hot magma rises

Questions

1. Earthquakes may have many causes, including the movement of the tectonic plates against each other, erupting volcanoes, and many artificial causes, including underground atomic explosions and even the collapse of old mine workings underground. Detecting earthquakes requires scientists to make measurements of tiny movements in the Earth's crust that happen as it shifts in the days and weeks running up to an earthquake. Some people think that predicting earthquakes is impossible – others think that this is not the case.

   Write a newspaper article explaining the cause of earthquakes, and describing whether or not you think predicting earthquakes is possible or not.

Key Ideas

- The movement of tectonic plates relative to one another provides explanations for earthquakes and volcanoes and many features of the Earth's crust, including the formation of ridges on the sea floor where the plates are moving apart.

Waves

3.12 End of chapter questions

1 In the diagram, the boxes on the left show some types of electromagnetic radiation.

The boxes on the right show some uses of electromagnetic radiation.

Draw a straight line from each type of radiation to its use.

The first one has been done for you.

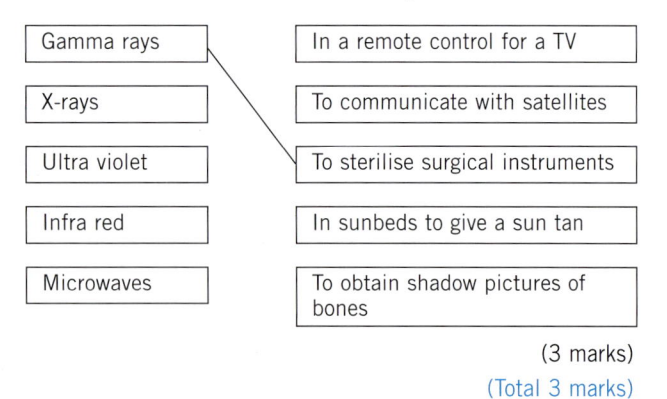

Gamma rays	In a remote control for a TV
X-rays	To communicate with satellites
Ultra violet	To sterilise surgical instruments
Infra red	In sunbeds to give a sun tan
Microwaves	To obtain shadow pictures of bones

(Gamma rays is connected to "To sterilise surgical instruments")

(3 marks)

(Total 3 marks)

2 Most young people can hear sounds in the frequency range 20 Hz to 20 000 Hz.

   a Which statement best describes frequency?

   A the maximum disturbance caused by a wave

   B the number of complete vibrations per second

   C the distance between one crest of a wave and the next one

   D the distance travelled by a wave in 1 second (1 mark)

   AQA specimen question

   b Diagram X shows a trace on an oscilloscope screen.

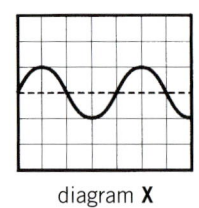

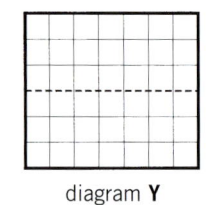

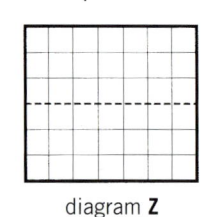

   diagram X   diagram Y   diagram Z

   i Draw a trace on a copy of diagram Y which has a higher frequency than that shown in diagram X.

   ii Draw a trace on a copy of diagram Z which has a larger amplitude than that shown in diagram X. (2 marks)

   c i Write down the name given to sound waves of frequency higher than 20 000 Hz.
      (1 mark)

      ii Write down **two** uses of these very high frequency sound waves.
      (2 marks)

   (Total 6 marks)

3 a The diagrams show rays of light. They are travelling inside Perspex and striking its edge.

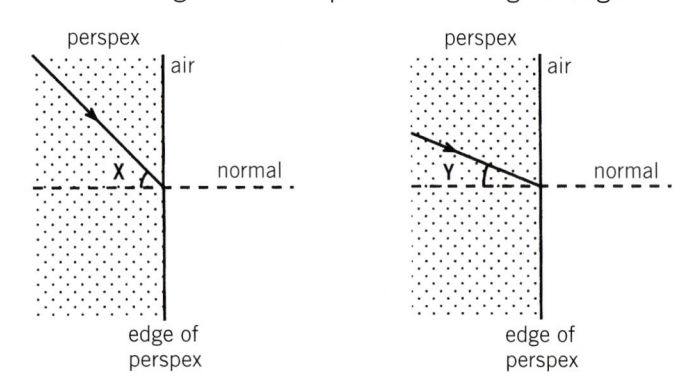

      i Angle **X** is bigger than the critical angle for Perspex. On a copy of the diagram complete the path of the ray as it leaves the edge of the Perspex. (1 mark)

      ii Angle **Y** is smaller than the critical angle for Perspex. On a copy of the diagram complete the path of the ray as it leaves the edge of the Perspex. (1 mark)

   b The diagram shows a ray of light passing through an optical fibre.

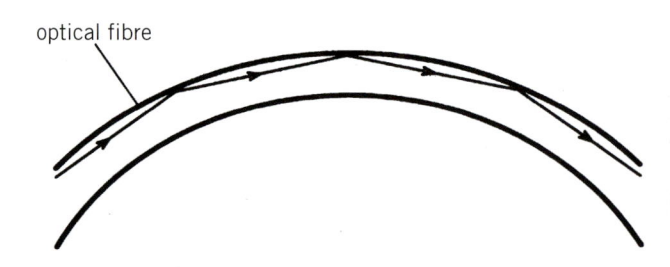

   Explain why the ray of light stays in the optical fibre. (2 marks)

   (Total 4 marks)

   AQA specimen question

Waves

4 a Copy and complete the following sentence about waves.

Waves travelling across the surface of water are .... waves.

The disturbance in the water is .... the direction in which the wave is travelling.

Sound waves in air are .... waves.

The disturbance of the air is .... the direction in which the waves are travelling.

.... waves can travel through a vacuum.

When a wave moves through a gap it spreads out. This is called ....
(6 marks)

b The diagram shows apparatus used to find the position of a flaw in a metal casting.

The cathode ray oscilloscope is producing a visual display to show how the ultrasonic waves are partly reflected at different boundaries.

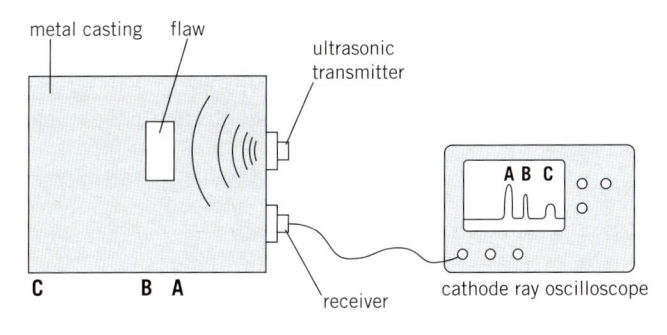

  i What causes trace **C**? (1 mark)

  ii What causes traces **A** and **B**? (1 mark)

  iii How could the position of the flaw be calculated? (2 marks)

(Total 10 marks)
AQA specimen question

5 Wegener's theory of continental drift is now generally accepted.

a Copy and complete the sentences below by adding the missing words.

At one time it was thought that mountains like the Cairngorms were formed because the Earth's crust shrank as the Earth .... It is now thought that the crust of the Earth is split into a number of pieces called .... which are moving because of .... currents in the Earth's mantle.
(3 marks)

To gain full marks in this question you should write your ideas in good English. Put them into a sensible order and use the correct scientific words.

b Wegener suggested that all the separate continents on Earth once formed a single land mass. Describe the evidence that supports this idea. (2 marks)

(Total 5 marks)
AQA specimen question

6 Information about the Earth's structure has been obtained by studying the shock (seismic) waves produced by earthquakes.

The diagrams show the paths of seismic waves through the mantle and the core.

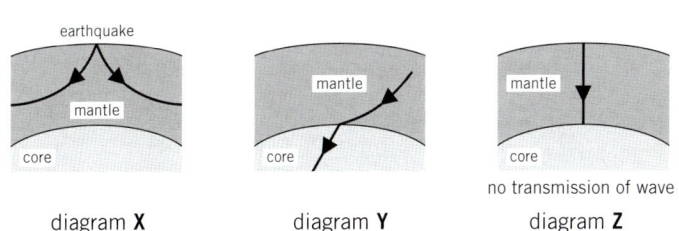

diagram **X**   diagram **Y**   diagram **Z** (no transmission of wave)

a Describe and explain what happens to the waves travelling through the mantle in diagram **X**.
(3 marks)

b Describe and explain what happens to the waves travelling from the mantle to the core in diagram **Y**.

State which type of wave is shown. (3 marks)

c Explain why the wave shown in diagram **Z** does not travel through the core.

State which type of wave is shown. (2 marks)

(Total 8 marks)

Waves

4.1 The Solar System

For thousands of years people have looked up at the night sky and wondered at its beauty. The stories that ancient people told about the patterns they saw in the heavens are still with us today, in the names of the **constellations** of stars – like 'The Plough', 'The Hunter' and 'The Great Bear'. To explain how the heavenly bodies moved, people put the Earth at the centre of the Universe, with the Sun, Moon and stars revolving round it.

Although the Earth-centred model of the Universe can explain day and night, and the movement of the stars around the Earth, the planets presented ancient people with a different problem. The planets appear like stars in the sky, but unlike stars they do not actually give out their own light – instead, they reflect light from the Sun. Their motion is different to the stars too. Instead of moving smoothly round the Earth, the planets wander around, sometimes moving faster than the stars, sometimes more slowly – and sometimes moving in the opposite direction.

The wandering motion of the planets (the word 'planet' comes from the Greek word meaning 'wanderer') is due to the fact that the Earth is not at the centre of the Universe, but orbits the Sun along with the other planets. This means that the position of the planets in the sky depends on where they are in their orbits, and where the Earth is in its own orbit around the Sun.

In ancient times people believed that the stars and other bodies must move in circles, because a circle (so they believed) was such a perfect figure. We now know that the orbits of the planets around the Sun are actually **ellipses**, which can be described as 'squashed circles'. In fact the orbit of the planet Pluto is so elliptical that it spends part of its time as the outermost planet in the Solar System, and part of its time closer to the Sun than its neighbour, Neptune.

The orbits of **comets** are even more elliptical – at some times a comet may come closer to the Sun than the Earth, while at others its orbit takes it far outside the Solar System. A comet is a small object made of ice and dust and surrounded by vapour.

To keep one object in orbit around another requires an unbalanced force – otherwise it would simply travel in a straight line, as we saw on page 30. This unbalanced force is provided by **gravity**, and the size of the gravitational force between two objects depends on the distance between them. As the distance between the objects gets bigger, the size of the gravitational force between them gets smaller. This decrease in force happens more quickly than the increase in distance – so doubling the distance between the objects actually decreases the force to one quarter of what is was before.

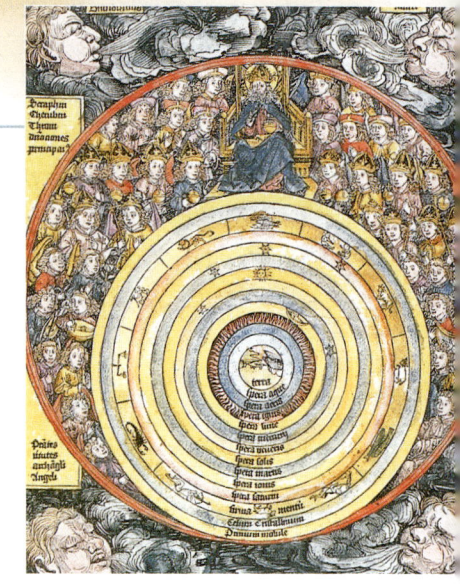

Figure 1: The Earth-centred model of the universe fitted nicely with the tendency of humans to put themselves at the centre of things.

Figure 2: (a) Day and night are not due to the movement of the Sun round the Earth, but to the rotation of the Earth on its axis once every 24 hours. The half of the Earth facing the Sun is in daylight, while the half away from the Sun is in darkness. **(b)** The motion of the planets around the Sun explains why the position of the other planets seen from Earth changes against the background of the stars. The Earth travels once round the Sun every 365 days.

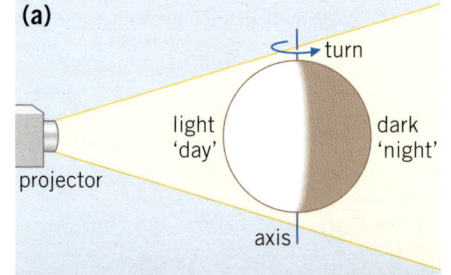

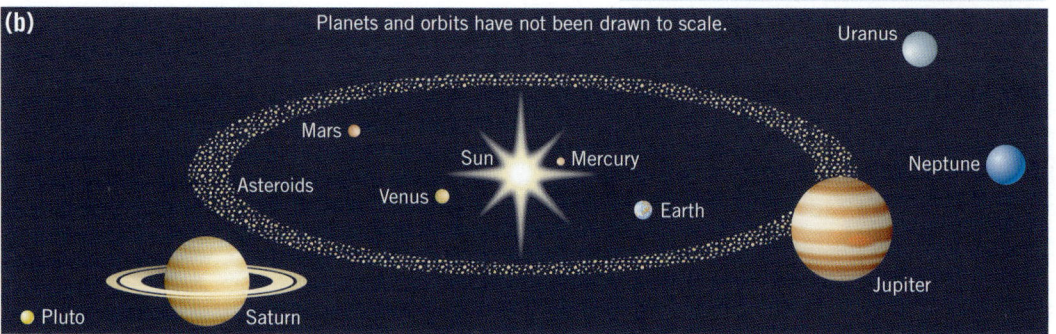

Ideas and Evidence

Comets

Figure 3: This is part of the 11th-century Bayeux Tapestry, showing the appearance of a comet prior to the invasion of England by the Normans.

In ancient times comets were often thought to be a sign foretelling disaster, appearing as part of the Earth's atmosphere, rather like clouds. However, in 1577 the Danish astronomer Tycho Brahe measured the distance of a comet from the Earth and showed that it was at least six times as far away as the Moon. One hundred years later Isaac Newton showed that comets obey the same laws as the planets in their orbits. About the same time, the Astronomer Royal Edmond Halley showed that the comet that appeared in 1682 was identical with those that had appeared in 1607 and 1531. He successfully predicted its return in 1758, when it became known as Halley's comet. Halley's comet passed the Earth early in 1986. As it headed away from the Sun, it was observed by two Soviet space probes, Vega 1 and 2, and by a European probe called Giotto, as well as by two Japanese probes.

Figure 4: Comet Hyakutake, which passed the Earth in 1996, was one of the brightest comets of the 20th century.

Questions

1 One day on Neptune lasts 16 Earth hours, while one year is 84 Earth years. How long does it take Neptune

   a to rotate once on its axis

   b to go once round the Sun?

2 The table shows some data for the planets. For each planet the length of the year and the average distance from the Sun is given relative to the Earth.

	Length of year	(Length of year)^2	Average distance from Sun	(Average distance from Sun)^3
Mercury	0.2408		0.388	
Venus		0.6152		0.724
Earth		1.0000		1.000
Mars		1.881		1.524
Jupiter		11.862		5.200
Saturn		29.457		9.540

According to Kepler,

$$(\text{length of year})^2 \div (\text{average distance from Sun})^3 = \text{constant}.$$

Do these figures support this law?

Science people

Tycho Brahe lived from 1546 to 1601, and spent a large part of his life making accurate observations of the stars and planets. He lost his nose in a duel with a mathematician, and had a new nose made out of metal.

Key Ideas

- The Earth spins on its axis once every 24 hours, and orbits the Sun once every 365 days.

- The planets move irregularly across the background of the fixed patterns (constellations) of stars.

- The orbits of planets and comets around the Sun are ellipses.

- The force keeping these bodies in orbit is gravitational attraction.

The Earth and beyond

4.2 Gravity grabs the planets

The planets are kept in orbit around the Sun due to gravity – the force which acts between two masses. To understand how gravity keeps a planet in orbit, think about whirling something like a conker around your head on the end of a string. The string keeps the conker moving in a circle around you by providing an unbalanced force on the conker that acts towards you. If the string breaks, the conker carries on moving in a straight line.

The string provides an unbalanced force acting on the conker in this direction.

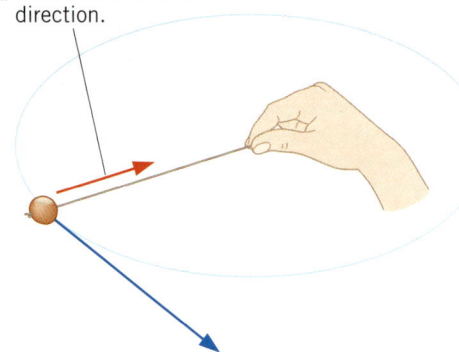

With no unbalanced force acting on it (if the string broke, for example) the conker would carry on moving in a straight line, like this.

→ **Figure 1:** The string provides the force to keep the conker moving in a circle. In the same way, gravity provides the force to keep the planets moving around the Sun.

Ideas and Evidence

Isaac Newton was the first to think about the way in which gravity pulls an object so that it orbits around another object. He carried out a 'thought experiment' in which he imagined a cannon firing a cannon ball from a cliff or the top of a high hill (Figure 2). After the cannon ball is fired it falls towards the Earth – and the faster it is fired, the further it will travel. Newton reasoned that because the surface of the Earth is curved, it falls away beneath the cannon ball, and so the ball will travel further than it would if the Earth was flat. If the cannon fires cannon balls at faster and faster speeds, eventually one of the cannon balls will fall towards the Earth at exactly the right rate to ensure that its height above the Earth remains constant – in other words it would be in orbit!

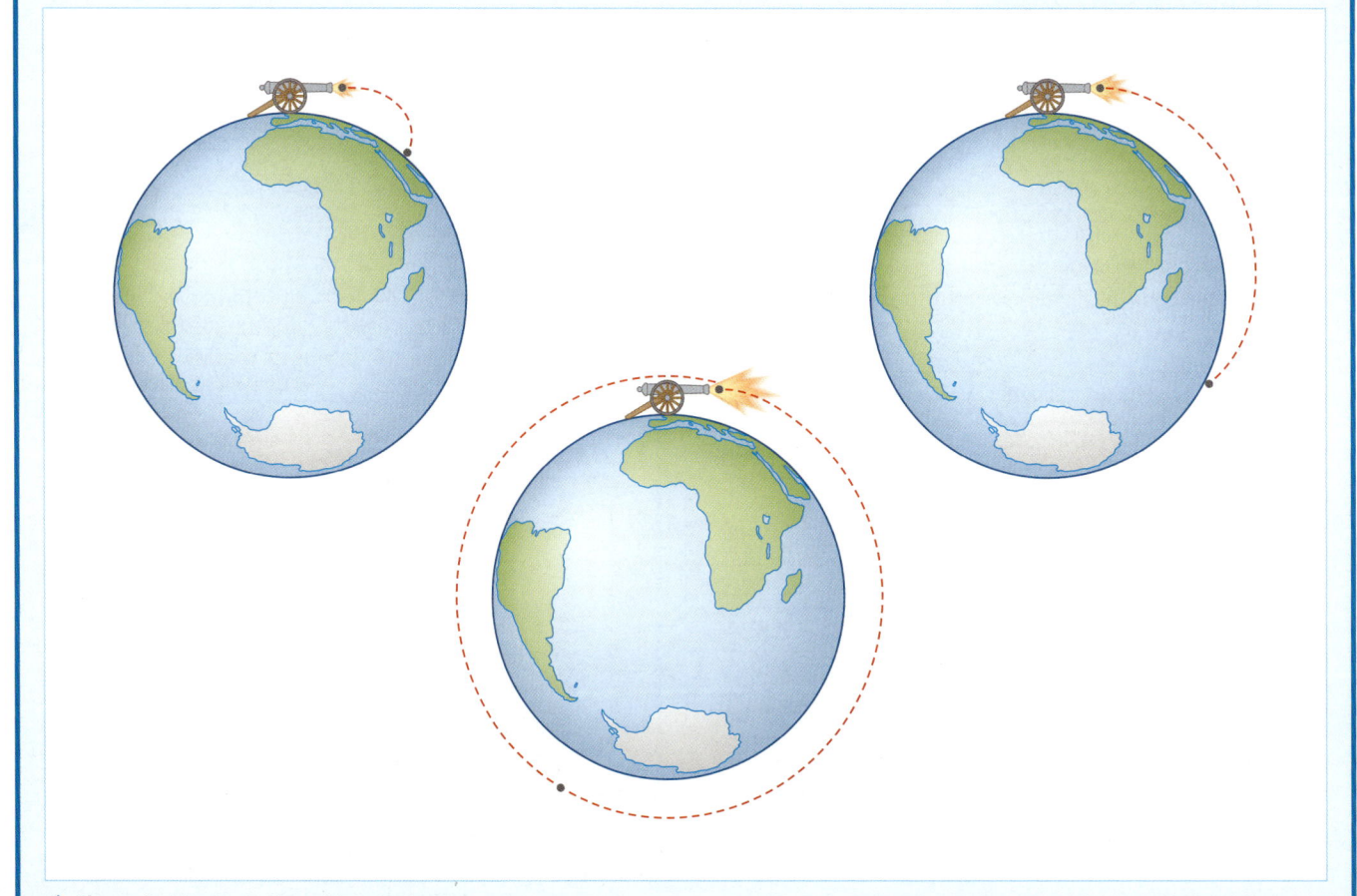

↑ **Figure 2:** Newton's thought experiment.

The Earth and beyond

Ideas and Evidence

Thought experiments

Thought experiments play an important part in developing scientific theories. This is especially true where it may be difficult to carry out a real experiment – the development of Einstein's theory of relativity is just one example of this.

When he was riding on a tram, Einstein noticed a clock as he passed a particular building. He imagined what would happen if the tram travelled at the speed of light. As he would be travelling at the same speed as the ray of light that left the hand of the clock at a particular time, no other rays of light would reach him, since they would be unable to catch up with the first ray. Since he would continue to see just the one ray of light from the clock, Einstein realised that this would mean that the clock would appear to have stopped. From this initial realisation came the theory that 'moving clocks run slow'.

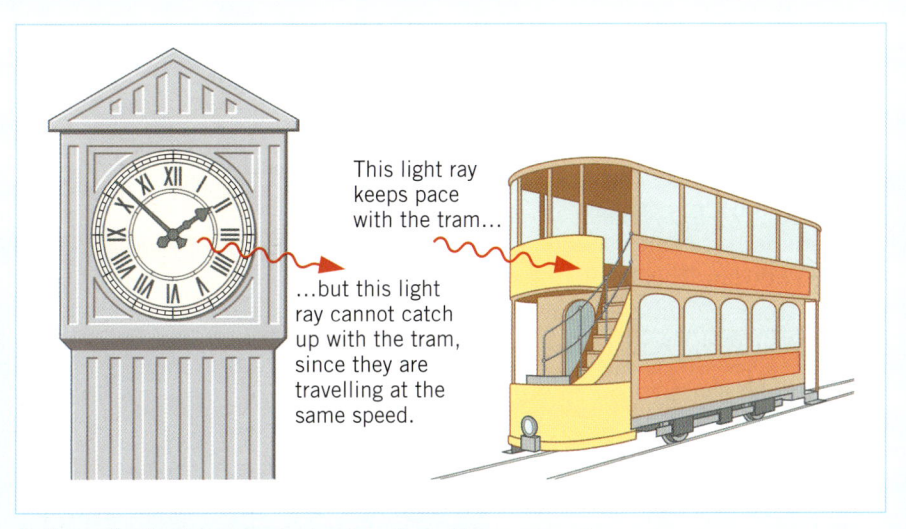

↑ **Figure 3:** Einstein's 'gedanken', or thought experiment.

Questions

1. The Moon orbits the Earth once every 28 days, while the Earth rotates on its own axis every 24 hours. High tide in a particular place on the Earth's surface gets about one hour earlier each day. Explain the behaviour of the tides by drawing a diagram showing the direction of rotation of the Earth about its axis and the direction of the Moon's orbit around the Earth.

2. Einstein's thought experiments were confirmed by experimental observations made by physicists some years after he first proposed his ideas. Imagine that you are the science reporter for a national newspaper writing an article about 'Ideas in Physics'. Explain as clearly and simply as you can to your readers:

   a. what a thought experiment is, and how it differs from a 'real' experiment

   b. why thought experiments require 'real' experiments to decide whether a theory is correct or not.

Key Ideas

- A small object will orbit a larger object if it travels at the right speed and at the right distance from the larger object.

The Earth and beyond

4.3 Artificial satellites

Apart from the planets in the Solar System, there are many other examples of orbits. Many of the planets have smaller bodies orbiting around them. A smaller object in orbit around a larger one is sometimes called a **satellite**, although natural satellites in orbit around a planet are usually called **moons**. The Earth has only one moon, but Mars has two (called Phobos and Deimos) and Uranus has seventeen!

In addition to its natural satellite, the Earth has many artificial satellites, launched for various purposes including:

- telecommunications – to send information between places that are a long way apart on the Earth's surface

- remote sensing – to make observations of the Earth to record the weather, changes in vegetation or even changes on the Earth's surface for military intelligence

- astronomy – to make observations of the Universe without the Earth's atmosphere getting in the way.

The rate at which a satellite orbits a larger body depends on the distance between them – the further apart they are the longer the time taken for one complete orbit. Telecommunication satellites are put into orbit above the equator at an altitude of 35 800 km. This means that they orbit the earth once every 24 hours, exactly the time that the Earth takes to rotate. Orbiting in the same direction as the Earth rotates, a communication satellite is always over the same place on the Earth's surface – in an orbit that is described as **geostationary**. This means that the satellite can always 'see' the same points on the Earth, and so provides uninterrupted communications between the ground stations it is linking. However, to avoid interfering with each other's signals, there is space for only about 400 geostationary satellites.

Remote-sensing satellites provide scientists with a powerful tool which can be used for many purposes, including weather forecasting and minerals exploration. Automatic picture-taking satellites provide data about cloud cover and other features of the atmosphere, while infra-red sensors allow measurement of cloud temperatures, providing information about their heights. Satellites now provide data of this kind for over half the Earth, making weather forecasting more accurate, and making longer-range weather predictions possible.

Many remote-sensing satellites are launched to cover large areas of the Earth's surface. To do this they may be put into relatively low orbits that pass over the Earth's poles. This means that the Earth spins underneath the satellite as it orbits, passing over each point on the Earth's surface every day or so. This **low polar orbit** enables greater detail to be recorded by the satellite, as well as providing complete coverage of the Earth.

↓ **Figure 1:** Telstar was one of the first telecommunications satellites. Launched in 1962, it transmitted the first live television images between the United States, Europe, and Japan.

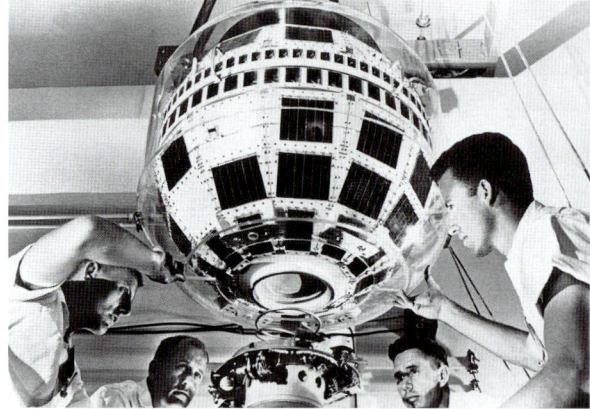

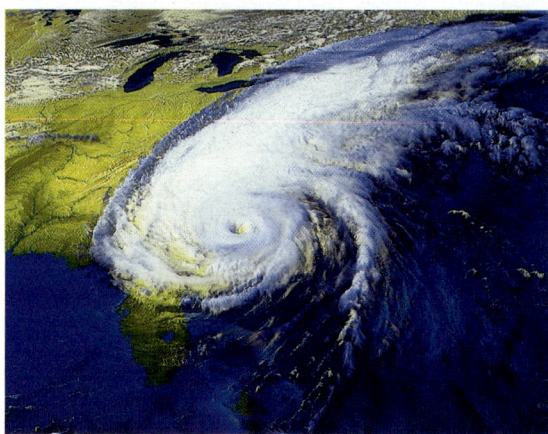

↑ **Figure 2:** Weather forecasters make great use of information from weather satellites. This computer image of Hurricane Floyd was produced using data from a US NOAA satellite.

↓ **Figure 3:** A geostationary orbit above the Equator (left) and a low polar orbit (right).

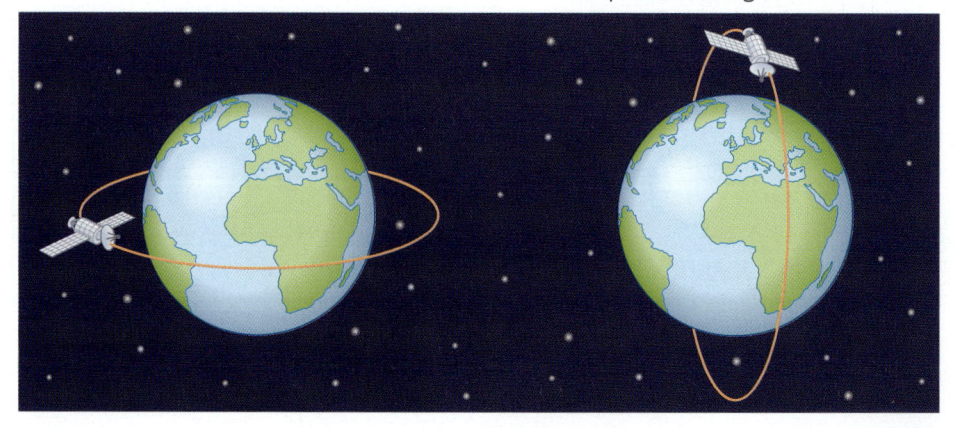

One of the problems with making observations of space from the surface of the Earth is that the Earth's atmosphere absorbs certain frequencies of electromagnetic waves so that they cannot be detected. In particular, astronomical satellites enable measurements of infra-red, ultra-violet and X-ray waves to be made, from which many important new features of the Universe have been discovered. Probably the most famous orbiting astronomical observatory is the Hubble telescope, which was launched in 1990. Another satellite called COBE (the COsmic Background Explorer) provided important evidence in support of the 'big-bang' theory of how the Universe was formed.

Science people

In 1945 the science fiction writer Arthur C Clarke first put forward the idea of artificial satellites in geostationary orbit above the Earth. Clarke is probably best known for his book *2001 – A Space Odyssey* which was also made into a film.

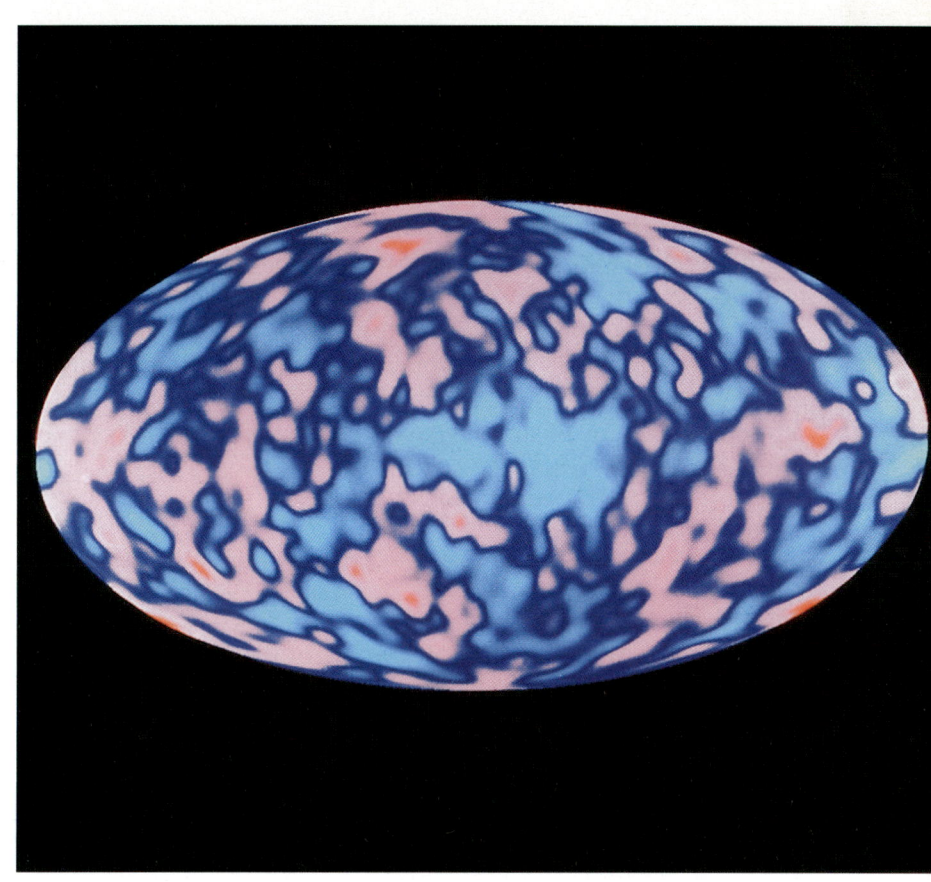

↑ **Figure 4:** Taken by the COBE satellite in 1992, this photograph provided scientists with important evidence about the origin of our Universe.

Questions

1. Why does Jupiter orbit the Sun more slowly that the Earth?

2. Use table in question 2 on page 65 to work out roughly how many times

   a Mercury

   b Saturn

   have orbited the Sun since you were born.

3. Why are satellites for broadcasting television signals put into geostationary orbits rather than low polar orbits?

4. A new satellite is to be built to observe space from an orbit round the Earth. It will cost many hundreds of millions of pounds to build and launch. A friend of yours says, 'That money would be better spent making medicines to cure people in poor countries.' Another friend says, 'It's important that we find out as much about space as we can – who knows when such knowledge may be useful?'

   Who do you agree with, and why?

Key Ideas

- Satellites can be put in orbit round the Earth for communications purposes, and for remote sensing of the Earth and space.

- Communications satellites are normally placed in geostationary orbits above the Earth's equator, so that they stay over the same place on the Earth's surface.

- Satellites designed to gather data about the Earth may be placed in low polar orbit in order to cover as much of the Earth's surface as possible.

The Earth and beyond

4.4 A star is born

Using powerful instruments, astronomers have measured a wide range of electromagnetic waves coming from space, including light and radio waves. From their observations, they know that our Sun is part of a group of stars known as the Milky Way galaxy, which contains between 100 and 200 billion stars. Enormous distances separate these stars. If you imagine that the distance from the Earth to the Sun is represented by the width of this book, the distance from the Sun to the nearest star is about 12 km, and the diameter of the Milky Way itself is the distance from the Earth to the Moon!

The Milky Way itself is just one of many galaxies in the Universe. Although there is no way to be sure, astronomers estimate that the number of galaxies may be as many as one billion. The Milky Way is one of a small group of about 30 galaxies called the **local group**.

Stars are formed by vast clouds of dust and gas in space being pulled together by gravitational forces. Once the star has begun to form the large mass of the star may attract smaller masses which become planets orbiting the star.

Figure 1: The Milky Way can be seen from the Earth as a faint band of stars stretching from the north-east to the south-east horizon at night. Its faintness is due to the light from stars that are too far away to be seen individually with the naked eye. The individual stars that we see in the sky are those in the Milky Way galaxy that are close enough to the Earth to be seen separately.

Although stars in the night sky appear as tranquil, twinkling dots of light, each one is a seething mass of hot, luminous matter. You can see this most clearly in our own Sun, which is so close to us that it appears very differently to the other stars in the sky. Made almost entirely of hydrogen and helium its diameter is about 1.4 million km (1.4×10^6 km), it has a mass of about 2 thousand billion billion billion kg (2×10^{30} kg) and a temperature at the surface of around 6000 °C which rises to about 16 million °C at the centre!

Figure 2: The astronomer Cecilia Payne-Gaposchkin was the first person to investigate the chemical composition of stars, by analysing the light from them.

The Earth and beyond

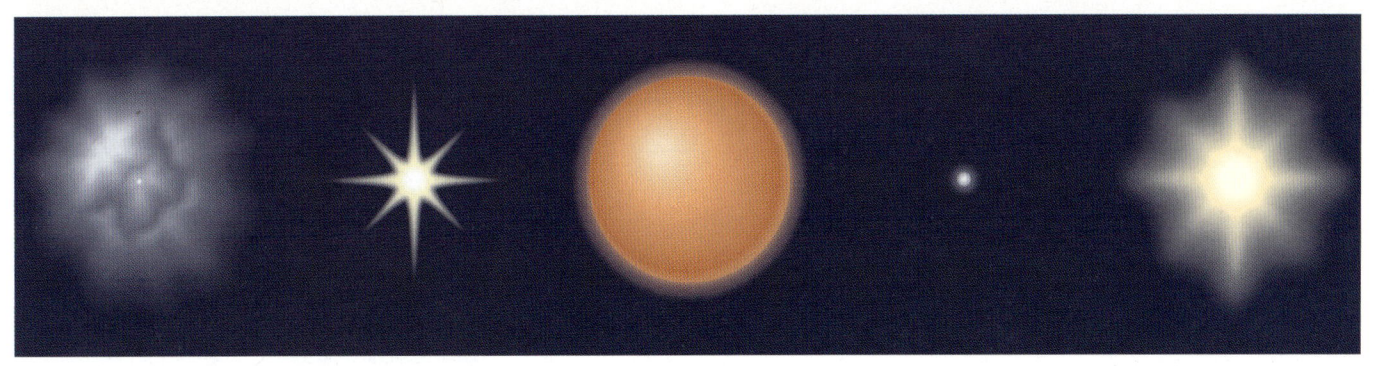

Stars form when a huge cloud of hydrogen gas in space begins to come together due to gravitational forces. As the cloud collapses under the influence of gravity, a protostar is formed. The protostar heats up as it collapses, and eventually becomes hot enough for atoms of hydrogen to smash into one another and join together – it is this that produces the energy which is radiated by stars.

Once the star that has formed enters a stable period in its life, it is known as a **main sequence star**. During this time the high temperatures in the star create enormous forces which tend to make the matter in it fly apart – but the enormous gravitational field caused by its vast size provides forces which oppose this so the star is held together. The Sun is at this stage of its life.

As the star gets older, the temperature at its core increases and the star begins to swell as the forces pushing its matter apart overcome the gravitational forces. The surface of the star cools, and it becomes a **red giant**.

As the star cools again it collapses under its own gravity and heats up, becoming a **white dwarf**. Because the atoms are forced together so strongly, the matter in a white dwarf is many millions of times denser than matter on Earth.

If a star has a mass much greater than the Sun it may end its life violently, contracting rapidly and then exploding as a **supernova**, in which dust and gas are flung far out into space. The gravitational forces as the star collapses are so strong that protons and electrons join together to form neutrons, and all the star's matter becomes squashed into a sphere about 10 km in diameter – a **neutron star**.

↑ **Figure 3:** The life of a star.

H As the matter in a very massive star collapses, the gravitational field may become absolutely enormous. It is then a **black hole**, surrounded by a spherical boundary called a horizon, through which matter and energy may enter but from which nothing – not even light – may leave. Because nothing can escape from black holes we cannot see them. However we can sometimes see the X-rays produced as matter near to a black hole is pulled into it in an enormous spiral, a bit like water draining away down the plughole of a bath.

The process that produces energy inside a star is called **nuclear fusion**. In nuclear fusion the nuclei of light atoms smash together and fuse to produce heavier atoms. Heavy elements are present in the Sun and in the matter of the inner planets of the Solar System. This suggests that the planets were formed from the matter left over when the Sun was formed. Surrounding the early Sun, astronomers think that dust containing heavy elements formed into the inner planets, while dust and gases formed into the outer planets.

Key Ideas

- Our Sun is one of billions of stars in the Milky Way galaxy.
- The Universe is made up of up to one billion galaxies.
- Stars form from dust and gases, which collapse under their own gravitational field.
- If it is massive enough, a collapsing star may form a **black hole** from which no matter or light can escape.
- A star produces energy through **nuclear fusion**, in which light elements combine to form heavier ones.
- Nuclei of heavier elements are present in the Sun and in the inner planets of the Solar System.

Questions

1. Why are dust clouds in space sometimes described as 'the nurseries of stars'?
2. Use the data in this section to calculate the average density of the Sun (the volume of a sphere is calculated from the formula $\frac{4}{3}\pi r^3$). How does it compare to the density of water?
3. **H** The Sun is converting hydrogen to helium at a rate of 600 billion kg per second. How much hydrogen has it converted to helium in your lifetime?

The Earth and beyond

4.5 Is there anybody there?

How would we know whether there is life elsewhere in the Universe? There are various ways that we might go about looking for life.

Looking for life

The enormous distances involved in space travel mean that our efforts to go looking for life will have to be limited to our own Solar System, at least until science fiction travel becomes science fact. Possible places to look include Mars, and the moon of Jupiter called Europa. Both of these seem to offer some possibility of life, in terms of the existence of water and in terms of the range of temperatures that can be expected there.

For more than 100 years some people have been convinced that intelligent life might exist on Mars. In 1877 the Italian astronomer Giovanni Schiaparelli noticed lines, on the planet, which he claimed were a planet-wide system of canals. Other people seized on this idea and saw them as proof of an attempt by intelligent life forms to irrigate the arid surface.

Scientists have used satellites to survey the surface of Mars from orbit around it, and have sent robotic probes to the surface of it. The probes have sent back pictures to Earth, and have analysed samples of the Martian soil and atmosphere. Based on this evidence, scientists now think that the likelihood of intelligent life ever having lived on Mars is very small indeed. The 'canals' are natural features, and changes in the colour of the surface, which some people have claimed to be due to seasonal changes in plant life, are actually due to dust storms in the thin atmosphere.

However some scientists believe that there is evidence for the existence of very *simple* life on Mars. This evidence exists in meteorites which fell to Earth in Antarctica about 12 000 years ago. It is believed that these meteorites were blasted from the surface of Mars by volcanic eruptions or the impact of other meteorites. The meteorites found in Antarctica contain pockets of gas with a composition almost identical to the Martian atmosphere today, together with traces of what appear to be fossil bacteria. Scientists remain deeply divided about whether the meteorites do indeed contain fossil bacteria, and resolving the question once and for all will probably take an expedition to Mars which collects samples of soil from below the surface for careful analysis.

↑ **Figure 1:** Are we alone in the Universe? The answer 'yes' to this question has often been given in books and films – but we shall not know for sure until we have made contact with other life, either directly or indirectly.

↑ **Figure 2:** Scientists believe that Europa may have a layer of ice kilometres thick that covers a layer of liquid water. This is an artist's impression of an undersea explorer probe on Europa.

Chemical evidence

Living organisms like those found on Earth carry out complicated chemical reactions in order to remain alive. These complex reactions affect the environment around the living things, so that chemicals are present which would not be there otherwise. (For example, there is more oxygen in the Earth's atmosphere than would be present if there were no plants on the Earth's surface.) The environment of a planet or other body could be sampled by sending a probe there. Alternatively, it might be possible to make predictions about the composition of the planet based on the wavelengths of electromagnetic radiation coming from it, since different chemicals absorb electromagnetic waves in different ways.

Detecting signals

Since about 1960 vast radio telescopes have been used to look for radio signals coming from outer space that might have been broadcast by intelligent life, in a project called SETI – Search for Extra-Terrestrial Intelligence. The stars and other bodies in space act as giant radio broadcasting stations. This means that detecting broadcasts that may come from intelligent civilisations is very difficult – a problem that is a bit like trying to detect the tune that someone is playing on a guitar among 100 000 chanting football fans!

However, the problem is not impossible, thanks to the fact that radio signals within a narrow band of frequencies are present at very low level, providing a 'hole' through which we may be able to detect the broadcasts of distant civilisations. It is almost as if the football fans in the football crowd are chanting using either very low or very high frequency notes, leaving the sound of the guitar to come through the gap in the middle of these!

To decide whether a signal comes from a natural object or from intelligent life, complex mathematical analysis needs to be carried out on the data collected by radio telescopes. Since the middle of 1999 the SETI@home project has enabled anyone with a computer connected to the Internet to join in this task by downloading special software from the SETI@home website. When the computer is running but not being used, this software downloads radio telescope data and processes it, then sends the results back to the SETI server. In this way over two million computer users around the planet are contributing to the search for extraterrestrial life.

Figure 3: Intelligent life may use technologies which produce large changes to the atmosphere in which they occur. Observing such changes may provide clues about life present on other planets.

Key Ideas

- If there is life elsewhere in the Universe we may find it by looking in three ways:
  - we might go looking for it ourselves or using robotic probes
  - we might look for chemical changes that provide evidence of life
  - we might be able to detect radio signals from other life.
- Radio signals from a limited range of radio frequencies are examined, since these contain little background noise.
- Despite 40 years of searching, there is still no evidence of life in the Universe other than on Earth.

Questions

1. Would life elsewhere in the Universe necessarily be like life on Earth? Explain your answer.

2. It may be very difficult to decide whether or not a signal has been sent by intelligent life. Why?

The Earth and beyond

4.6 How did it all start? H

If you have ever been standing at the side of the road when an emergency vehicle rushes past, you will almost certainly have noticed how the pitch of the siren rises as it approaches you and then falls as it goes past. Physicists call this the **Doppler effect**, which was first described by Christian Doppler more than 150 years ago. This effect can be explained by thinking of the sound waves in front of a moving object being 'squashed', reducing their wavelength and so increasing their pitch. In the same way, we can think of the sound waves behind a moving object being 'stretched' – this increases their wavelength and so reduces their pitch.

Nearly 100 years ago astronomers looking at distant stars in other galaxies noticed how the wavelengths of the light coming from the stars were very similar to the light coming from nearby stars in our own galaxy, except for one thing. Light from the distant stars seemed to have longer wavelengths than expected, with the result that it appeared more red than light from stars that are nearer to us, in our own galaxy. This observation quickly became known as the 'red shift', and it was noticed that the further away a star was, the greater was the red shift – that is, the more the wavelength of light coming from it was 'stretched'.

Astronomers explain the pattern of red shift in the light from distant stars using the Doppler effect. The light from distant stars is shifted to the red end of the spectrum because these stars are rushing rapidly away from us. The further away the stars are, the more rapidly they are moving – which explains why the red shift increases the further away the star is.

To explain why stars should be moving apart in this way, astronomers think about what happens when a firework explodes. As this happens, fragments of firework fly apart in all directions with different speeds. A certain time after the explosion the situation might look like Figure 3, with fragments flying in all directions. Some fragments will have travelled further than others – and obviously the fastest will have travelled furthest.

Our observations of the Universe suggest that it may have started off in a gigantic explosion, which scientists call the **big bang**. In this explosion the Universe somehow exploded out of an infinitely small point. The red shifts of stars that we see today are a result of this explosion – just like the firework, the parts of the Universe that are travelling fastest are those that are furthest from the explosion.

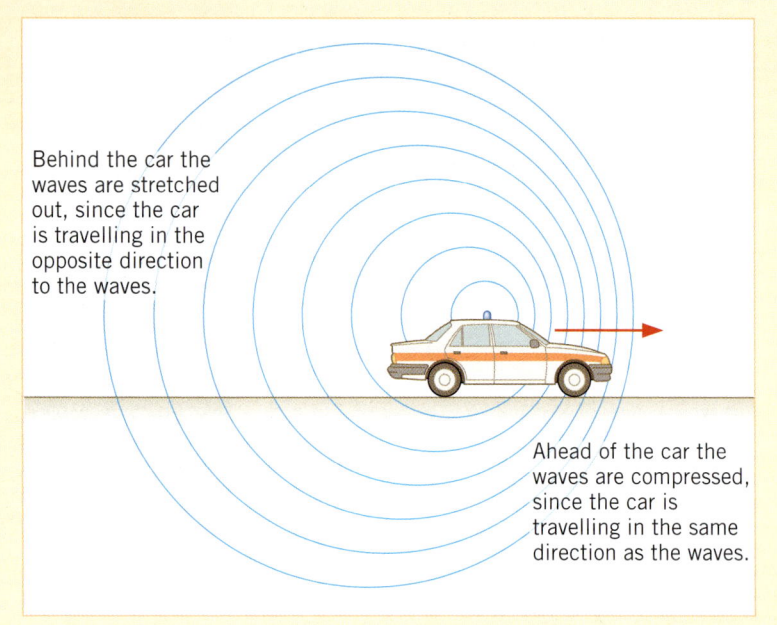

Behind the car the waves are stretched out, since the car is travelling in the opposite direction to the waves.

Ahead of the car the waves are compressed, since the car is travelling in the same direction as the waves.

↑ **Figure 1:** The Doppler effect applies to all waves, not just to sound waves.

Sun's spectrum

Distant star's spectrum

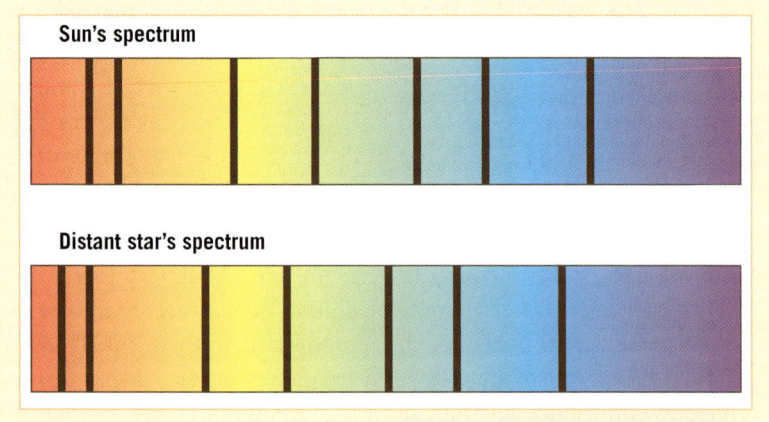

↑ **Figure 2:** The dark lines in the spectrum of the Sun show where helium atoms have absorbed light of certain wavelengths. The spectrum of light from a distant star contains a similar set of lines – but shifted towards the red end of the spectrum.

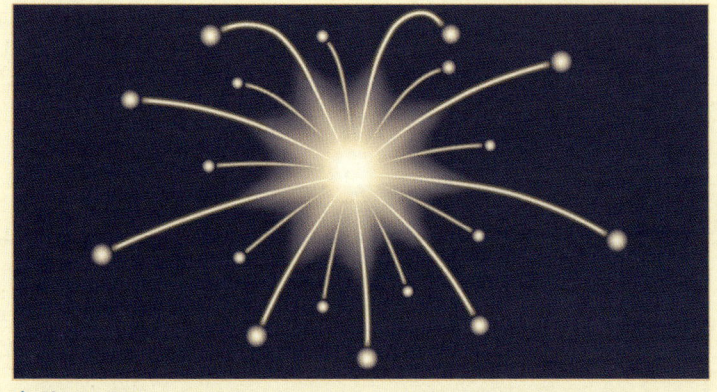

↑ **Figure 3:** An exploding firework sends fragments in all directions – this suggests that the Universe came from an explosion too.

The Earth and beyond

The big bang was not really like a firework though – this is just a simple model for helping us to understand it. The big bang was not an explosion of a lump of matter in space – in the explosion space and time as well as matter and energy were formed, and exploded out of the fireball. It makes no sense to ask, 'What was there before the big bang?' because there was no time (or space!) before it!

Scientists are unsure how the Universe will end. Will space carry on expanding, or will it eventually come to a halt? Or maybe it will start to contract again, and there will eventually be what some scientists have called a 'big crunch'. Which of these endings is the right one depends on how much matter there is in the Universe – and astronomers cannot yet measure this accurately enough to decide just what will happen.

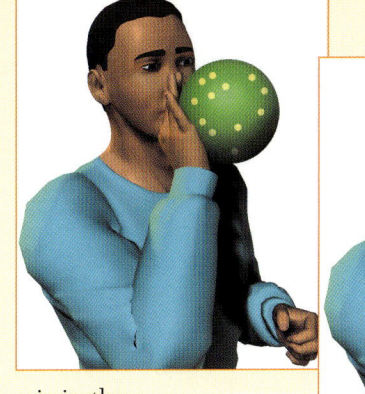

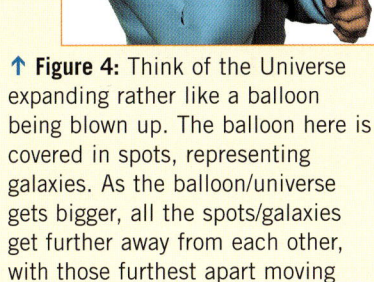

↑ **Figure 4:** Think of the Universe expanding rather like a balloon being blown up. The balloon here is covered in spots, representing galaxies. As the balloon/universe gets bigger, all the spots/galaxies get further away from each other, with those furthest apart moving away from each other most quickly.

Ideas and Evidence

It's just a theory

The theory that the Universe began with a gigantic explosion is just that – a theory. But this does not mean that the idea of the big bang is just a guess, as the word 'theory' often does in everyday language.

A theory in science is not a guess, but a very carefully worked out explanation for many experimental observations and results. The big bang theory is not just based on observations of the red shift of light from distant galaxies but on many other pieces of evidence as well, including the evidence from the COBE satellite (Figure 4, page 69). These pieces of evidence form a web of support for the theory – the more support there is from evidence from different sources, the more confident we can be about the theory.

Questions

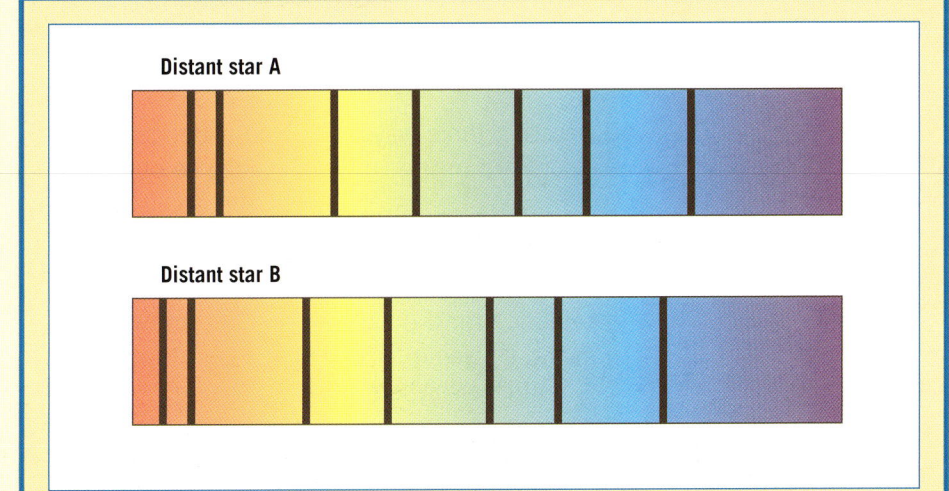

↑ **Figure 5:** The spectra of light from two distant stars.

1 Look at Figure 5, which shows the spectra of light from two distant stars. Which of the two stars is further away? Why?

2 One model for the expansion of the Universe is an exploding firework, while another is an inflating balloon. Which of these two models is better? Give your reasons.

Key Ideas

- Light from distant galaxies is shifted towards the red end of the spectrum – the further away the galaxy, the greater the red shift.

- Astronomers believe that the observed red shift of galaxies is because the Universe was formed in a gigantic explosion called the Big Bang many billions of years ago.

- This suggests that the whole Universe is expanding. It may carry on expanding, or it may stop, when it may then collapse again, eventually forming a Big Crunch.

The Earth and beyond 75

4.7 End of chapter questions

1 The table shows data about some of the planets in our Solar System.

Planet	Time to orbit Sun once (years)	Time to rotate once on axis (days)	Gravitational field at surface (N/kg)	Approximate average distance from Sun (million km)
Mercury	0.24	59	4	58
Venus	0.6	243	9	110
Earth	1.0	1	10	150
Mars	1.9	1	4	230
Jupiter	12	0.4	26	780
Saturn	30	0.4	11	1430
Pluto	248	6	4	5900

   a Which planet takes longest to go round the Sun? (1 mark)
   b Which planet has the longest day? (1 mark)
   c On which planet would you weigh most? (1 mark)
   d A spacecraft has a mass of 3500 kg. How much would it weigh on
      i Mars (2 marks)
      ii Jupiter? (2 marks)
      (Total 7 marks)

2 The diagram shows circular orbits for two satellites around the Earth.

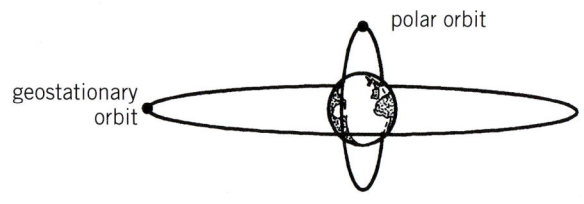

   a i How long does it take a geostationary satellite to complete an orbit? (1 mark)
      ii How is the orbital time of the polar satellite shown in the diagram different to that of the geostationary one?
         Explain your answer. (2 marks)
   b The Hubble telescope is in orbit around the Earth.
      What is the advantage of this telescope over ground-based telescopes on Earth? (1 mark)
      (Total 4 marks)
      AQA specimen question

3 The diagram shows an orbiter, the reusable part of a space shuttle. The data refers to a typical flight.

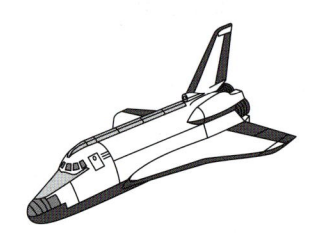

Orbiter data	
Mass	78 000 kg
Orbital speed	7.5 km/s
Orbital altitude	200 km
Landing speed	100 m/s
Flight time	7 days

   a Calculate the kinetic energy, in joules, of the orbiter while it is in orbit. (2 marks)
   b i Give the equation that links acceleration, force and mass. (1 mark)
      ii Calculate, in newtons, the force needed to bring the orbiter to a halt after it has landed. After landing the orbiter decelerates at 2 m/s^2. Show clearly how you work out your answer. (1 mark)
      (Total 4 marks)

4 Some scientists are searching for evidence of life in other parts of the Universe.
   a Describe **three** ways in which evidence for life elsewhere in the Universe might be obtained. (3 marks)
   b As at July 2001 the SETI project ('Search for Extra Terrestrial Intelligence') had found no evidence for the existence of life elsewhere in the Universe. Does this suggest that there is no life elsewhere in the Universe? (3 marks)
      (Total 6 marks)

The Earth and beyond

5 *To gain full marks in this question you should write your ideas in good English. Put them into a sensible order and use the correct scientific words.*

a The Sun is at the stable stage of its life.

Explain, in terms of the forces acting on the Sun, what this means. (3 marks)

b At the end of the stable stage of its life a star will change.

Describe and explain the changes that could take place, for a star:

i to become a white dwarf (3 marks)

ii to become a black hole. (3 marks)

(Total 9 marks)

AQA specimen question

6 The graph shows how the time for a satellite to make one orbit round the Earth varies according to its height above the Earth's surface.

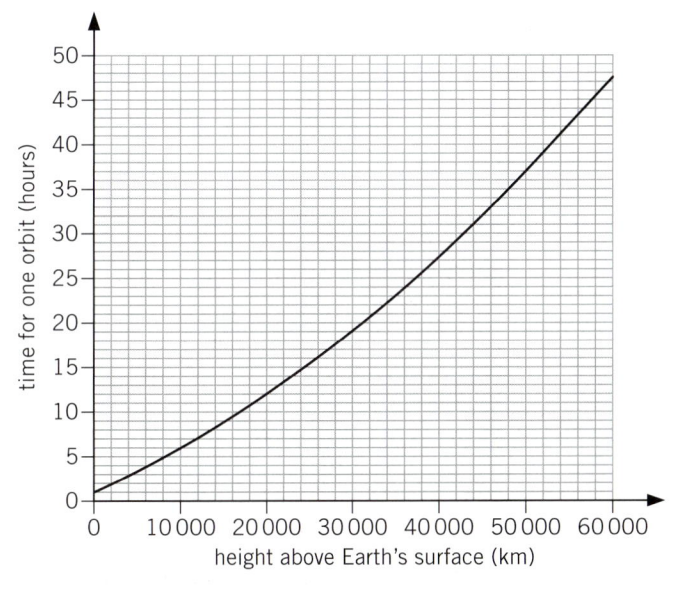

a Some satellites may be placed in a **low polar orbit**. Give **two** advantages of this kind of orbit for satellites used to observe the Earth's weather. (2 marks)

b A team of scientists wishes to launch a satellite so that it orbits the Earth three times each day.

i How long would this satellite take to orbit the Earth **once**? (1 mark)

ii Use the graph to find out the height of this satellite above the Earth when it is in orbit. (1 mark)

c Telecommunications satellites are usually placed in **geostationary** orbits.

i Give **one** reason why this kind of orbit is used for communications satellites. (1 mark)

ii Write down the time taken for a geostationary satellite to orbit the Earth **once**. (1 mark)

(Total 7 marks)

iii Use the graph to work out the height of a geostationary satellite's orbit above the surface of the Earth. (1 mark)

(Total 7 marks)

5.1 Transferring heat energy

Figure 1: Energy flows from a place where the temperature is high to a place where the temperature is lower. In solids this is called **conduction**, while in liquids and gases the flow of energy is usually through a mechanism called **convection**, in which the liquid or gas carries energy as it moves. Energy is also transferred to and from objects by means of electromagnetic radiation.

As we have already seen, electromagnetic radiation is all around us and has many different wavelengths. Objects that are hot emit electromagnetic radiation mainly in the infra-red region of the electromagnetic spectrum. As the temperature of an object increases, the wavelength of the electromagnetic radiation it emits gets shorter, and eventually the object may give off light as well as infra-red radiation. You can see this if you slowly increase the current through a filament lamp. At first the filament does not glow, then it glows a dull red colour, then orange, then yellow and eventually white as wavelengths throughout the visible spectrum are produced.

When we talk about energy being 'transferred by radiation' it is usually infra-red radiation that we are talking about. Photographs taken with cameras that are sensitive to infra-red radiation can reveal similar effects in a surprising way, as Figure 2 shows.

When an object absorbs electromagnetic radiation of any type its temperature increases. The energy carried by the electromagnetic wave makes the atoms of the material vibrate more, and so its temperature rises. Electromagnetic waves of all wavelengths behave like this, but infra-red radiation is particularly good at heating.

When an object absorbs infra-red radiation, its surface is the most important factor affecting the rate at which the radiation is absorbed. You can observe this effect using two pieces of card, one black and the other white. If you put the two pieces of card outside on a sunny day, after 15 minutes or so the black card will feel much warmer than the white card – it has absorbed more infra-red radiation.

As a general rule, dull (or **matt**) black surfaces are the best absorbers of infra-red radiation, while shiny silver surfaces are the worst. White surfaces are also bad absorbers. This means that white clothing is much cooler to wear in sunny weather than dark clothing, and that dark buildings will absorb more energy from the Sun than light buildings.

Figure 2: This false colour photograph of a man, woman and child shows how different areas of the body are at different temperatures. The white areas are hottest and are emitting large amounts of infra-red radiation with short wavelengths, while the purple areas are coldest, and emit far less infra-red radiation, which has a longer wavelength.

The emission of infra-red radiation also depends on the surface of the object emitting the radiation. One way to show this is to use a light bulb with one side painted matt black (Figure 3). When the bulb is switched on you can clearly feel that energy is being emitted from the black side of the bulb at a greater rate than from the unpainted side.

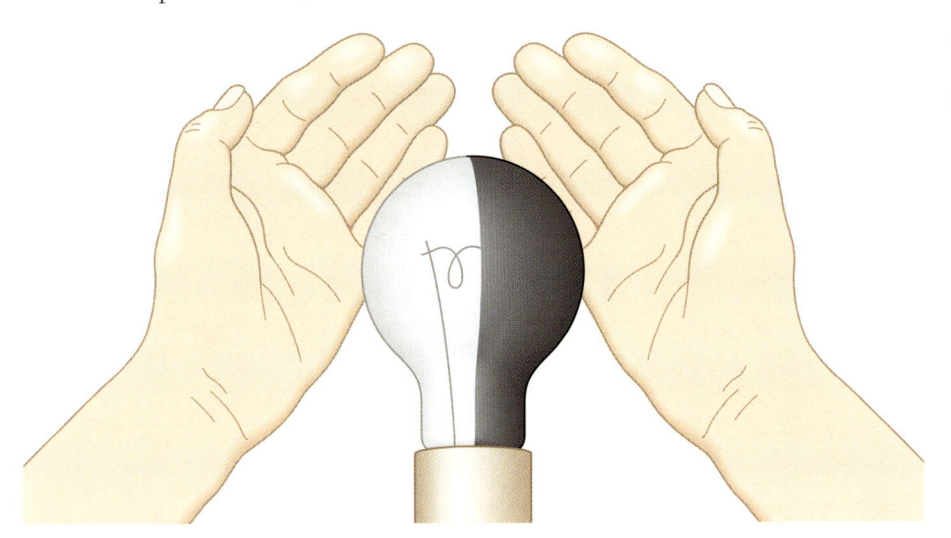

← **Figure 3:** Dull, dark surfaces are better emitters of energy than shiny white surfaces.

The rule for emitting infra-red radiation is the same as the rule for absorbing radiation; that is, as a general rule, dull (or matt) black surfaces are the best emitters of electromagnetic radiation, while shiny silver surfaces are the worst. White surfaces are also bad emitters.

Science people

The unit of energy is named after the British scientist James Prescott Joule, who was born in Salford, Lancashire nearly 200 years ago. Joule is remembered for his research on heat and work, which he carried out with his fellow scientist William Thomson. Thomson later became Lord Kelvin of Largs, and made a large amount of money as a scientific adviser to companies manufacturing and laying undersea telegraph cables. Kelvin gave his name to a unit of temperature.

Key Ideas

- The hotter an object is, the more energy it radiates.
- Dark, matt surfaces emit more radiation than light, shiny surfaces at the same temperature.
- Dark, matt surfaces are good absorbers of radiation, while light, shiny surfaces are poor absorbers of radiation.

Questions

1. Two cars are identical except for their colour – one is black, the other white. Which is likely to be cooler to travel in during the summer and why?
2. Central heating radiators are usually painted white. Does their colour really matter?
3. Figure 4 shows a thermos flask. Explain carefully how each of the features of the flask help to slow down energy transfer by conduction, convection and radiation.

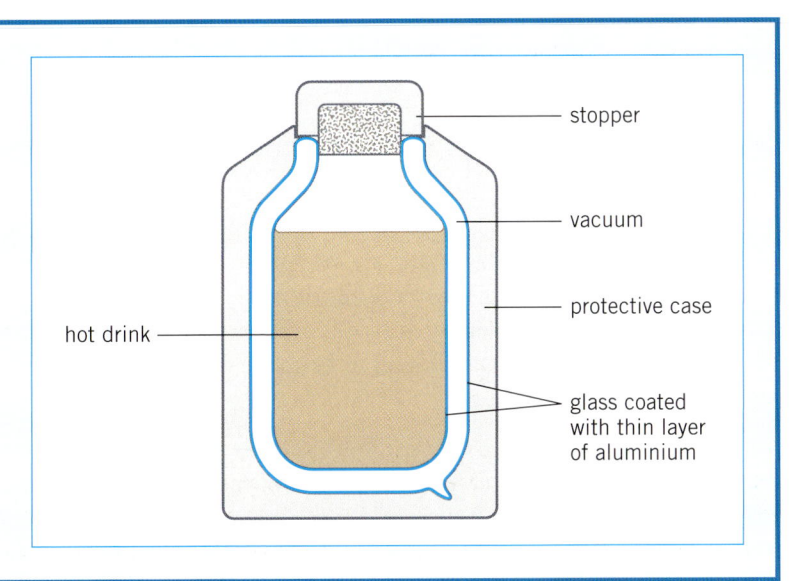

→ **Figure 4**

(labels: stopper, vacuum, protective case, hot drink, glass coated with thin layer of aluminium)

Energy resources and energy transfer

5.2 Less energy by design

Scientists estimate that almost half the energy used in Western Europe goes to heat and light the buildings in which we live and work – our homes, shops, offices and schools. With concerns about supplies of fossil fuels running low (see page 88), it is very important to think about ways in which we can construct buildings which use as little energy to heat and light them as possible.

Think about the way in which energy enters and leaves a building like a school. Obviously energy is used to heat the building, either by burning oil or gas (or perhaps even coal), or by using electricity. Electricity is also used to light the building, and to power machines like computers, televisions, photocopiers and so on inside it. But energy also enters and leaves the building through the walls, roof and windows. Whether energy enters or leaves depends on whether the temperature inside the building is higher or lower than the temperature outside the building. If the inside of the building is warmer than the air outside, then energy will flow out of the building – exactly what we do not want to happen in the middle of winter!

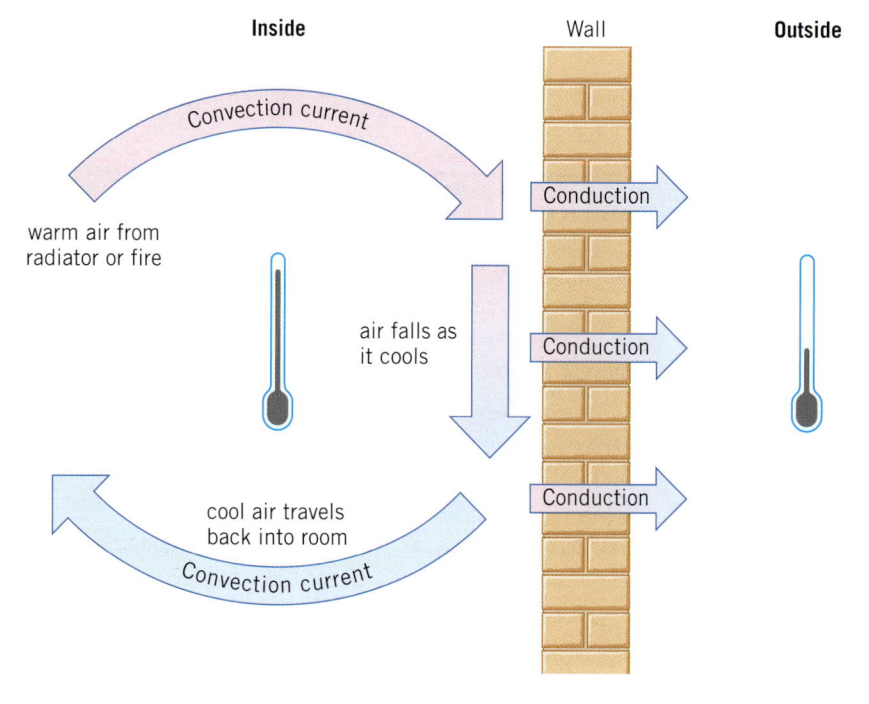

Figure 1: Two fairly typical schools – just how energy-efficient are they?

Figure 2: Energy always tends to flow from a warm place to a cold one, whether by conduction or convection.

To prevent energy flowing too quickly from the warm air inside the building to the cold air outside, we can do several things. First, we can make the walls of the building from materials that are very poor conductors of heat. The concrete building blocks used for the inside walls of modern houses are an example of such a material. However, these blocks are not very pretty to look at, so the outside walls of houses still tend to be made of materials like brick, which are not such good insulators.

Second, we can build the house using techniques that slow down the rate of energy transfer even further. The outer walls of modern buildings are actually made of two walls, with a space or 'cavity' about 10 cm wide between them. The air in this cavity can carry energy by convection, but heat loss this way can

Energy resources and energy transfer

be prevented by filling the cavity with foam or with tiny plastic beads. The roof of the building also needs to be insulated in order to slow down the rate at which energy flows through it. A lot of energy may flow out through the roof, so the insulation here must be particularly thick – building regulations in the UK currently require roof insulation in new houses to be 200 mm thick.

Double-glazing also helps to stop energy leaving the building through the windows. It does this by trapping a thin layer of air between two sheets of glass about 1 cm apart – air is about 30 times less good as a conductor than glass. With a thin layer of air there is not enough room for convection currents to be set up – so energy flows very much more slowly though double-glazed windows than through single glazed ones.

Energy is also transferred between a building and its surroundings by radiation. On a night with no cloud cover, the Earth rapidly radiates its energy into outer space, which may lead to heavy dew in summer (as moisture in the air condenses on the cold ground) and a frost in winter (as the moisture which condenses on the ground freezes). In the same way, a warm building will also radiate energy to its surroundings. Since we know that light, shiny objects are much worse radiators than dark, matt objects, it might seem a good idea to paint all buildings in light, glossy colours – but this is not necessarily the case! We may sometimes want a building to absorb as much infra-red radiation as possible – for example, on a cold winter's day when the Sun is out. In this case the building will need to be a dark matt colour in order to maximise the amount of radiation that it absorbs.

Deciding on the colour of a building in order to get the best advantages from energy transfer by radiation will depend on many things. A dark building will absorb a good deal of infra-red radiation on sunny days – which may be useful during cold winter days, but is likely to be much less so on hot summer ones! And a dark building will also radiate more energy at night, making it cool down more rapidly than it would do if it were light coloured. While this may not be important if the building is unoccupied at night (for example, if it is a school) a house that got cold quickly at night would not be a pleasant building in which to live.

Windows can also play an important part in energy transfers through radiation. Glass allows infra-red radiation from the Sun to pass through without absorbing very much of its energy, while infra-red radiation emitted by objects at or around room temperature (which has a lower frequency) cannot pass through glass. This means that windows act as a kind of 'energy valve', allowing energy to radiate into a building, but preventing it radiating out again.

Double glazing

Cavity wall insulation

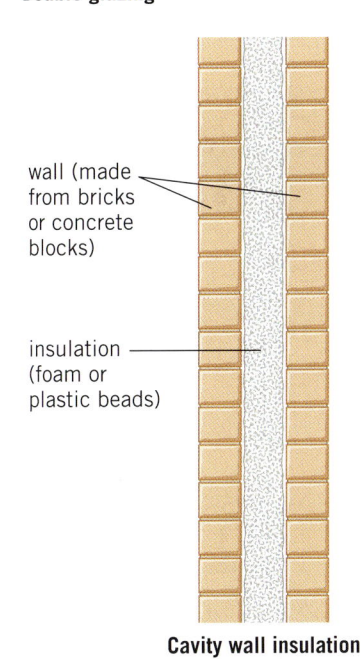

↑ **Figure 3:** Clever yet simple construction techniques can minimise the rate at which energy flows out of a building.

? Questions

1. Look at the photograph of the house in Figure 4. This has been taken using an infra red camera, which shows the hottest parts of the house as white and the coolest as purple.

    a Which parts of the house seem to be warmest? Which are coolest?

    b Suggest what could be done to reduce the rate at which energy is transferred from the warm house to the cool surroundings.

    ↑ Figure 4

    c Which of the measures you have suggested in part (b) do you think should be taken first and why?

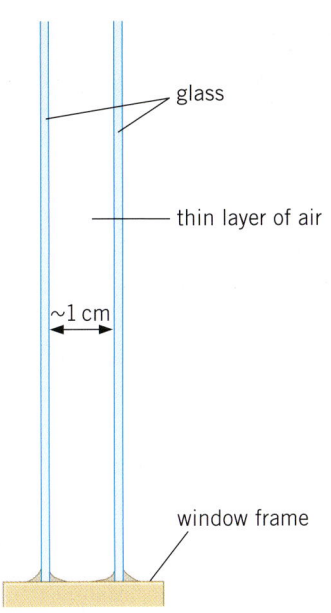

Key Ideas

- Energy-efficient buildings can be designed based on our understanding of energy transfers by conduction, convection and radiation.

Energy resources and energy transfer

5.3 Designs for energy efficient living

Marshmead School, Australia

This school was built in 1991 with no mains electricity supply due to its isolated location, in the Croajingalong National Park in Victoria. As well as a diesel generator, electricity is supplied by a wind turbine and photovoltaic cells, which transfer light energy to electrical energy. The buildings are designed to ensure that as much energy as possible is transferred from the surroundings to the buildings, and that as little energy as possible is transferred in the opposite direction. This is done using three main features:

- The floor, ceiling and external walls are all heavily insulated.
- Internal walls are made of special mud-bricks, able to store large amounts of energy.
- There are large north-facing windows, provided with shading.

Figure 1: Marshmead School, Australia. The wind turbine provides some of the electricity for this energy efficient building.

Energy resources and energy transfer

Living underground

Underground, or **earth-sheltered** houses are built with most of the house below the ground's surface. The earth surrounding the house is at a fairly constant temperature throughout the year, and provides natural insulation. This makes this kind of house inexpensive to heat and cool.

Clever use of windows ensures that an earth-sheltered house can be almost as light as a conventional house built above the ground, while the thick earth walls provide excellent insulation. The best place to put an earth-sheltered house is on a well-drained hillside which faces south.

→ **Figure 2:** An earth-sheltered house in West Yorkshire.

Questions

1 The Australian school has large north-facing windows – why?

2 Here is some information about the cost of building a house in two different ways.

	Conventional building method	**Super energy-efficient method**
Building cost	£75 000	£85 000
Yearly cost of heating	£800	£300
Likely lifetime of house	50 years	75 years

Is it worth building the super energy-efficient house? Explain your answer.

3 The best place to put an earth-sheltered house is on a well-drained hillside which faces south. Explain why this is.

4 The following is adapted from a letter to the Global Ideas Bank written by Dr Julian White of Cambridge:

1 power station = 100,000 energy-efficient houses

If £3 billion is taken as the average construction cost of a modern power station, then if this money were used to build energy efficient houses, by taking a rough value of £30 000 as the construction cost of a medium-sized mass-produced house, 100 000 houses could be constructed for the same price as the power station.

For construction on this scale the houses could have all the most recent resource efficient measures included (insulation to Scandinavian standards, low energy lighting, super low flush toilets and showers to reduce water consumption, reversible heat pumps to both heat the houses in winter and to cool them in summer). Then you get 100 000 families who are living in the worst housing and you re-house them in this accommodation and demolish their previous dwellings.

So what have you gained by doing this as opposed to building the power station? Well you have got rid of 100 000 of the worst houses as far as energy consumption and just plain living conditions are concerned, probably more than saving the amount of electricity generated by the power station. In the process the amount of resources (gas, coal, oil, and pure water) has been reduced. Most of all, one of the greatest ills of society – that of inadequate housing and homelessness – has been greatly eased. With this one simple act all these different acute modern-day crises have been eased simultaneously. The lives of the poorest members of society have been drastically improved; and in a caring modern day society, the benefits afforded by society as a whole should always go to those who need them most.

Do you agree with the ideas put forward by the writer of this letter? Give your reasons.

Energy resources and energy transfer

5.4 More about conduction, convection and radiation

Conduction

Of all solids, metals are particularly good conductors of electricity. Non-metals are usually poor conductors and gases are very poor.

H The model for a metal consists of a grid of metal atoms, each of which gives up some of its electrons, forming a sort of 'electron soup'. (See page 19.) Those parts of a piece of metal which are at a high temperature contain metal ions which have a lot of kinetic energy as they vibrate vigorously. Some of this energy is transferred to electrons as they collide with the metal ions. Since the electrons can move freely, the energy is transferred to cooler parts of the metal, as the electrons travel through the metal ions, colliding with them and other electrons.

Non-metals have no free electrons. Conduction happens as vibrating atoms pass energy from one to another, rather like someone jostling at one end of a queue might cause a disturbance which reaches the other end. This is a much slower process than the transfer of energy by free electrons – which is why non-metals are much poorer conductors of heat than metals.

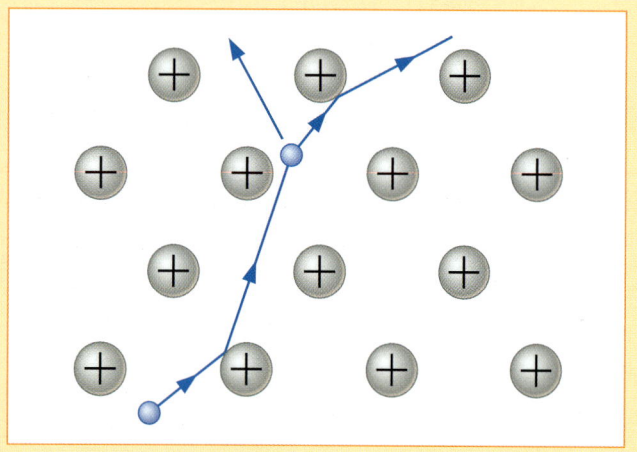

↑ **Figure 1:** Freely moving electrons transfer thermal energy quickly throughout a piece of metal.

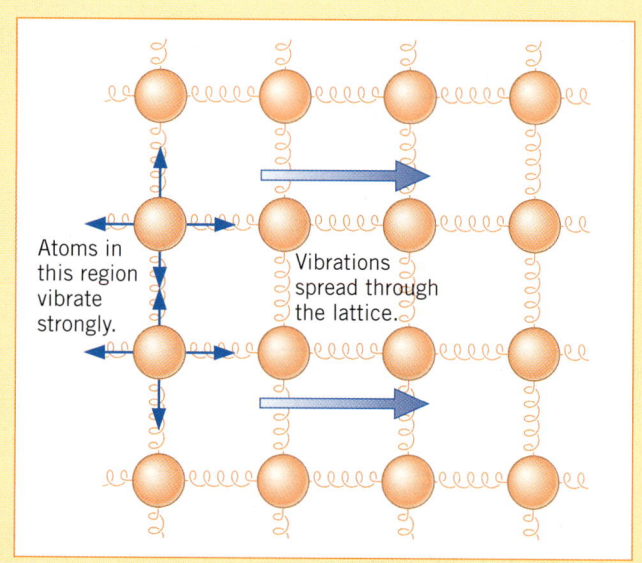

↑ **Figure 2:** There are no free electrons in non-metals. Conduction through these materials is due to vibrations being passed from one atom to another.

Convection

Convection is an important mechanism for energy transfer in fluids – liquids and gases, which are able to **flow**.

H When a substance is heated, the particles in it acquire more energy and begin to move more vigorously. In a solid this motion is in the form of vibrations, with the particles moving around about a fixed position. In the case of fluids the increased movement of particles is in the form of random motion, in which the particles move increasingly rapidly from one place to another as more and more energy is supplied. The result of this more vigorous movement, whether in a solid or a fluid, is **expansion** – an increase in the average distance between particles.

It is the expansion that happens when a fluid is heated which causes convection. Figure 3 shows what happens. The region of the fluid (in this case the water in a saucepan) being heated becomes warmer and expands as it does so. The density of a substance is calculated from the relationship **density = mass/volume**. Because this part of the

Energy resources and energy transfer

fluid has expanded its volume has increased, so its density has decreased. Being less dense than the fluid around it, the warm fluid rises, and is replaced by colder fluid – producing a **convection current**.

Convection currents may be enhanced by forcing the warm fluid to mix with the colder fluid – by stirring with a spoon in the case of the water in the saucepan, or by using an electric fan, in the case of an electric room heater. This is **forced convection**.

→ **Figure 3:** Convection currents are produced whenever one part of a fluid is warmer than another part.

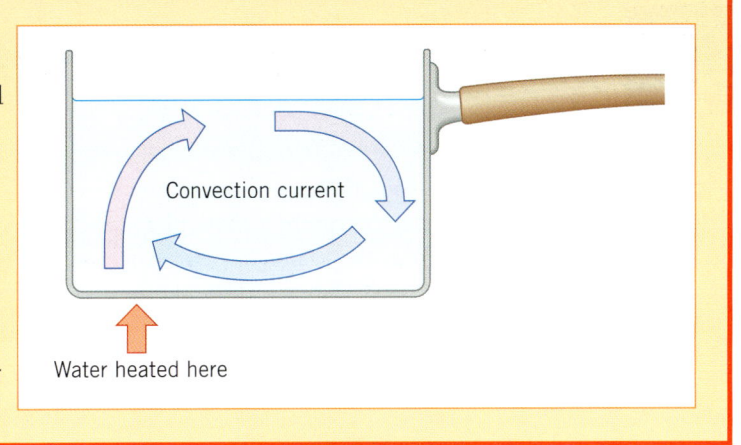

Radiation

The transfer of energy by radiation involves electromagnetic waves, as we have seen. Since waves transfer energy from one place to another without any movement of matter, this makes radiation a very important method of energy transfer. It is the only means of heat transfer through a vacuum.

H Most importantly, infra-red radiation is an electromagnetic wave, which can travel through a vacuum. This is the only way that energy from the Sun can reach the Earth, without which the Earth would be a very cold and inhospitable place – colder even than the outer planets of the Solar System.

Radiation is also important in heating our homes and in many types of cooking. The warmth that you feel when you stand next to a bonfire or an open flame fire indoors is due to energy transfer through radiation. When you make toast (whether in an electric toaster or under a grill) or cook food on a barbecue, the energy transferred to the food happens through radiation.

↑ **Figure 4:** A Crookes radiometer. Each vane in the radiometer has one side painted black, and the other painted white or silver. There is virtually no air in the glass bulb, so energy reaches the vanes only through radiation. When placed in bright light, the vanes rotate rapidly.

Questions

1 Why are gases poor conductors?

2 Why does most insulation work by trapping a still layer of air?

3 Architects and builders use 'U-values' to calculate the amount of energy transferred by conduction through different building materials. The rate at which energy is conducted through a particular material is given by the relationship:

**rate of energy transfer =
U-value × area × temperature difference**

Two different building materials A and B have U-values of $1.5\,\text{W/m}^2/°C$ and $1.0\,\text{W/m}^2/°C$ respectively. Calculate the rate at which energy flows through two walls, one constructed from A the other from B, each with an area of $25\,\text{m}^2$ and a temperature difference of $20\,°C$ across them.

4 In 1987 a hurricane battered the southern counties of England. Explain how energy from the Sun provided the energy for this.

Key Ideas

- Conduction in metals happens quickly due to the presence of free electrons which are able to carry energy quickly from one part of the metal to another.

- Convection occurs in liquids and gases (fluids) due to the decrease in density that results as one part of the fluid heats up. This part of the fluid then rises, and is replaced with colder fluid.

- Thermal radiation involves the transfer of energy by wave.

Energy resources and energy transfer

5.5 Energy transfers – useful and useless

When we use energy to do something – for example, when we switch on a lamp at home – we want to transfer energy in a particular way. In the case of the lamp, we want electrical energy from the mains to be transferred to light energy, so that we can see. Figure 1 shows how we can represent energy transfers.

Unfortunately not all of the energy from the mains gets transferred to light energy, as you will know if you have ever put your hand near a light bulb that has been switched on for some time. Whenever energy is transferred some of it is always transferred to places and forms that we do not want. In particular, some energy is always wasted as its heats up the device that we are using.

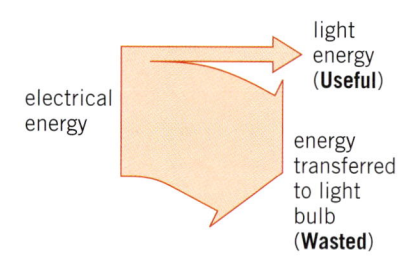

Conventional light bulbs, which use a white-hot wire filament to produce light, are particularly bad at transferring electrical energy into light energy. As Figure 2 shows, only a tiny proportion of the electrical energy from the mains supply ends up as light energy – an energy transfer that we can describe as *useful*. Most of the energy transferred from the mains goes to heating up the light bulb, increasing its temperature to a point which could cause you quite a painful burn if you were to touch it for any length of time.

By contrast, a modern 'low energy' light bulb is much better at transferring energy from the mains supply to light energy, producing much more useful energy and much less wasted energy (Figure 3).

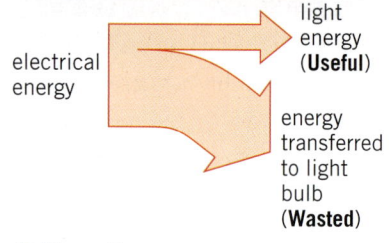

Virtually all energy transfers involve energy wasted as heat, and may also involve small amounts of energy wasted as sound.

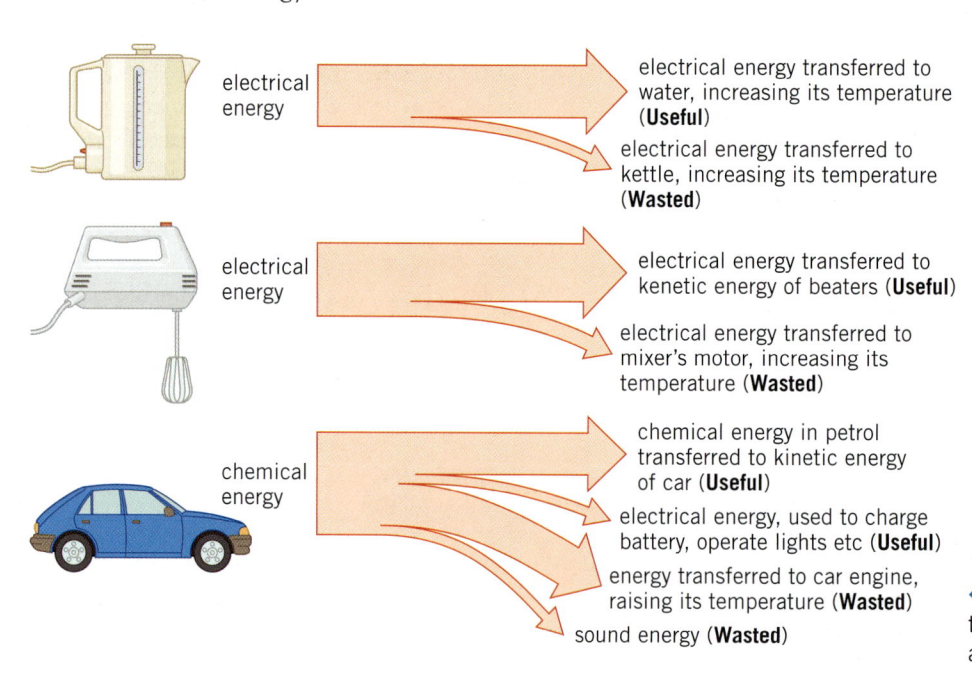

↑ Figure 1

electrical energy → light energy

↑ Figure 2

electrical energy → light energy (**Useful**) / energy transferred to light bulb (**Wasted**)

↑ Figure 3

electrical energy → light energy (**Useful**) / energy transferred to light bulb (**Wasted**)

electrical energy → electrical energy transferred to water, increasing its temperature (**Useful**) / electrical energy transferred to kettle, increasing its temperature (**Wasted**)

electrical energy → electrical energy transferred to kenetic energy of beaters (**Useful**) / electrical energy transferred to mixer's motor, increasing its temperature (**Wasted**)

chemical energy → chemical energy in petrol transferred to kinetic energy of car (**Useful**) / electrical energy, used to charge battery, operate lights etc (**Useful**) / energy transferred to car engine, raising its temperature (**Wasted**) / sound energy (**Wasted**)

← Figure 4: Some energy transfers involving useful and wasted energy.

Devices in which most of the energy supplied to the device is transferred as useful energy are described as efficient, while those in which a lot of the energy supplied is transferred as wasted energy are described as inefficient.

We can calculate the efficiency of a device if we know the amount of energy transferred:

$$\text{efficiency} = \frac{\text{useful energy transferred by the device}}{\text{total energy supplied to the device}} \times 100\%$$

Energy resources and energy transfer

Energy spreads out

Whether it has been transferred as useful energy or as wasted energy, ultimately all transferred energy ends up being transferred to the surroundings, which become warmer as a result. To see why this is, think about an electric lamp in a room.

The hot bulb transfers energy to the air around it, making it hotter. This warmer air then transfers energy around the room by convection, its place being taken by cooler air which carries more energy away from the hot bulb. The bulb also emits heat radiation, making the room warmer. As the room gets warmer, energy is transferred through the walls, ceiling and floor to the room's surroundings – and so the energy supplied to the lamp continues to spread out.

However, the effect of one light bulb on the temperature of the whole house will simply not be noticed. Energy always behaves like this – the more spread out it becomes, the less useful it is for other energy transfers. This is why fuels are so important – they are locked up stores of concentrated energy.

Example 1

An electric lamp is supplied with 80 J of electrical energy and produces 4 J of light energy. Calculate its efficiency.

We know that

$$\text{efficiency} = \frac{\text{useful energy transferred by the device}}{\text{total energy supplied to the device}} \times 100\%$$

The useful energy transferred by the lamp is 4 J, while the total energy supplied to it is 80 J, so

$$\text{efficiency} = \frac{4}{80} \times 100\% = \mathbf{5\%}$$

Example 2

An electric motor has a power input of 2.5 kW. It transfers useful energy at a rate of 1.5 kW. What is its efficiency?

We know that

$$\text{efficiency} = \frac{\text{useful energy transferred by the device}}{\text{total energy supplied to the device}} \times 100\%$$

The information in the question tells us that energy is supplied to the motor at a rate of 2.5 kW, while the motor transfers useful energy at a rate of 1.5 kW. This means that

$$\text{efficiency} = \frac{1 \cdot 5}{2 \cdot 5} \times 100\% = \mathbf{60\%}$$

Notice how we can use the **rate** at which energy is transferred (measured in watts) as well as the **amount** of energy transferred in calculating the efficiency of something. This is possible because the rate at which energy is transferred tells us how much energy is transferred each second – so dividing the useful energy transferred each second by the total energy supplied each second tells us the efficiency.

Questions

1. a. For every 3000 J of energy supplied to an electric motor, 2250 J of useful energy is transferred. Calculate the efficiency of the motor.
   b. Energy is supplied to the engine of a lawnmower at a rate of 1.4 kW. The engine transfers useful energy at a rate of 0.84 kW. What is the efficiency of the engine?

2. A filament lamp is 5% efficient, while a replacement 'ecolamp' is 60% efficient. If both lamps produce light energy at a rate of 3 W, at what rate does each lamp produce wasted energy?

3. Here is some information about the running costs for electric lamps:

	Purchase cost	Rate at which energy must be supplied for required light output	Estimated life of lamp
Lamp 1	50 p	100 W	1000 hours
Lamp 2	£5.00	10 W	3000 hours
Lamp 3	£20.00	2 W	5000 hours

If the cost of 1 Unit of electricity is 6p, which lamp would you buy? Explain your answer.

Key Ideas

- Whenever energy is transferred only some of it is transferred as useful energy – the rest of it is transferred in some other way, and is wasted.
- The more energy supplied to a device that is transferred as useful energy, the more efficient that device is.
- All of the energy supplied to a device ends up being transferred to the surroundings, which become warmer.
- As energy spreads out it becomes increasingly more difficult to use for further useful energy transfers.

Energy resources and energy transfer

5.6 Electricity from fuels

One of the most versatile sources of energy for modern life is electricity. The convenience of electricity is the way in which it can supply energy that can be transferred in many different ways – including heating, lighting and movement. At present, most of the energy resources that we rely on are fossil fuels, which are non-renewable. These release vast amounts of energy when they are burnt, and so are very convenient for us to use. Unfortunately the supplies of these fuels are limited, and they produce gases which scientists are concerned may damage our environment. Because of this, scientists and engineers are investigating other ways of producing electricity in order to supply the energy we need for our way of life.

↑ **Figure 1**: Most of our energy comes from fossil fuels, either directly or as a source of electricity.

How a power station works

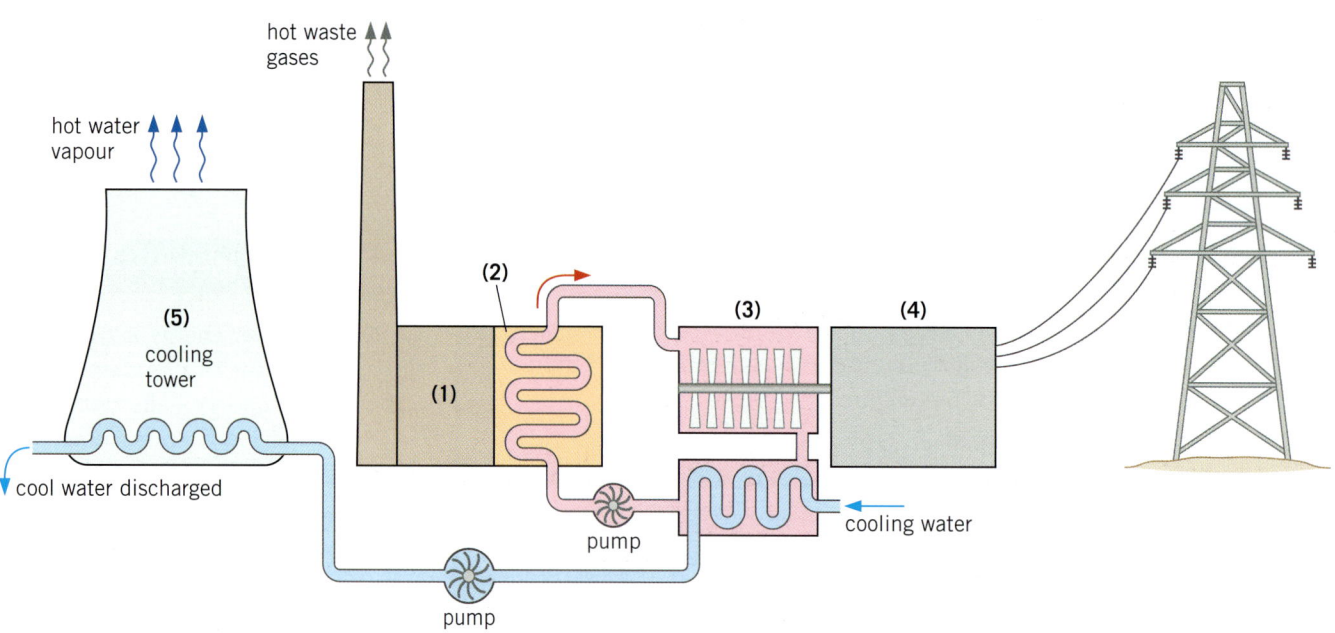

↑ **Figure 2**: In most power stations water is boiled to produce steam, which drives huge turbines connected to generators.

In many power stations the energy is supplied by burning a fossil fuel (oil, coal or gas). This energy is used to heat water in the boilers (1) to produce steam at a very high pressure and temperatures, up to about 800 °C (2). This high-pressure steam then drives a turbine (3), connected to a generator (4). Careful control of the turbine keeps the generator spinning at exactly 50 revolutions per second, producing electricity with a frequency of 50 Hz. After driving the generators the steam is condensed and returned to the boilers – it is the job of the huge cooling towers (5) at the power station to transfer the energy from the steam to cooling water circulating through the towers.

Energy resources and energy transfer

It is not always a burning fuel that provides energy to produce steam. In nuclear power stations a nuclear fuel, uranium or plutonium, is the source of the energy used to heat the water in the boilers.

Efficiency

Just like any other energy transfer device, a power station is not 100% efficient – in fact it is much less than that, with an overall efficiency of about 35%. This means that to produce 35 Units of electricity we need the equivalent of 100 Units of electricity in fuel – almost three times as much!

Most of the energy in the fuel, whether fossil or nuclear, is actually used in heating up parts of the power station that we do not want to heat. In a coal-fired power station as much as 15% of the energy supplied goes in heating up the gases which pass out of the furnace and up the chimney. As much as 45% of the energy in the low pressure steam coming out of the turbines is transferred into the cooling water, while about another 5% goes in heating up parts of the turbines and generators due to friction and electrical heating in the wires.

Figure 3: Energy transfer from the re-circulated steam causes huge clouds of water vapour to rise from the cooling towers of a power station.

Questions

1. Use the figures in the text above for the efficiency of a power station to draw an 'energy arrow' diagram for a power station, showing where and how much energy is wasted.

2. Most power stations generate electricity using fossil fuels. Why is it a bad idea to use this electricity for heating?

3. A power station uses the energy stored in fossil fuels to produce electricity. The table shows the total energy input and outputs in megajoules per second.

Input energy	Output energy	
From burning coal 4800	Electrical energy	1900
	Heating cooling water	2400
	Hot gases up chimney	400
	Electrical energy used to run power station	100
	Total	4800

   a. Draw a suitable graph to show how the total energy output is made up.
   b. What percentage of the input energy is transferred as useful energy?
   c. What percentage of the input energy is wasted in heating the cooling water?
   d. The power station is modified so that 50% of the energy originally wasted in heating the cooling water is now used to heat homes and offices near the power station. What percentage of the energy input is now transferred as useful energy?

Key Ideas

- In most power stations a fuel is used to heat water to produce steam. This fuel may be a fossil fuel or a nuclear fuel.
- The steam produced by the fuel drives turbines connected to generators which produce electricity.
- The efficiency of a power station is around 35%.

Energy resources and energy transfer

5.7 Electricity from wind and water

At present the vast majority of our electricity is generated using energy resources that are **non-renewable**, especially in Britain. However it is possible to generate electricity using **renewable** energy resources that do not depend on energy locked up in fuels.

Hydroelectric energy

Hydroelectric power stations use the flow of water from a higher level to a lower level to produce electricity. Water is trapped behind a dam from where it flows downhill to a turbine. This turbine is coupled to a generator, which produces electricity in exactly the same way as the fossil fuel powered station.

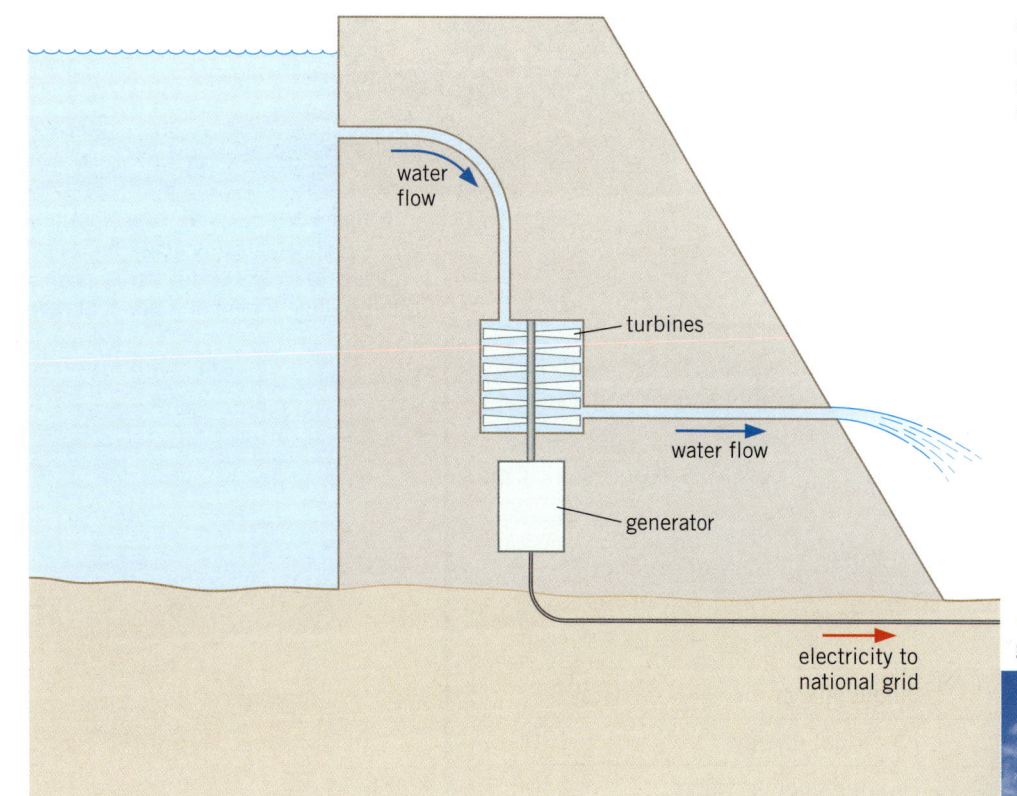

← **Figure 1**: Generating electricity using the energy stored in a raised body of water – hydroelectricity.

↓ **Figure 2**: A group of wind generators is known as a **wind farm**.

Wind energy

For many hundreds of years windmills have been used to drive machinery to grind corn or to pump water. More recently new designs of windmills have been developed which are able to drive generators to produce electricity – although these owe very little to the kind of windmills that people from times past would recognise. The reason for this is the need to transfer as much energy as possible from moving air to electricity. Scientists have estimated that up to ten per cent of the world's electricity could be provided by wind generators. Modern windmills usually begin generating electricity when the wind reaches speeds of about 20 km/h, produce electricity most efficiently at wind speeds of about 45 km/h, shutting down when wind speeds exceed about 100 km/h to avoid damage to the rotors and other components. For large-scale electricity generation windmills have rotors with diameters up to 30 m.

Energy resources and energy transfer

Using the sea (1) – tidal energy

The rise and fall of the sea as the tides flow in and out is another way of generating electricity. The principle of **tidal power** is very similar to hydroelectric generation, with water flowing through turbines connected to generators. Water flows first one way as the tide comes in and then in the opposite direction as the tide goes out. Electricity is generated in both cases.

Using the sea (2) – wave energy

While the rise and fall of water due to the tides happens slowly, the rise and fall of water due to waves on the surface of the sea happens much more quickly, and in a much less regular way. For this reason the production of electricity from waves is very difficult – the first commercial wave generated power station opened on November 21 2000 on the Island of Islay off the West Coast of Scotland.

The ways of generating electricity described above do not have the disadvantages of fossil or nuclear fuels – but this is not to say that they have no disadvantages at all. Remember that fuels are **concentrated** sources of energy. When we burn fuels this energy is released so that it can do useful things – such as boil water to make steam to drive turbines connected to generators that produce electricity. Although the total amount of energy from a fuel is not destroyed when it is burnt, the energy spreads out, becoming less and less useful as it does so. This is why renewable energy schemes (such as wind farms) often need to take up large areas of space.

↑ **Figure 3:** This tidal power station across the River Rance in north-west France went into operation in 1966.

→ **Figure 4:** The LIMPET (Land Installed Marine Powered Energy Transformer) power station, which generates 500 kW of electricity using renewable energy.

Questions

1. A remote farmhouse uses electricity generated from wind power to charge batteries so that electricity is always available. The farmer connects an electric drill to the batteries. Draw energy arrows to show the energy transfers involved when this drill is used to drill a hole in some wood. Start with the energy in the wind, and include all the places where useful energy is lost.

2. Power stations that use renewable energy sources have to be large in order to 'capture' energy that is very 'spread out'. One estimate suggests that much of the electricity needs of the UK could be met by a large array of wave-generated power stations down the west coast of Britain. Draw up a table listing the advantages and disadvantages of such a scheme.

Key Ideas

- Electricity can be generated from renewable energy resources.
- Some renewable resources can drive turbines directly. These include hydroelectric energy, wind energy, tidal energy and wave energy.

Energy resources and energy transfer

5.8 Using solar and geothermal energy to produce electricity

Geothermal energy

The temperature of the Earth's core is estimated to be around 6500 °C. This high temperature is maintained by the decay of radioactive elements inside the Earth. In areas of intense geological activity the results of the Earth's high internal temperature can clearly be seen, as molten rock is pushed out of the Earth through volcanoes.

The high temperature within the Earth can be used to generate electricity by boring down into the crust. In certain areas of the world water and steam at depths of 3000 m can be reached in this way. After purification at the top of such wells the steam is piped to turbines and used to generate electricity in exactly the same way as a fossil or nuclear-fuelled power station. As an alternative to using water and steam found below the surface, water may be injected into hot, dry rock structures, and returned to the surface as steam.

← **Figure 1:** A geothermal power station, near Geyserville in California. 'The Geysers' can supply most of the electricity needed by the city of San Francisco, 170 km south of the power station.

Electricity from the Sun

Electricity can be produced by transferring energy from the Sun, either directly or indirectly. The indirect route involves transferring the energy first to water, to produce steam, which is then used to drive a turbine attached to a generator. The electricity generated using this method is called **solar thermal electricity**. All designs for solar thermal electricity generating plants work by concentrating the Sun's rays onto a 'boiler' in order to produce steam. Because of the Sun's motion across the sky the reflectors used in the concentration process have to be capable of tracking the Sun, requiring complex control systems.

Energy resources and energy transfer

Direct generation of electricity by transferring energy from the Sun's rays to electrical energy is called **photovoltaics**. Photovoltaic cells, or **solar cells**, produce varying amounts of electricity, depending on how much light is falling on them – the more light, the greater the current they can produce, up to a limit. The electricity from solar cells is direct current, although special equipment may be used to turn this into alternating current if necessary.

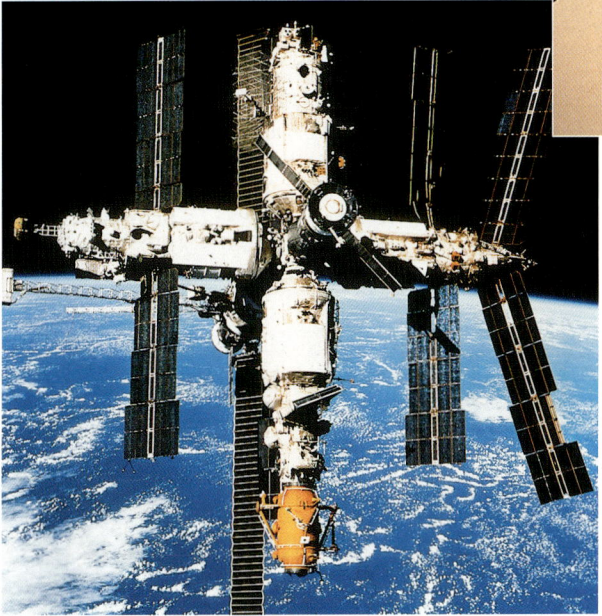

Figure 2: A solar thermal electricity generating plant in California. The plant has 650,000 computer-controlled mirrors which track the Sun across the sky.

Figure 3: Solar cells are used to provide electricity in spacecraft.

Questions

1. The angle between a solar panel and the ground affects the amount of energy it receives at different times of the year. The table shows how different angles affect the amount of energy received by the panel during the summer.

Month	Maximum daily energy input for a 1 m² panel (megajoules)					
	Angle of tilt of panel to the horizontal					
	20°	30°	40°	50°	60°	70°
April	23.8	24.9	24.8	24.1	22.7	20.5
May	28.4	28.8	27.4	25.2	23.0	19.8
June	29.2	29.2	27.4	25.2	22.3	19.1
July	28.8	29.2	27.4	25.6	23.0	20.2
August	25.6	25.9	26.3	24.8	22.7	20.5
September	20.5	21.6	22.3	22.7	21.6	20.5

   a. Plot this information on a suitable graph.

   b. Use your graph to suggest the most suitable angle for the panel for the months from April to September.

Key Ideas

- Renewable resources can be used to generate electricity include geothermal energy and solar energy.

Energy resources and energy transfer

5.9 Electricity on demand

Switch on the light, the television, the toaster or your CD player – we take the instant availability of electricity for granted. Different power stations are available for producing electricity at different times, depending upon the energy resource that is used to transfer energy to electrical energy – so planning for continuous electricity supply that can meet all demands is a far from simple process.

Transferring energy from fuels

The overwhelming majority of electricity around the world is generated from fuels, whether these are fossil fuels (coal, oil and gas) or nuclear fuels (principally uranium). Power stations that use coal are generally designed to operate at a rate that is fairly constant, since it is difficult to bring about rapid changes in output when using coal as a fuel. At the other extreme, power stations that produce electricity using gas turbines can be started up and shut down very quickly. This makes them very suitable to use as stand-by generators of electricity, to provide electricity when there are sudden surges in demand. Between these two extremes lie oil-fired power stations. The output of an oil-fired power station can be increased more rapidly than the output from a coal-fired power station, but not as rapidly as the output from a gas turbine station. The output from a nuclear power station can also be changed rapidly by changing the position of the control rods (see page 142). However nuclear power stations take far longer to build and to commission than conventional power stations due to the elaborate safety features that must be built into them.

The ability of a country's electricity supply to adapt to such changes in demand is very important – if sudden increases in demand cannot be met, this may lead to power cuts. For this reason it is not just the cost of the electricity produced by a power station that must be taken into account when electricity supply is being planned – the ability of the power station to respond to changes in demand may be important too.

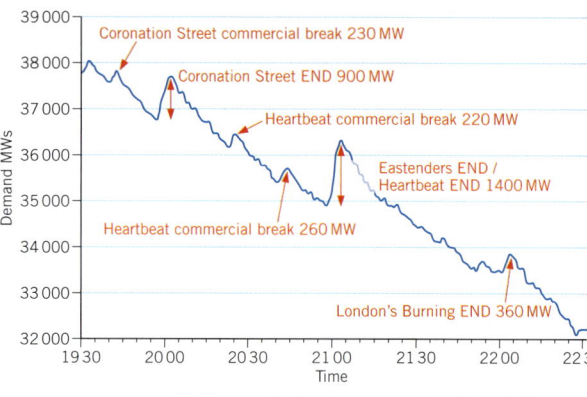

↑ **Figure 1:** An increase in electricity demand is called a **pickup**. This graph shows the pickups during the evening of February 20 2000 due to various television programmes.

Hydroelectric power

Hydroelectric power stations can be started up very quickly, and they can be used as a way of storing energy when surplus electricity is produced – for example, at night. Large quantities of electricity cannot be stored as electrical energy – instead the surplus electricity is used to pump water from a lower reservoir to an upper one. This is called 'pumped storage'. When a sudden demand for electricity occurs, water from the upper reservoir can be allowed to flow back down into the lower reservoir, flowing through turbines connected to generators producing electricity.

↑ **Figure 2:** Pumped storage requires a height difference of at least 300 m between the two reservoirs. There are pumped storage power stations at Dinorwig and Ffestiniog in Wales, and Cruachan and Foyers in Scotland. The upper reservoir of a pumped storage power station typically takes about five or six hours to fill, and the power station can be brought on-line in a matter of a few minutes.

Wind power

The amount of electricity produced by wind generators depends on the strength of the wind. This may vary a great deal from day to day, which can make this method of electricity generation unreliable. For local electricity supplies (for example, to a group of isolated houses) these problems may be overcome by transferring surplus electricity generated to chemical energy stored in batteries, or by having an

Energy resources and energy transfer

alternative electricity supply in the form of a diesel-powered generator. For large-scale electricity generation, wind farms need to be sited in places where there is a relatively constant wind – like on a west-facing coast or hilltop in the UK.

Using the sea – tidal power and wave power

The amount of electricity that can be produced using a tidal barrage varies according to the state of the tide. The water level is the same on each side of the barrage twice during each day, as one level falls and the other rises. When this happens the barrage cannot produce electricity, since water will only flow through the barrage when the water levels are different. The electricity produced by a tidal barrage varies throughout a 24-hour period as the graph in Figure 3 shows. Although this variation is not ideal, the behaviour of the tides is predictable, and so it is possible to predict accurately when a tidal power station will be unable to produce electricity and to make arrangements for electricity to be supplied by other means.

The issues with wave power are very similar to those for wind power, since the waves on the surface of the sea are largely caused by the wind.

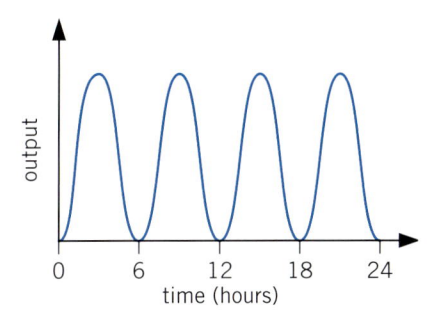

Figure 3: The variation in output of a tidal power station during a 24-hour period.

Using the Sun

As with tidal power, the Sun is only available at certain, predictable times – and even then it may be covered by cloud during the day. This means that using the Sun to generate electricity for heating water and homes is a problem, since the time at which most energy is needed is the time at which least energy is available.

Transferring energy from the Sun's rays to electrical energy can be done very efficiently using photovoltaic cells. However, these cells are very costly, which makes electricity generated in this way very expensive. If alternating current is required, the cost of converting the direct current output from the cells into alternating current must also be added to this cost. Despite the high cost of electricity generated by photovoltaic cells they are often the best way of generating electricity in remote places or where only small currents and low voltages are needed (for example in watches and calculators).

Key Ideas

- Energy resources differ in how readily they are available for generating electricity.

Questions

1. The island population of a small island in the North Atlantic use a diesel generator to supply all of their electricity needs. They wish to find another method of generating electricity in order to reduce their reliance on diesel fuel, which is delivered by the supply ship which calls once a month. Details of the island are shown in figure 4.

   What advice would you give the islanders about suitable ways of generating electricity that are economic but which do not leave them without enough generating capacity when they need it most?

Figure 4: The island – what advice would you give?

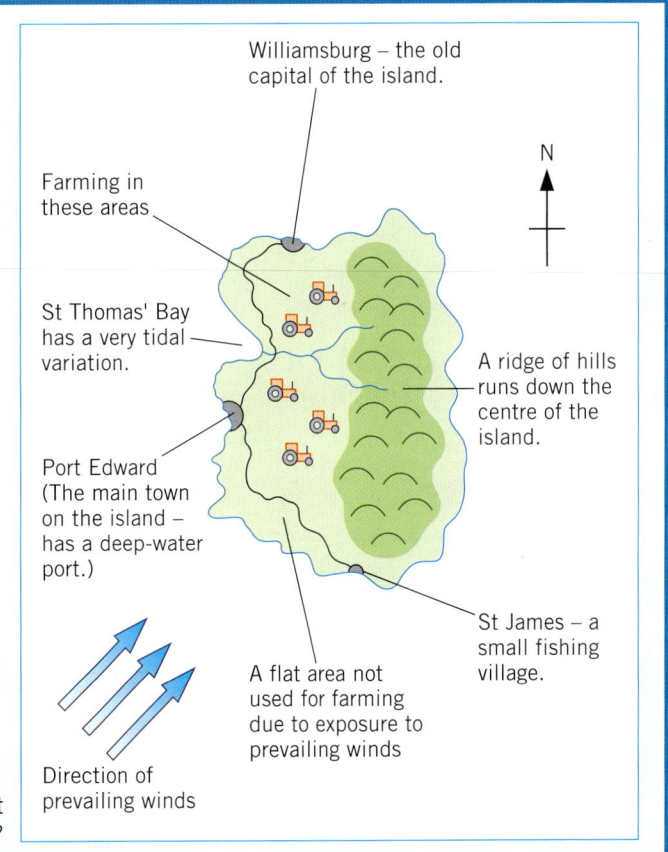

Energy resources and energy transfer

5.10 Electricity and our environment

In their different ways, the different methods for generating electricity all have some kind of impact on our environment. In some cases they may have a very local impact that is restricted to the area immediately around the power station. In other cases the impact may be more widespread, affecting things on a regional or even a global scale. And, in certain cases, the impact may be felt many thousands of years into the future.

Fossil fuels

When fossil fuels burn, the chemical elements in them combine with oxygen, producing water and carbon dioxide. There is strong scientific evidence to suggest that the carbon dioxide produced by burning fossil fuels may be adding to the greenhouse effect and contributing to an increase in temperatures around the world, known as global warming.

Since there is no way to prevent the carbon dioxide produced by burning fossil fuels from entering the Earth's atmosphere, scientists and engineers have sought to find ways to reduce the amount of carbon dioxide produced when a given amount of electricity is generated. One way of doing this is to use oil rather than coal to generate electricity, since oil produces less carbon dioxide than coal when the energy from the fuel is transferred to one Unit of electricity. Natural gas is even better than oil, as Figure 1 shows.

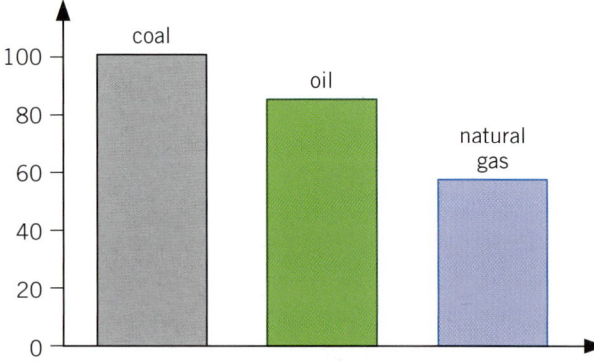

↑ **Figure 1:** Relative amounts of carbon dioxide produced per Unit of electricity for coal, oil and natural gas (coal = 100).

Natural gas has another advantage over coal and oil, since it contains very little in the way of sulphur compounds. The compounds produce sulphur dioxide when the fuel is burnt, leading to the production of acid rain. The effect of this may be felt many hundreds of miles away from where the fuel was burnt. It is possible to remove the sulphur compounds from the fuel before it is burnt, or to remove the sulphur dioxide from the waste gases before they leave the chimney of the power plant and enter the Earth's atmosphere – but both of these alternatives increase the cost of the electricity being generated.

Nuclear fuels

Nuclear fuel does not burn, and does not contribute to the production of carbon dioxide or sulphur dioxide – nuclear power stations do not therefore contribute to global warming or acid rain. Indeed, when a nuclear power station is running normally it emits very little radiation or radioactive material into its surroundings. However, in an accident, large quantities of radioactive material can be given off by a nuclear reactor, and this may spread over a wide area, as it did following the accident at Chernobyl.

Although nuclear fuels do not burn, they do produce waste. Some of this waste is highly radioactive and must be stored for many thousands of years under conditions where it may be monitored. The disposal of this 'high level waste' presents many problems, and is one of the principal issues when the pros and cons of nuclear power are discussed.

↑ **Figure 2:** A spruce forest in Poland damaged by acid rain.

Energy resources and energy transfer

Renewable resources

As we have seen in Sections 5.5, the spreading out of energy explains why methods of generating electricity which use renewable resources have to be so big – because they are 'harvesting' low quality energy which is extremely spread out. It is the sheer size of schemes designed to generate electricity from renewable energy resources that can be their downfall.

To produce an amount of electricity comparable to a fossil fuel power station, a wind farm may consist of several thousand wind turbines spread over an area of many square kilometres. Such a large concentration of wind turbines produces a significant amount of noise, and the rotating blades may also interfere with radio and television signals. These two problems of 'noise pollution' and 'radio signal pollution' may not be a significant problem where the wind farm is sited in a remote place far away from human settlements. However, there may still be concerns about the visual pollution of the countryside if the site is somewhere that may attract people because of its beauty.

Tidal barrages and hydroelectricity schemes also have an impact due to their size. Tidal barrages may cause enormous changes to the estuaries in which they are built, changing the way in which water flows and altering vital features such as mud flats. This may have an enormous effect on wildlife, including migrating birds, which make use of estuaries as stopping off points during their long journeys. In the same way, hydroelectric schemes involve damming river valleys, trapping large amounts of water behind the dam. This can have large effects at a local level, flooding land that may previously have been used for agriculture or forestry, or even flooding villages. Large hydroelectric schemes can even have effects on the local climate, since the large surface area of water reflects a greater proportion of the Sun's rays than the terrain it replaced.

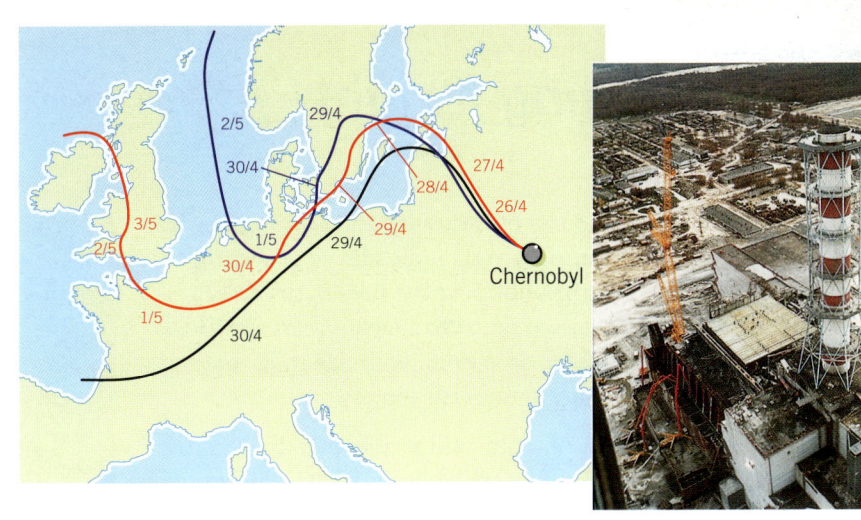

Figure 3: A chemical explosion at the Chernobyl power station in the Ukraine in April 1986 blew the lid off the building housing the reactor, and many tonnes of radioactive material escaped into the atmosphere, travelling hundreds of miles.

Figure 4: Wind power production does not add to global warming or produce gases that cause acid rain – but it still has an impact on the environment around where the wind farm is sited.

Questions

1. Use the information about renewable energy resources in Sections 5.7, 5.8 and 5.9 to draw up a table showing the advantages and disadvantages of using each energy resource in the UK.

Key Ideas

- Using different energy resources has different effects on our environment.
- Fossil fuels produce carbon dioxide when burnt – this contributes to global warming.
- Fossil fuels may also produce sulphur dioxide when burnt – this helps to produce acid rain.
- Nuclear fuels do not produce gases which contribute to the greenhouse effect or which lead to acid rain. However they do produce nuclear waste, which has to be stored safely for thousands of years.
- Power stations that use renewable resources must be large in order to harvest a large amount of low-quality energy. The size of these power stations may lead to environmental effects.

Energy resources and energy transfer

5.11 Getting it right (H)

Generating huge amounts of electricity using tidal power has been talked about for many years – the idea of generating electricity using the rise and fall of the tides in the Severn Estuary was first discussed more than eighty years ago. Tidal power has been in use for centuries, with tide mills, used to grind corn, dating back to the 11th century.

The modern version of a tide mill is a barrage built across an estuary. In the UK there are eight possible sites for such a barrage, across the Severn, the Mersey, the Wash, the Humber, the Dee, Morecambe Bay, the Solway Firth and the Thames. Of these possibilities, the Severn is the most favoured since the rise and fall of the tides in the estuary is very large – the second largest in the world.

Plans for the development of a tidal power scheme across the Severn have been drawn up by a group of six engineering and construction companies who believe that the construction of a tidal barrage makes sense, financially and environmentally, and is technically possible. They have made the following estimates of the positive impact of the Severn barrage:

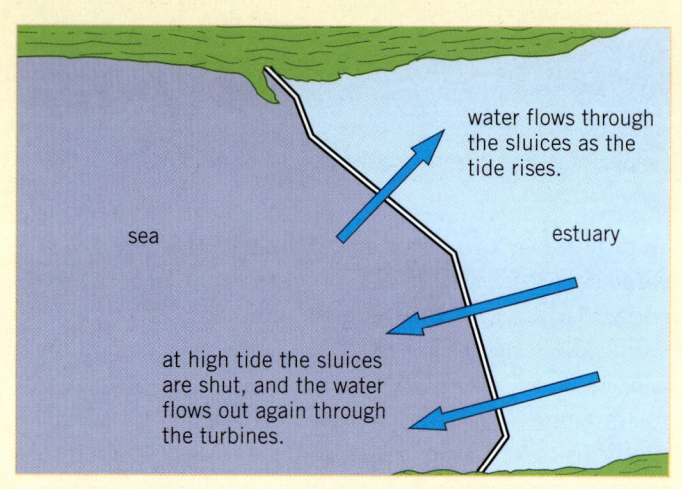

Figure 1: A tidal barrage across the Severn would be over 15 km long.

Figure 2: An artist's impression of the Severn Barrage.

Generating capacity	17 billion kWh each year (6% of the total demand for electricity in England and Wales)
Economic benefits	Construction of the barrage would produce about 200 000 person years of employment – about 35 000 jobs at the peak of construction. Many of these would be in areas away from the barrage site, in the manufacturing regions of the UK. In addition it is estimated that another 40 000 jobs would be created in the region around the Severn estuary in the longer term.
Environmental benefits	If electricity from the barrage were to replace electricity from coal-fired power stations it would enable the UK to reduce its carbon dioxide emissions by about 3%.
Planning	Unlike other renewable energy resources, tidal power is predictable. With reasonable maintenance the barrage would have a long life. It could therefore play a significant part in long-term energy policy for the UK.

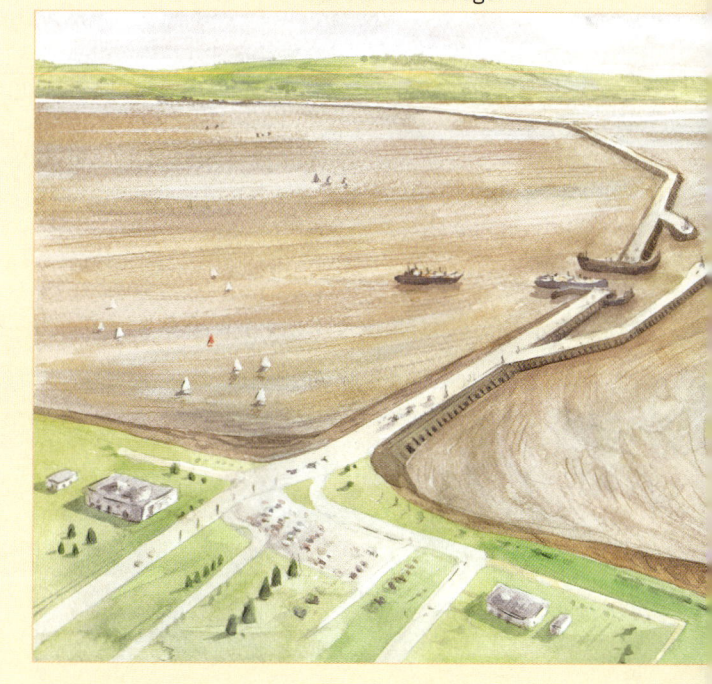

Money well spent?

The estimated cost of the Severn Barrage is around £10 billion. This is such a large sum of money that it is likely that the Government would have to contribute at least some of it, since it would be difficult to raise this much money from private investors. Once the high initial cost of the scheme is paid for, the electricity could be produced very cheaply indeed. This electricity would not use any fossil or nuclear fuels, and so would not produce any carbon dioxide, acid rain or radioactive waste. The creation of so many new jobs would also have a beneficial effect on the country's economy.

Energy resources and energy transfer

Or money down the drain?

Big civil engineering projects often cost much more than planned – for example, the Thames Barrage, built to protect London from flooding, cost six times more than the original estimate. The money spent building the barrage could be used to clean up Britain's fossil fuel power stations and encourage energy-saving measures, like better insulation for houses. The barrage would undoubtedly have a large environmental impact on the Severn Estuary, which is an important stopping point for birds migrating from the Arctic to West Africa and beyond – in winter the estuary regularly holds more than 80 000 birds.

It's our choice

The Severn Barrage problem shows just how difficult it is to find the right answer to problems of pollution and our growing demands for energy.

- Should we opt for a clean way of generating electricity which may upset the ecology in one part of the world, and which will be very costly to build?
- Should we go for fossil-fuelled power stations which can be built quite cheaply but which produce carbon dioxide or other substances which may affect the Earth's atmosphere?
- Should we opt for nuclear power stations? These can be built and operated quite cheaply, and produce little pollution during their lifetime. But they leave behind waste that must be kept for many thousands of years. And these power stations require expensive decommissioning once their useful life is over in order to get rid of the dangerously radioactive parts of the plant.
- Or should we simply use less electricity?

Questions

1. In the Severn Barrage scheme, where would the energy to generate electricity come from?
2. Apart from its effect on birds, what other environmental impact might the barrage have?
3. The graph in Figure 3 shows electricity demand in the UK throughout a typical day in winter.
   a. Why does demand vary like this?
   b. Would the Severn Barrage be able to supply electricity in this way? Suggest how the supply could be made to match the demand more closely.

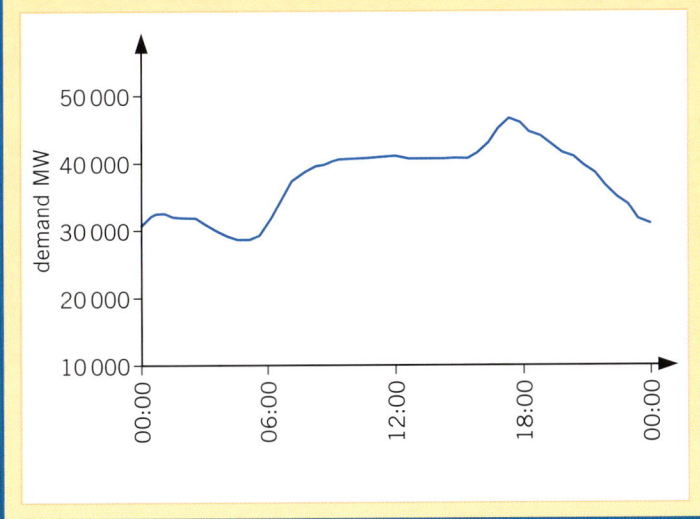

Some of the arguments for and against building the Severn Barrage are given in the text above. Some are based on science, some are based on economics, and some may simply be people's opinions based on very limited information. Try to answer the following questions using the information given, together with your own knowledge and ideas.

4. The barrage would use fossil fuels while it was being built. Why?
5. Electricity from the barrage might be more expensive than electricity from fossil-fuelled or nuclear-fuelled power stations. Why?
6. 'The Severn Barrage means damage to our own back yard – more coal-fired power stations mean damage to our neighbours' back yards.' What did the person who said this mean?
7. Some people argue that the welfare of thousands of birds is more important than electricity for homes, schools and hospitals. Other people think the opposite. Which point of view do you think is right – is it possible to decide?

← **Figure 3:** Electricity demand during a 24-hour period in winter.

Energy resources and energy transfer

5.12 Energy calculations

Transferring energy and doing work

Think about a very simple situation in which George travels upwards in a lift (Figure 1) while Pandit climbs the stairs. Both Pandit and George have the same mass, 60 kg. We know that their weights (the downward force acting on each of them) can be calculated from the relationship that we met on page 36:

    weight = mass × gravitational field strength
  (newtons, N) (kilograms, kg) (Newtons/kilogram, N/kg)

Since the gravitational field strength at the surface of the Earth is about 10 N/kg, both George and Pandit have a weight of 60 × 10 N = 600 N.

As the lift travels upwards at a constant speed it must apply an upwards force to George which exactly balances his weight acting downwards – in other words, an upwards force of 600 N. If the lift raises George a vertical distance of 15 m, we can calculate the energy transferred by the lift motor – this energy transferred is called the **work done** by the motor:

  energy transferred = work done = force applied × distance moved in direction of force
    (joules, J)   (joules, J)   (newtons, N)   (metres, m)
    = 600 × 15 J = 9000 J (= 9 kJ)

↑ **Figure 1:** If we take the lift, the lift motor transfers the energy – if we climb the stairs, it is our muscles that do it.

Pandit walks upstairs rather than taking the lift, so it is his muscles that do the work rather than the lift motor. The same amount of work has to be done to raise Pandit a vertical distance of 15 m as had to be done to raise George, but the lift can raise George more quickly because it is more **powerful** than Pandit's muscles – it can transfer energy more quickly:

$$\text{power (watt, W)} = \frac{\text{work done or energy transferred (joules, J)}}{\text{time taken (seconds, s)}}$$

If the lift raises George a vertical distance of 15 m in 3 s while it takes Pandit 30 s to run up the stairs, we can compare the power produced by the lift motor and the power produced by Pandit's muscles:

$$\text{power of lift motor} = \frac{9000}{3} \text{ W} = 3000 \text{ W}$$

$$\text{power of Pandit's muscles} = \frac{9000}{30} \text{ W} = 300 \text{ W}$$

The lift motor is more powerful than Pandit's legs so it can transfer energy (or do work) more rapidly.

Gravitational potential energy

Anything that is lifted up against the pull of the Earth's gravity gains gravitational potential energy – even George and Pandit! We can calculate the energy transferred to gravitational potential energy – this is the amount of work done:

  energy transferred = work done = force applied × distance moved in direction of force

The force that must be applied to raise an object at a constant speed is equal to its weight, so that:

  change in gravitational = weight × change in vertical height
    potential energy
    (joules, J)   (newtons, N)   (metres, m)

Energy resources and energy transfer

In George and Pandit's case, raising each of them a vertical distance of 15 m increases the gravitational potential energy of each of them by 9000 J.

Example 1

How much gravitational potential energy can be transferred as 1 kg of water falls a vertical distance of 150 m as it travels through a hydroelectric power station?

To solve this problem we use the relationship:

**change in gravitational = weight × change in
potential energy   vertical height**

The water has a weight of 1 × 10 N = 10 N, so

change in gravitational = 10 × 150 J = **1500 J**
potential energy

Elastic potential energy

Elastic potential energy is the energy stored in something due to a change in its shape – the energy stored in a stretched rubber band is an example of this.

↑ **Figure 2:** Elastic potential energy!

Kinetic energy

Moving objects have energy because of their motion. The amount of kinetic energy a moving body has depends on its mass and speed:

kinetic energy = $\frac{1}{2}$ ×   mass   ×   speed^2
(joules, J)   (kilograms, kg) ((metres/second)^2, (m/s)^2)

Example 2

Which has a greater kinetic energy: a 1 kg ball travelling at 30 m/s or a 1000 kg car travelling at 1 m/s?
We know that:

kinetic energy = $\frac{1}{2}$ × mass × speed^2

so we can write:
kinetic energy of ball = $\frac{1}{2}$ × 1 × 30^2 J

= $\frac{1}{2}$ × 900 J

= 450 J

and
kinetic energy of car = $\frac{1}{2}$ × 1000 × 1^2 J

= 500 J

The car has more kinetic energy than the ball.

? Questions

1 A person pushes a supermarket trolley in a 20 m straight line applying a force of 25 N.

   a Calculate the amount of work they do.

   b The person stops pushing the trolley and it stops. What has happened to the energy transferred to it?

2 A tractor pulls a plough, applying a force of 15 000 N. The tractor and plough travel a distance of 300 m in a straight line in a time of 150 s. Calculate the power output of the tractor.

3 A racing car has a mass of 750 kg and a kinetic energy of 2 400 000 J. How fast is it travelling?

4 A marble with a mass of 0.02 kg is dropped from the top of the Eiffel Tower, 300 m above the ground.

   a Calculate the gravitational potential energy gained by the marble when it is taken from ground level to the top of the tower.

   b What is the kinetic energy of the marble just before it hits the ground?

   c At what speed does the marble hit the ground?

   d Does the mass of the marble affect the speed at which it hits the ground? Explain your answer.

Key Ideas

- When a force moves an object, energy is transferred and work is done
- Work done = energy transferred.
- Work done = force applied × distance moved in direction of force
- Power = work done/time taken
- Gravitational potential energy is the energy stored in an object because of the height to which an object has been lifted against the force of gravity.
- Change in gravitational potential energy = weight × change in vertical height.
- Elastic potential energy is the energy stored in an object due to its change in shape.
- Kinetic energy = $\frac{1}{2}$ × mass × speed^2

Energy resources and energy transfer

5.13 End of chapter questions

1. The hairdryer transfers electrical energy to heat energy and kinetic energy.

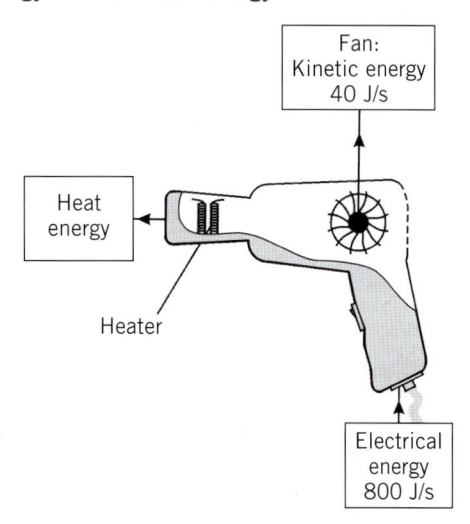

   Fan: Kinetic energy 40 J/s
   Heat energy
   Heater
   Electrical energy 800 J/s

   Calculate the efficiency of the hairdryer in transferring electrical energy into heat energy.

   (2 marks)
   (Total 2 marks)
   AQA specimen question

2. The drawing shows an investigation using a model steam engine to lift a load.

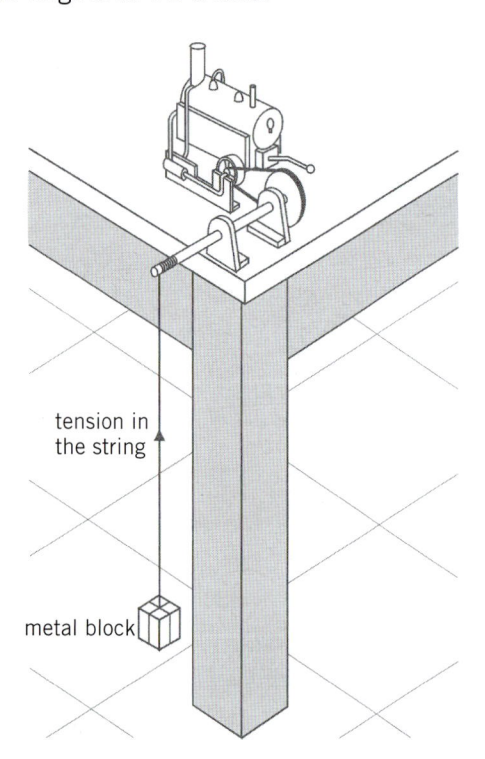

   tension in the string
   metal block

   In part of the investigation, a metal block with a weight of 4.5 N was lifted from the floor to a height of 90 cm.

   a Explain what causes the weight of the metal block. (2 marks)

   b i Calculate the work done in lifting this load. Write the equation you are going to use, show clearly how you get to your answer and give the unit. (3 marks)

      ii How much useful energy is transferred to do the work in part (b) (i)? (1 mark)

   (Total 6 marks)
   AQA specimen question

3. The diagram shows an experimental solar-powered bike.

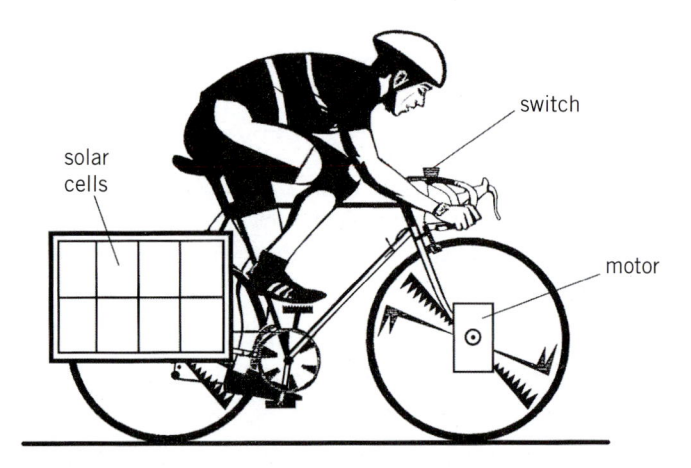

   solar cells
   switch
   motor

   A battery is connected to the solar cells.

   The solar cells charge up the battery.

   There is a switch on the handlebars.

   When the switch is closed, the battery drives a motor attached to the front wheel.

Energy resources and energy transfer

a Use words from the list to complete the following sentences. Words may be used once, more than once, or not at all.

chemical   electrical   heat (thermal)   kinetic

light   potential   sound

  i The solar cells transfer .... energy to .... energy.

  ii The motor is designed to transfer .... energy to .... energy.

  iii When the battery is being charged up .... energy is transferred to .... energy.

  (6 marks)

b Name **one** form of wasted energy which is transferred when the motor is running.

  (1 mark)

  (Total 7 marks)

  AQA specimen question

4 In a power station energy is used to generate electricity.

  a Name **three** fuels which are commonly used in power stations to produce this energy. (3 marks)

  b The diagram shows three boxes. Each box represents a major part of a power station. The first box represents the boiler.

  | boiler |—| |—| |

    i Use words from the list to label the other two boxes. (2 marks)

    generator   motor   solar panel   turbine

    ii What is the job of the boiler? (1 mark)

c Electrical energy can be produced using wind power.

    i Describe **two** advantages of using wind power compared to burning fuels. (2 marks)

    iii Describe **two** disadvantages of using wind power compared to burning fuels. (2 marks)

  (Total 10 marks)

  AQA specimen question

5 The table shows the rate at which electrical energy is generated by a wind turbine at different wind speeds.

Wind speed (m/s)	0	2.5	5	10	15	20	25
Rate of energy transfer (kW)	0	50	150	800	1600	1800	1900

  a Plot a graph of these data. Plot wind speed on the *x*-axis and rate of energy transfer on the *y*-axis. (4 marks)

  b Explain the shape of your graph. (2 marks)

  c Would the wind turbine generate much more electricity at higher wind speeds? Explain your answer. (2 marks)

  d Wind power is a **renewable energy resource** while coal and oil are **fossil fuels**. Explain the terms in bold letters. (2 marks)

  e Give one advantage and one disadvantage of relying on wind power to generate all of our electricity supplies. (2 marks)

  (Total 12 marks)

Energy resources and energy transfer

6.1 Magnets from electricity

We explain the behaviour of magnets by saying that a magnet is surrounded by a **magnetic field**. The magnet exerts a force on any magnetic material (including iron and steel and other magnets) when they are in the magnetic field. When one magnet is brought into the magnetic field of another magnet, it is repelled if two like poles (north and north, or south and south) are brought together, or attracted if two opposite poles (north and south) are brought together.

A coil of wire carrying a current also behaves like a bar magnet — it is called an **electromagnet**. Just like a bar magnet, an electromagnet has one end which is a north-seeking pole, and another end which is a south-seeking pole. When the current through an electromagnet is reversed, the magnetic poles of the electromagnet are reversed — so the north pole becomes a south pole and vice versa.

A wire carrying an electric current does not have to be in a coil in order to behave like a magnet — you can show this using a simple investigation like the one in Figure 1. If the apparatus is arranged exactly as shown in the diagram, when the power supply is switched on, the loose wire resting across the other two wires is catapulted horizontally out from between the two magnets.

The distance that the wire is catapulted depends on the size of the force acting on it. A careful investigation shows that the force can be increased by:

- increasing the strength of the magnetic field
- increasing the size of the current.

Investigation also shows that the **direction** of the force is reversed if either the direction of the current or the direction of the magnetic field is reversed.

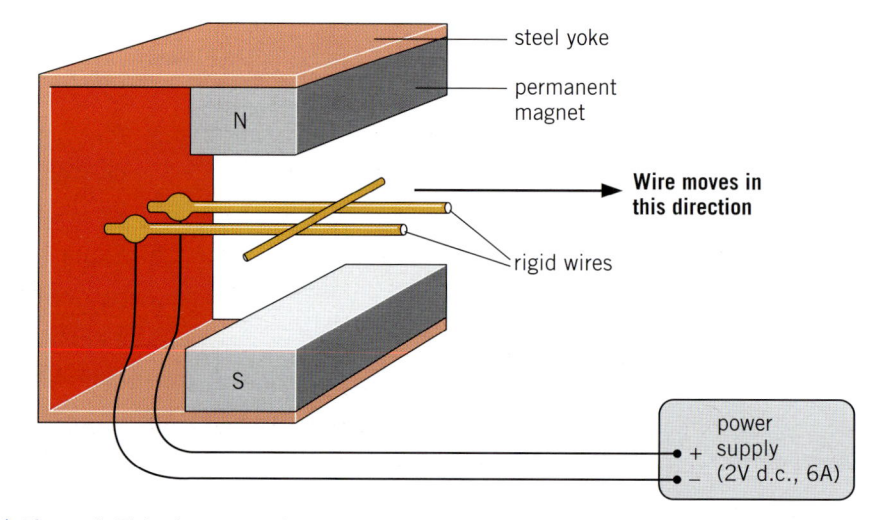

↑ **Figure 1:** This demonstration shows the 'catapult effect' (sometimes called the 'motor effect').

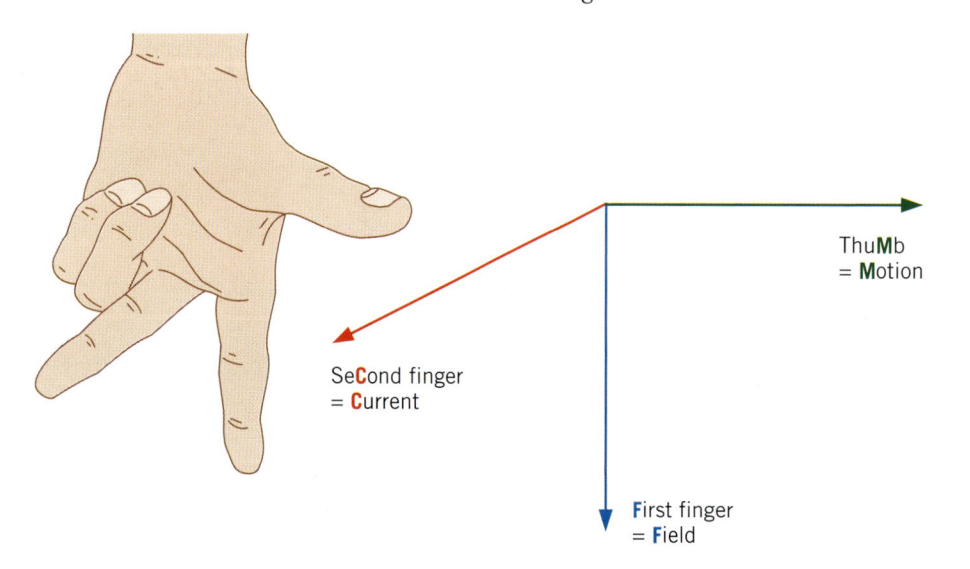

← **Figure 2:** The force acting on a wire, the current through it and the magnetic field are all at right angles to each other. The 'left-hand rule' predicts the direction of each.

ThuMb = Motion
SeCond finger = Current
First finger = Field

104 Electricity and magnetism

Science people

The story of electricity and magnetism cannot be told without mentioning two great figures of the 19th century – the Briton Michael Faraday (1791–1867) and the American Joseph Henry (1797–1878). The two men had contrasting backgrounds. While Henry received a good education, Faraday's origins were much more humble, his career beginning as an apprentice to a bookbinder.

Both men worked to explore the relationship between electricity and magnetism. While Faraday was concerned to develop scientific understanding, Henry focused on the ways in which electricity and magnetism could be employed in practical ways that would change people's lives.

Faraday's work spanned a huge area of science. Building on the work of other scientists, he made huge contributions to our understanding of electricity and magnetism, and to the area of science we now call electrochemistry. Work in his later life also led to the development of an important area of physics now known as field theory, which helps to explain how gravity behaves.

Henry designed a new and better electric motor, and developed the first telegraph system, which led eventually to the invention of the telephone. At the start of the 19th century messages took many days to cross a country. By the end of the century, messages could be sent over enormous distances in fraction of a second. Although Henry discovered electromagnetic induction before Faraday he did not publish his results straight away. Faraday published his results first, and is generally credited with the discovery.

Later in their lives both men achieved great honour in the scientific community: Faraday became Director of the Royal Institution in London and Henry was Director of the Smithsonian Institute in Washington.

↑ **Figure 3:** The apparatus which Faraday used in his work on electricity and magnetism. According to one story, Faraday would always carry a small iron bar and a coil of wire in his pocket so that he could use a spare moment to carry out an experiment!

Questions

1 Describe what would happen to the wire in Figure 1 if:

   a the direction of the current is reversed

   b the direction of the magnetic field is reversed

   c the directions of both the current and the magnetic field are reversed.

Key Ideas

- A magnet exerts a force on any piece of magnetic material near it.

- A coil of wire acts like a bar magnet when a current flows through it. One end of the coil becomes a north-seeking pole, the other a south-seeking pole.

- Reversing the current through an electromagnet reverses its poles.

- A wire carrying a current in a magnetic field experiences a force. The size of the force can be increased by increasing the magnetic field or by increasing the current.

- The direction of the force is reversed if either the direction of the current or the direction of the magnetic field is reversed.

Electricity and magnetism

6.2 Using electromagnets

Electric motors

An electric motor consists of a coil of wire in a magnetic field. When a current flows through the coil it rotates – Figure 1 shows why this happens.

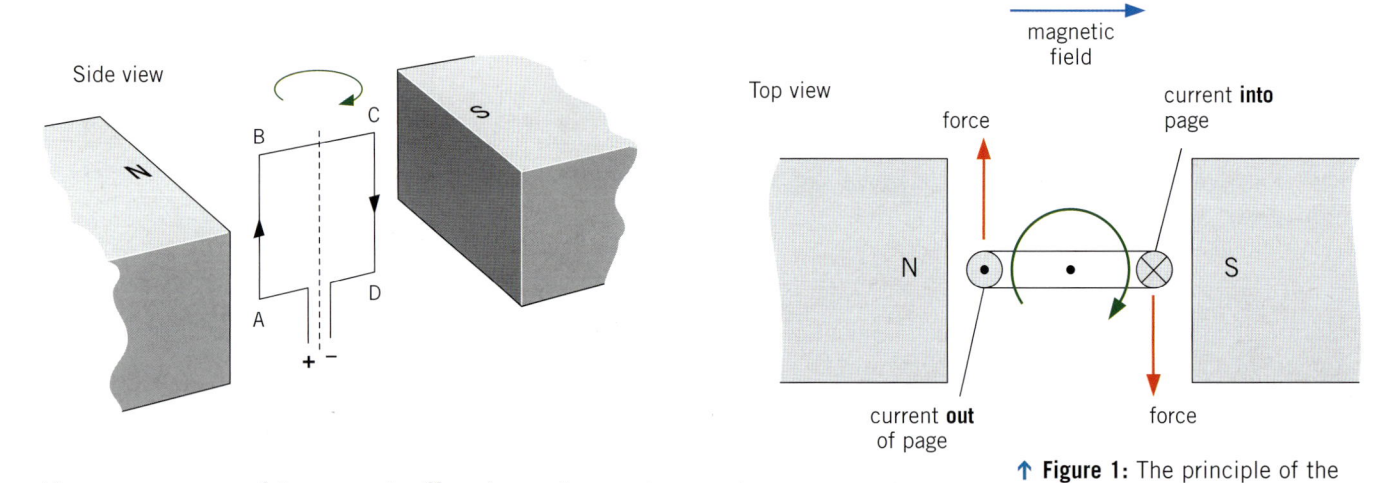

↑ **Figure 1:** The principle of the electric motor.

The investigation of the catapult effect shows that a wire carrying a current in a magnetic field experiences a force, and that the direction of the force can be predicted using the left-hand rule. Side AB of the coil in Figure 1 experiences a force in one direction, while side CD experiences a force acting in the opposite direction. The effect of these forces is to make the coil turn in the direction shown by the green arrow.

A practical electric motor requires a device called a **commutator** to allow the coil to rotate freely and to keep the current flowing through the coil in the correct direction.

Circuit breakers

Two types of circuit breakers use electromagnetism to limit the damage that electric currents may do. The first of these is sometimes called a **resettable fuse**, and is placed in the live conductor of the power supply. The live conductor is wound around an iron core, next to an iron rocker. A spring holds the rocker so that the current passes through the contacts and the rocker, and then flows through the wire wound around the iron core. If the current flowing gets too big, the electromagnet becomes strong enough to pull the rocker against the spring, which breaks the circuit. A manual reset button can be used to restore the current once any fault has been cleared.

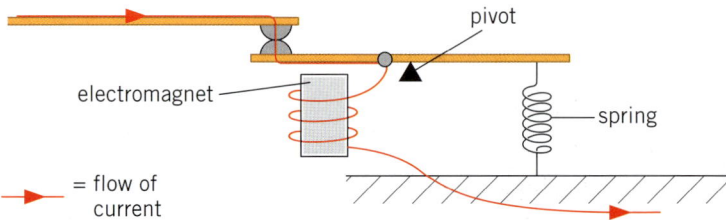

Another type of circuit breaker, called a **residual current device** (RCD) helps to keep people safe. If someone mows the lawn using an electric lawnmower, there is a real danger that they may cut through the power cord and electrocute themselves. In the UK, around 50 people each year are taken to hospital as a result of electrical accidents in the garden. Figure 3 shows how the current flows when someone cuts through the flex connected to a mower. Notice how current flows through the live conductor in the flex but not through the neutral conductor – instead, the current flows to earth through the mower, and through the person holding the end of the flex.

↑ **Figure 2:** Resettable fuses have largely replaced fuse wires in mains wiring because of their convenience.

Electricity and magnetism

The fact that the current through the live and neutral conductors is different allows the RCD to protect the person cutting the lawn. The RCD monitors the current through the live and neutral conductors of the supply to an appliance, and cuts off the supply very quickly if it detects a difference between these two currents. Figure 4 shows how the live and neutral conductors in a circuit breaker pass through an iron core. Normally the current through the live conductor is the same size as the current through the neutral conductor, but in the opposite direction. The current through the live conductor and the current through the neutral conductor each cause a magnetic field in the iron core. Because the currents are equal in size but opposite in direction, the two magnetic fields are also equal in size but opposite in direction – so there is no overall magnetic field in the coil. When something goes wrong and current flows from the live conductor to earth, the live and neutral currents no longer balance. This induces a magnetic field in the core, causing a current to flow in the secondary coil. The trip relay then shuts off the supply to prevent any further current flowing to earth.

Figure 3: When someone cuts through the flex connected to a lawnmower or other power tool, electricity may flow to earth through the tool, through the person or both. In certain conditions the current through the person may be enough to kill them.

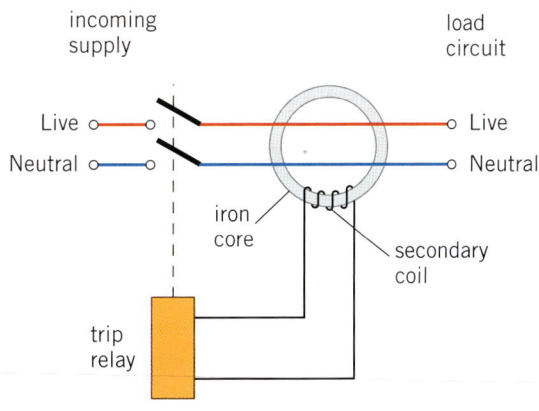

Figure 4: Circuit breakers may be installed as part of the wiring in a home. Portable circuit breakers can also be bought and plugged in where needed. This design is simply plugged into a 13 amp socket, and the appliance is plugged into the front of it using a standard 13 amp plug.

? Questions

1. Explain why a d.c. motor needs a device to change the direction of the flow of current every half turn.

2. A person is cutting their lawn using an electric lawnmower. They cut through the flex connecting the lawnmower to the mains electricity supply. They may be electrocuted – write down as many things as you can that might increase the likelihood that this would happen.

Key Ideas

- A resettable fuse is a kind of circuit breaker that breaks the circuit if the current through it is too large.

- Another kind of circuit breaker is called a residual current device (RCD). This breaks the circuit if the current through the live and neutral wires are not the same.

Electricity and magnetism

6.3 Electricity from magnets

Electricity and magnets are closely connected. Just as electric currents can be used to produce magnetic fields, so magnetic fields can be used to produce electric currents. The mains electricity that powers our homes, schools, offices and factories is produced in this way.

Figure 1 shows a simple investigation using a bar magnet, a coil and a galvanometer (a sensitive ammeter). When this investigation is carried out it shows that:

- No current flows when the magnet and the coil are stationary.
- The galvanometer shows that a current flows when the magnet is moved into or out of the coil (physicists call this an induced current).
- The direction of the induced current depends on two things: the direction that the magnet is moving in, and the pole of the magnet that is moved into the coil.

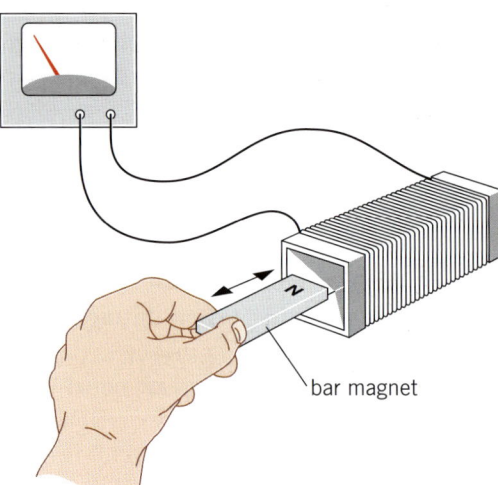

Figure 1: A simple investigation to show the relationship between electricity and magnetism.

Pole of magnet moved nearer to the coil	Direction of magnet's motion	Direction in which galvanometer needle moves
north	into coil	to left
north	out of coil	to right
south	into coil	to right
south	out of coil	to left

As a wire moves through the magnetic field around a magnet it passes through and 'cuts' the magnetic field lines. A voltmeter, connected between the ends of the wire as it cuts through the field, shows that a potential difference exists between the ends of the wire – this potential difference is sometimes called an **induced voltage**. If the ends of the wire are connected together to produce a complete circuit, the induced voltage causes a current to flow. The situation is the same if it is the magnet rather than the wire that is moving, since the wire still cuts through the magnetic field.

Generating electricity

A generator is similar in construction to a motor. As the coil rotates, the opposite sides of the coil cut through the magnetic field in opposite directions – side AB moves up while side CD moves down, producing a voltage across the ends of the coil.

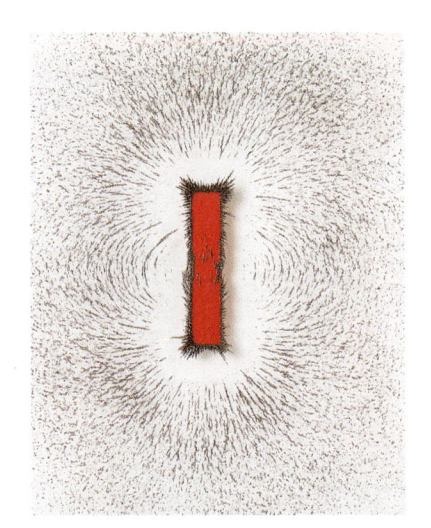

Figure 2: The lines seen in the iron filings here show the pattern of the magnetic field around the magnet.

Using a simple generator, investigation shows that the induced voltage increases when:

- the coil rotates more quickly (so the rate at which the wire cuts through the magnetic field is greater)
- the number of turns of wire on the coil is increased (so there is more wire cutting through the magnetic field)
- the area of the coil is made bigger (this also means that there is more wire cutting through the magnetic field)
- the strength of the magnetic field is increased (this also increases the rate at which the wire cuts through the magnetic field).

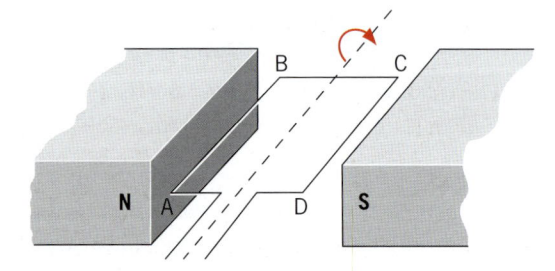

Figure 3: The principle behind the generator, used to produce electricity.

Electricity and magnetism

Instead of rotating a coil in a magnetic field produced by a stationary magnet, electricity can just as well be generated by rotating a magnet inside a stationary coil. This arrangement has the advantage that electrical connections to the coil are much simpler, since it is not rotating.

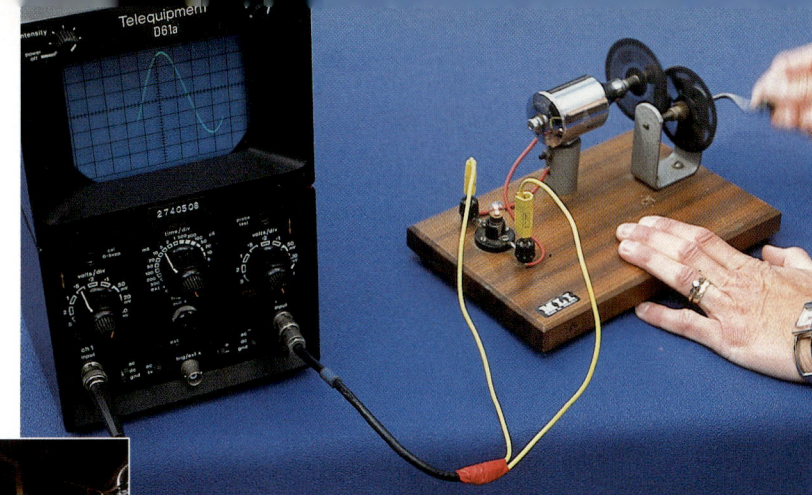

Figure 4: Investigating the factors affecting the size of the induced voltage.

Figure 5: The generator in a power station.

? Questions

1. Pushing the north pole of a magnet into a coil of wire induces a current to flow through the coil, which is connected in a complete circuit. How could you induce the *same* current to flow using the **south** pole of the *same magnet*?

2. Draw energy transfer diagrams to show the energy transfers taking place in a motor and a generator.

3. A generator consists of a coil of wire rotating in a magnetic field. Using the idea of energy transfer, explain why making the coil rotate faster increases the voltage and current produced by the generator.

4. The two ends of a coil are connected to a galvanometer. The needle of the galvanometer deflects two units to the left when the north pole of a bar magnet is pushed into the coil at a rate of 5 cm/s. Predict what happens in the following investigations:

    a the north pole of the bar magnet is pushed into the coil at a rate of 10 cm/s

    b the south pole of the bar magnet is pushed into the coil at a rate of 5 cm/s

    c another identical magnet is placed alongside the first magnet, so that their north poles lie next to one another and so do their south poles. The north pole of this combined magnet is pushed into the coil at a rate of 5 cm/s.

    d Another coil is wound with the same number of turns as the first coil but with a diameter 1.4 times larger. It is connected to the galvanometer and the south pole of the first bar magnet is pushed into it at a rate of 5 cm/s.

Key Ideas

- A magnet moving into a coil of wire induces a voltage across the ends of the wire. The induced voltage causes a current to flow if the wire is part of a complete circuit.

- The direction of the induced voltage and the induced current depend on the direction of movement of the magnet.

- Electricity can be generated by a coil of wire rotating in a magnetic field, or by rotating a magnet inside a coil of wire.

- The size of the voltage induced in a wire or coil increases when:
    - the speed of movement increases
    - the strength of the magnetic field is increased
    - the number of turns on the coil is increased
    - the area of the coil is increased.

Electricity and magnetism

6.4 Electricity – from the power station to your home

As we have seen, the vast amounts of electricity that we use each day are supplied by power stations – huge devices designed to transfer other forms of energy to electrical energy. But generating electricity is only the first part of the story – after it has been generated, the electricity has to be distributed to homes, schools, offices and factories. This is the job of the **National Grid**, a network of power lines and cables which receives electricity from power stations of all kinds and transmits it to where it is needed, often far away from where it was generated.

Because electricity must be transmitted over long distances, **energy losses** must be controlled carefully. As an electric current flows through a wire, the resistance of the wire causes some of the electrical energy to be transferred, heating up the wire. (This is how an ordinary electric filament lamp works.) The electrical energy can be transmitted either using a low voltage with a large current, or by using a high voltage with a small current. The heating effect increases rapidly with the size of the current, so very high voltages are used. This reduces the current flowing through the wire, and minimises the energy losses.

Transformers are used to convert electricity from one voltage to another, but they work only with alternating current, not with direct current – which is why mains electricity is alternating current. Transformers play a vital part in the distribution of electricity. At the power station, **step-up transformers** increase the voltage of the electricity produced to 400 000 volts, which is the voltage used for distribution over long distances through the National Grid. Once the electricity reaches the area where it is to be used, **step-down transformers** then decrease the voltage to useable levels for local distribution – 33 000 volts or 11 000 volts. The exact voltage that the final consumer uses varies – homes, schools and small offices will usually have a supply at 230 volts, while the supply to large offices and to factories may be higher than this. Even though transmitting electricity safely at very high voltages requires tall pylons and huge insulators, this is still far cheaper than paying for the energy losses that would occur if low voltages were used instead.

↑ **Figure 1:** Much of our electricity is transmitted at very high voltages over power lines like these.

↙ **Figure 2:** The National Grid, transmitting electricity at high voltages keeps the current low, which reduces energy losses.

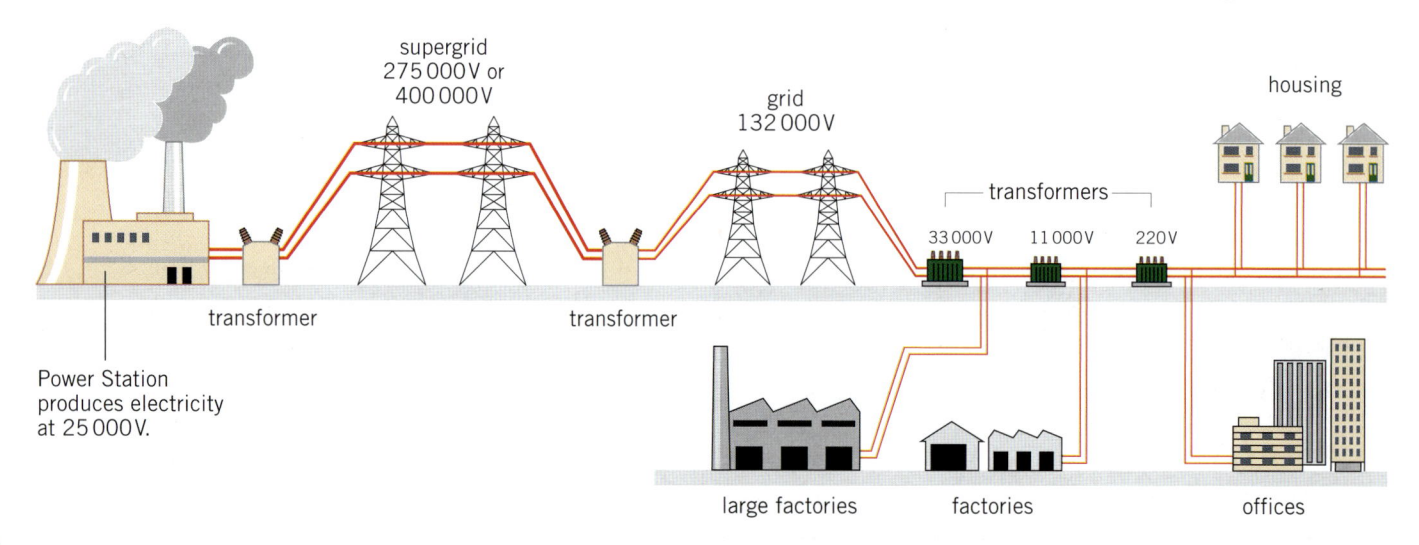

Power Station produces electricity at 25 000 V.
transformer
supergrid 275 000 V or 400 000 V
transformer
grid 132 000 V
transformers
33 000 V — 11 000 V — 220 V
housing
large factories
factories
offices

Electricity and magnetism
110

→ **Figure 3:** Insulators like these are needed on pylons which carry electricity at 400 000 volts.

Ideas and Evidence

Why a.c. and not d.c.?

The development of electricity supply in the UK followed a haphazard pattern. During the late 19th and early 20th centuries, power stations were installed to produce electricity for towns and cities, although no system for distributing electricity over long distances existed. As a result of these local developments, no standards for supply voltages existed, and some supplies were direct current while others were alternating current. Many power stations even included large sets of batteries so that the generators could be turned off at night and the batteries used to supply the small amount of electricity that customers required!

Later in the 20th century a grid system began to develop, allowing electricity to be distributed over larger distances. This led to the need for standardised supply voltages, the use of alternating current to produce the high voltages for transmission by means of transformers, and the demise of the many tiny local power stations in favour of more efficient large power stations capable of supplying the electricity demands of large cities. Further standardisation between the UK and continental European countries has enabled electricity supplies between the countries to be linked, with cross-channel cables carrying electricity in either direction, depending on where the generating surplus is found.

Questions

1 Why do we use alternating current rather than direct current in our electricity supply?

2 Why is it much more expensive to transmit electricity at low voltages than at high voltages?

3 A factory uses electrical energy at a rate of 40 000 watts. Calculate the current that flows through the wires supplying the factory if the voltage of the supply is:

   a 230 volts

   b 400 000 volts.

   Comment on your answer.

Key Ideas

- Transformers are used to change the voltage of an a.c. supply.
- At power stations, transformers are used to produce very high voltages before the electricity is fed into the National Grid.
- Local transformers reduce the voltage of the electricity from the National Grid to safe levels.

Electricity and magnetism

6.5 More about electricity distribution H

Generators

We can make a simple generator (Figure 1) by rotating a coil of wire in a magnetic field, as we saw on page 106.

The ends of the coil are connected to a pair of **slip rings**. Each slip ring rubs against a **brush**, which makes good electrical contact with the ring, enabling current to flow from the coil to the circuit connected to it. As the coil rotates in the magnetic field an alternating voltage is induced across its ends. This causes an alternating current to flow through any circuit connected to the coil (Figure 2).

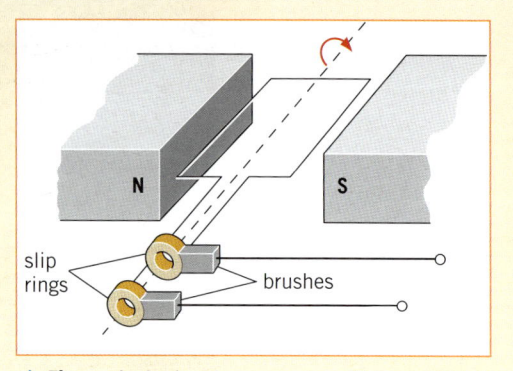

↑ **Figure 1:** A simple generator. This produces an alternating current, induced in the coil as it rotates in the magnetic field.

(a)
(i) As the coil cuts through the magnetic field a current is induced in it which flows in this direction.
(ii) The current passes through the slip rings and the brushes, and flows clockwise through the circuit containing the bulb.

(b) At this point the coil is at right angles to the field. The wires of the coil are moving in the same direction as the magnetic field, so they are not cutting through the field – so no voltage is induced in the coil and no current flows.

(c)
(i) The wires of the coil are once again cutting through the magnetic field, producing a current which flows in the same direction as before.
(ii) The current passes through the slip rings and brushes. Because the coil has rotated through 180°, the current now flows anticlockwise through the circuit containing the bulb.

(d) Once again the coil is at right angles to the field. The wires of the coil are moving in the same direction as the magnetic field, so they are not cutting through the field – so no voltage is induced in the coil and no current flows.

(e) The trace on an oscilloscope shows how the voltage induced in the coil increases to maximum, decreases again to zero, increases to a maximum in the opposite direction, decreases to zero again and so on.

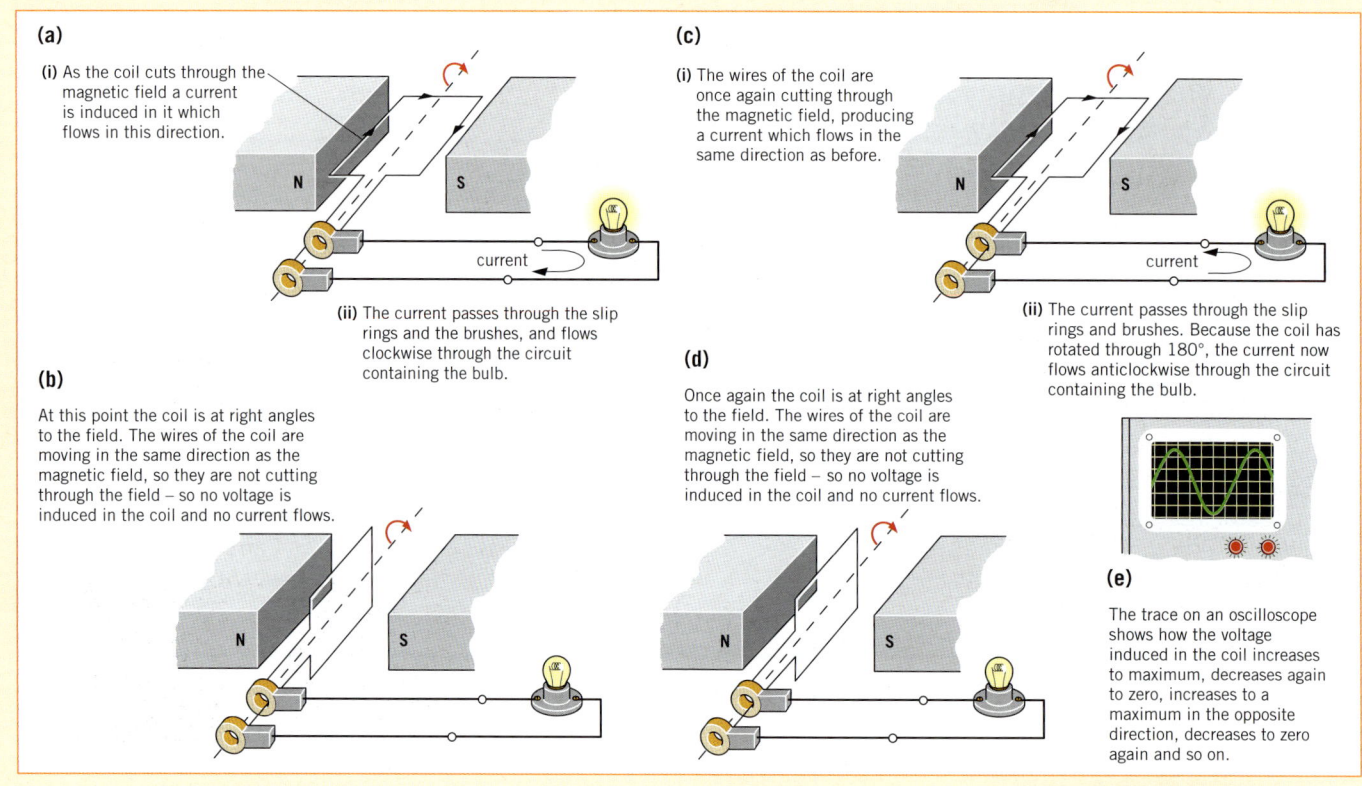

↑ **Figure 2:** The rotation of the coil produces an alternating current.

Large generators that produce high voltages, like those used in power stations, do not use a rotating coil like this, since it would be difficult to design an arrangement of slip rings and brushes that would not produce sparks. Instead of using a rotating coil inside a stationary magnetic field, these generators use a magnet that rotates inside a stationary coil.

From generator to user – energy losses

The energy losses that occur when electricity is transmitted over long distances are due to the resistance of the wires carrying the current. The rate at which energy is lost due to resistance, increases more rapidly as more current flows through the wire:

rate at which energy is transferred to heat = (current through wire)^2 × resistance of wire

This means that if we increase the current through the wire by a factor of 2 we increase the rate at which energy is lost by a factor of $2^2 = 4$.

Electricity and magnetism

The rate at which electrical energy flows through a wire is the electrical power, which is calculated using the relationship:

power = current × potential difference

Thus, if we want to transfer electrical energy through a wire as fast as possible, it does not matter whether we use a large current or a large voltage. However, it is obviously better to use a large voltage, since this reduces the energy losses due to heating.

Transformers

Transformers perform the task of increasing and decreasing the voltage used in electricity supply and distribution. A simple transformer consists of two coils of wire wound together over an iron core (Figure 3). An alternating voltage across the **primary coil** causes a current to flow through it, which produces an alternating magnetic field around the coil. The **secondary coil** is inside this alternating magnetic field, and induces an alternating voltage across the ends of the coil.

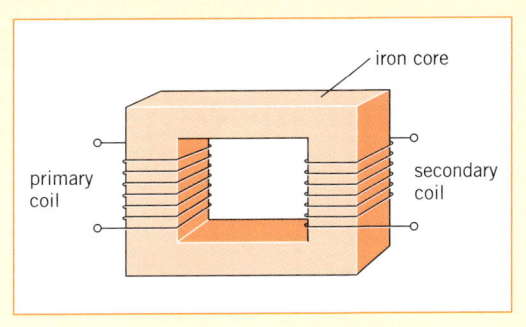

Figure 3: The principle of the transformer.

The relationship between the voltages across the primary and secondary coils of the transformer depends on the relative number of turns of wire on each coil:

$$\frac{\text{voltage across primary coil (volts, V)}}{\text{voltage across secondary coil (volts, V)}} = \frac{\text{number of turns on primary coil}}{\text{number of turns on secondary coil}}$$

A transformer in which the voltage across the secondary coil is bigger than the voltage across the primary coil is called a **step-up** transformer, while one in which the voltage across the secondary coil is less than the voltage across the primary coil is called a **step-down** transformer.

Key Ideas

- A simple a.c. generator uses a rotating coil inside a magnetic field.
- High voltage generators use a rotating magnet inside a stationary coil.
- Electricity is transmitted and distributed at high voltages to reduce energy losses.
- Transformers are used to increase and decrease the voltages used in electricity transmission.
- The ratio of the voltages across the primary and secondary coils depends on the ratio of the number of turns on the two coils.

Questions

1. The two graphs in Figure 4 show the voltage produced by an a.c. generator displayed on an oscilloscope. Describe as fully as you can how the rotation of the coil in (b) is different from the rotation of the coil in (a).

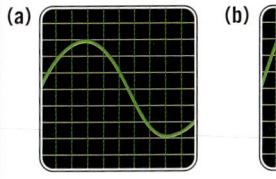

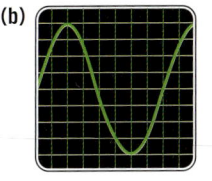

   Figure 4 (a) (b)

2. The table shows details of some transformers. Copy and complete the table.

	Turns on primary coil	Turns on secondary coil	Voltage across primary coil	Voltage across secondary coil	Step up or step down?
Transformer A	3600	180	240		
Transformer B	1000		16 000	400 000	
Transformer C	285	285	220		

3. The table shows the electrical power carried by an electricity cable, the current through the cable, the voltage at which electricity is transmitted through the cable, and the energy losses from it. Copy and complete the table and comment on your answers.

Power (watts)	Current (amps)	Voltage (volts)	Power loss (watts)
100 000	400	250	40 000
100 000		1000	
100 000	1		
200 000		100 000	

Electricity and magnetism 113

6.6 Tesla – unsung genius of electrical power

Ideas and Evidence

In the village of Smiljan in what is now Yugoslavia, at exactly midnight during the night of July 9 1856, a son was born to Djouka Tesla and her pastor husband Milutin. Given the name of Nikola, the boy was one of five children growing up in an agricultural community high up in the Velebit Mountains, part of a mountain chain which stretches from Switzerland to Greece. From this apparently inauspicious background came one of the most brilliant electrical engineers the world has seen.

The young Tesla showed many of the talents that were to play a role in his later life, excelling in mathematics and other technical subjects, and his childhood followed similar patterns to that of other children in the village. Nevertheless certain childhood incidents played a very important part in shaping Tesla's way of thinking – the story of the snowball is one example.

One winter Tesla was walking in the mountains with some friends. Getting bored with making snowmen, the boys began throwing snowballs down the steep slopes of a mountain. Most of the snowballs just rolled a little way, grew a bit bigger and then slowed down and stopped. But eventually one snowball found just the right conditions. The small ball of snow rolled and rolled until it had become a large ball, when it spread out, gathering up snow and becoming like a giant carpet. Suddenly the moving snow became an avalanche, which carried snow, rocks, soil and trees before it. After a descent of terrifying power the snow landed in the valley below the boys with a stupendous boom.

Figure 1: Nikola Tesla lived from 1856 to 1943.

The descent of the tiny snowball and its metamorphosis into a huge avalanche made a great impression on Tesla, convincing him that enormous forces of nature may be unlocked through the use of tiny amounts of force acting as triggers. During his later life he was always seeking such triggers in his many experiments.

Figure 2: Thomas Alva Edison developed the first practical electric light bulb, the direct current electricity generating system and the phonograph (a sound-recording device). Edison patented over 1000 inventions.

As a young man, Tesla studied electrical engineering and then went to work in France for the Continental Edison Company, a French company which manufactured dynamos and motors, and installed lighting systems under patents filed by the American inventor of the electric lamp, Thomas Alva Edison. Tesla had a passionate belief in the superiority of alternating current over direct current, but could not convince anyone in France that his ideas were worth following up. With no money of his own to set up a workshop, in 1884 Tesla decided to emigrate to the USA where he thought that Edison and other inventors and engineers might be willing to give his ideas a try.

Five years before Tesla arrived in America, Edison had demonstrated the first electric light bulb to use a glowing filament to produce light – earlier electric lights produced light by making a spark jump between two carbon electrodes, which were not practical for use in homes and offices. Following this great invention, Edison planned and built the world's first large-scale power station in New York which became operational in 1882, generating and distributing direct current to hundreds of homes over a small radius. Tesla was impressed with Edison and all he had been able to achieve, and was happy when Edison offered him a place on his staff.

Electricity and magnetism

Tesla worked hard for Edison, working for 18 hours a day, seven days a week, and undoubtedly made Edison's company a great deal of money. However Tesla soon argued with Edison over money, and resigned his job.

Scraping money together with the help of a fellow electrical engineer who had also fallen on hard times, Tesla set up his own workshop and laboratory and set about demonstrating the superiority of alternating current to direct current. His lucky break came in 1888, when he gave a lecture to the American Institute of Electrical Engineers. Through this he met George Westinghouse, head of the Westinghouse Electric Company. Westinghouse was completely convinced by Tesla's arguments for the use of alternating current, and offered Tesla generous terms to work with him to develop the use of alternating current supplies as a superior alternative to Edison's direct current. This deal made Tesla wealthy, and set in place the development of an electricity supply system that grew directly into the systems used around the world today.

This is not quite the end of Tesla's story, however. In 1890 the New York State authorities introduced the electric chair to execute prisoners who had been condemned to death. The electric chair used alternating current to achieve the high voltage required for electrocution, although direct current would have been just as deadly. When Tesla found out about this, he accused Edison of encouraging the use of alternating current for the electric chair as a way of discouraging its use in homes – after all, who wants to think of the sort of electricity they use at home being used to kill people too? There can be little doubt that the choice of alternating current was due to the ease with which it could produce the high voltages needed, but, in the battle between alternating and direct current, the appeal to emotion was just as important in its way as the appeal to bare scientific facts.

↑ **Figure 3:** The electric chair, used to execute prisoners condemned to death in some states of the USA. Tesla believed that Edison had publicised the use of alternating current in the electric chair in order to increase public approval for direct current.

? Questions

1 In his scientific work Tesla seems to see the snowball incident as a metaphor for the way that developments in scientific understanding affect the world. Describe an example of where a development in scientific understanding has had an enormous effect. In your example:

   a Explain the theory behind the new idea.

   b Name the scientists who developed the ideas.

   c Describe the reaction to these new ideas.

   d Explain how these ideas have changed life for ordinary people.

2 Tesla believed that Edison had tried to associate alternating current with capital punishment in order to make people feel badly about using it. Why was alternating current used for the electric chair rather than direct current? Why is it used now for supplying homes and industry?

3 'In the battle between alternating and direct current the appeal to emotion was just as important in its way as the appeal to bare scientific facts.' Are emotions important when scientific arguments are decided? Give examples to support your view.

Key Ideas

- Alternating current replaced direct current as a means of supplying electricity due to the fact that it enabled electricity to be transmitted over longer distances.

Electricity and magnetism

6.7 End of chapter questions

1   a   The diagram shows a magnet being moved into a coil of wire.

   The reading on the meter is shown in the diagram.

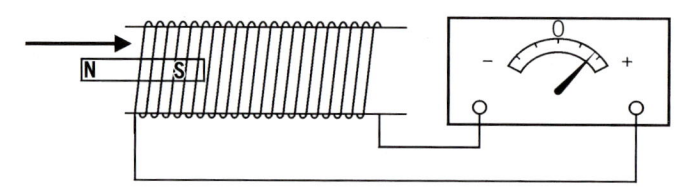

   On a copy of each diagram draw the meter reading that you would expect to get in each of the following cases.

   i The magnet is at rest inside the coil.

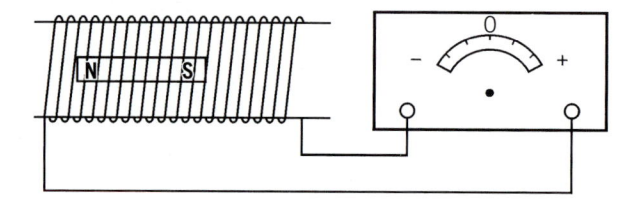

   ii The magnet is moved out of the coil.

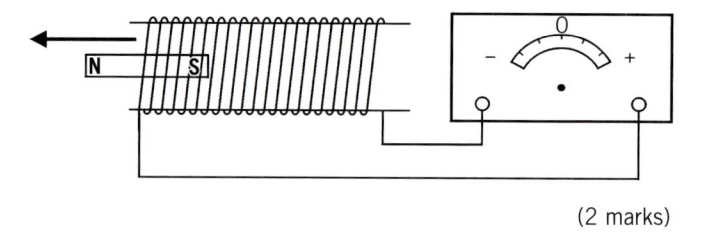

   (2 marks)

   To gain full marks in this question you should write your ideas in good English. Put them into a sensible order and use the correct scientific words.

   b   The diagram below shows a bicycle dynamo and part of the wheel.

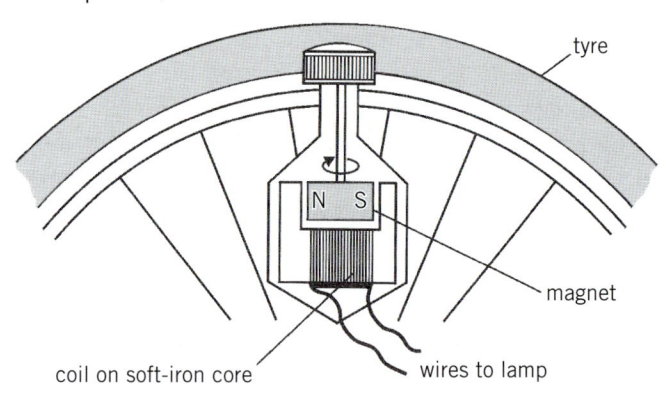

   Explain, as fully as you can, why a current flows through the bicycle lamp when the wheel of the bicycle turns. (4 marks)

   (Total 6 marks)

   AQA specimen question

2   a   Electrical energy is distributed around the country by a network of high voltage transmission cables.

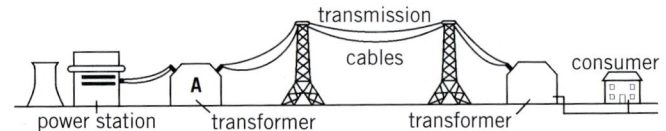

   i For the system to work the power is generated and distributed using alternating current rather than direct current. Why?

   (1 mark)

   ii Transformers are an essential part of the distribution system. Explain why. (2 marks)

   (Total 3 marks)

116   Electricity and magnetism

b The power station generates 100 MW of power at a voltage of 25 kV. Transformer **A**, which links the power station to the transmission cables, has 44 000 turns in its 275 kV secondary coil.

  i Write down the equation which links the number of turns in each transformer coil to the voltage across each transformer coil.
  (1 mark)

  ii Calculate the number of turns in the primary coil of transformer A. Show clearly how you work out your answer. (2 marks)
  (Total 6 marks)
  AQA specimen question

3 The figure shows a simple generator. When the coil rotates between the magnets an alternating voltage appears across the wires connected to the brushes.

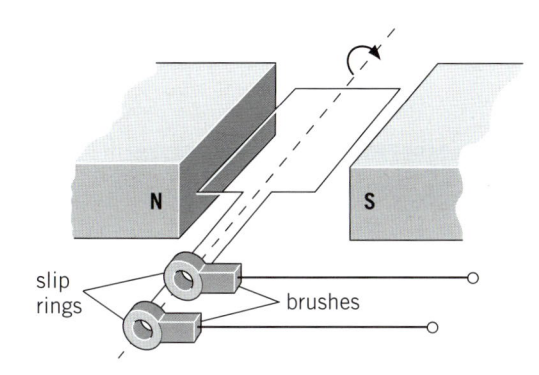

a Explain why the generator requires brushes and slip rings. (1 mark)

b With the aid of a diagram, explain what is meant by the term **alternating voltage**.
(2 marks)

c Describe **two** ways in which the voltage produced by the generator could be increased **without** changing the rate at which the coil rotates. (2 marks)

d The rate at which the coil rotates is doubled. Describe how this affects the voltage produced by the generator. (2 marks)
(Total 7 marks)

4 The generators in a power station produce electricity at a voltage of 25 000 volts. To transmit this electricity over long distances, the voltage is increased to 400 000 volts.

a Explain why the voltage is increased in this way.
(2 marks)

b A transformer with 2000 turns in its primary coil is used to increase the voltage.

  i Write down the equation which shows how the number of turns on each coil is related to the voltage across it. (1 mark)

  ii Calculate the number of turns in the secondary coil of this transformer. (2 marks)

c The figure shows a comparison between aluminium and copper. Copper wires are used to conduct electricity to where it is needed around our homes, schools and places of work. Aluminium is used to conduct electricity through overhead cables running over long distances.

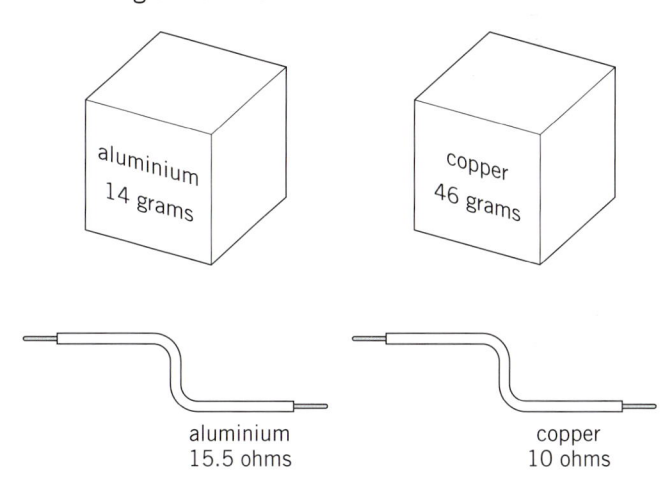

aluminium
14 grams

copper
46 grams

aluminium
15.5 ohms

copper
10 ohms

  i Why is copper used to carry electricity around the home? (1 mark)

  ii Why is aluminium used as the conductor in overhead power lines? (2 marks)
  (Total 8 marks)

Electricity and magnetism 117

7.1 Introducing radioactivity

At the end of the nineteenth century, just after Röntgen had discovered X-rays, the French physicist Antoine-Henri Becquerel was exploring the effect of sunlight on certain minerals. He called these minerals 'phosphorescent', and thought that they gave off X-rays when they had been exposed to the Sun's rays. To find out whether this was true, Becquerel placed a piece of a uranium salt on a sealed photographic plate and then exposed it to sunlight. On one day when he was doing this the Sun did not shine, so Becquerel placed the uranium salt and the photographic plate in a dark drawer for a few days. When the plate was developed it was blackened, showing that the uranium salt was giving off radiation that affected the plate. Other scientists soon became interested in Becquerel's discovery. They quickly found that uranium compounds give off radiation all the time, no matter what is done to them. The radiation was given the name 'radioactivity' – materials that give off radioactivity are said to be **radioactive**.

It is not just uranium that is radioactive – there are many other elements that are radioactive too. These sources give off three different types of radiation, called alpha, beta and gamma radiation.

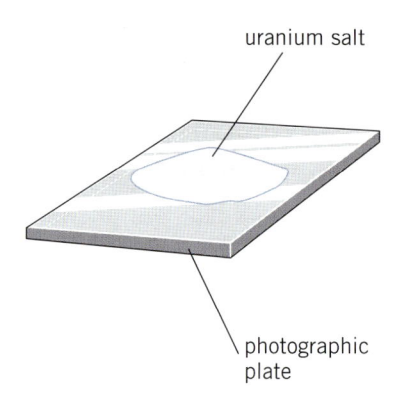

↑ **Figure 1:** Becquerel placed a uranium salt on a photographic plate. Even when the plate and the salt were kept in the dark, the plate still became blackened.

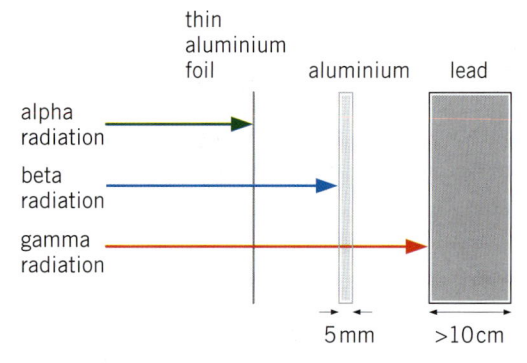

↑ **Figure 2:** The very different properties of alpha, beta and gamma radiation.

Ideas and Evidence

Alpha (α), beta (β) and gamma (γ) are the three first letters of the Greek alphabet. The scientists who discovered the properties of radioactivity over one hundred years ago would all have been educated in schools and colleges where they learnt at least some Latin and Ancient Greek. Because of this, it would have seemed very natural to use the Ancient Greek alphabet to give names to the three types of radiation.

If these three types of radiation had been found today, their names might have been very different. For example, in the second half of the twentieth century scientists naming six types of tiny particles described them as having six 'flavours' – up, down, strange, charmed, bottom and top!

Alpha, beta and gamma radiations have very different properties, as Figure 2 shows. Radiation travelling through a material can be absorbed. Alpha radiation can travel only a few centimetres through air before it is absorbed, and even a thin piece of tissue paper is enough to stop it. Beta radiation is much less easily absorbed, and can travel readily through air or paper. To absorb most of the beta radiation from a source it is usually enough to use a few millimetres of a metal such as aluminium. Gamma radiation is the hardest radiation to absorb. Like beta radiation it travels easily through air, but it will also pass easily through metals like aluminium. Gamma radiation will even travel some way through a metal like lead, so absorbing most of the gamma radiation from a source requires many centimetres of lead, or even metres of a material like concrete.

The absorption of radiation by materials can be used in industrial processes. One of these involves controlling the thickness of a plastic sheet as it is produced. Figure 3 shows a sheet of plastic being produced by squeezing hot plastic between two rollers. The force exerted on the plastic by the two rollers has to be carefully controlled in order to ensure that the sheet produced is exactly the right thickness. This is done by measuring radiation to control the force exerted by the rollers.

- The control system is set up so that, when the plastic sheet has the right thickness, the sheet absorbs the correct level of radiation from the source. The rest of the radiation passes through the sheet and reaches the detector.

- If the sheet becomes too thick, it absorbs more of the radiation from the source, so the amount of radiation reaching the detector decreases. This decrease activates machinery, which pushes the rollers closer together so they exert a greater force on the plastic.

- The opposite process happens if the sheet becomes too thin. In this case it absorbs less of the radiation from the source, so the amount of radiation reaching the detector increases. This increase activates machinery, which moves the rollers further apart so they exert a smaller force on the plastic.

Figure 3: Controlling the thickness of a material using radiation.

Questions

1. Becquerel was the first scientist to explore the properties of radioactive materials.
   a. What was his hypothesis about how radiation is produced?
   b. How was Becquerel testing this hypothesis?
   c. What happened to change this test?
   d. How did this affect Becquerel's hypothesis?
   e. Some people might think that Becquerel was lucky. What do you think?

2. Figure 4 shows packets of tea passing along a conveyor belt. As the belt moves along, the packets pass through the beam of beta particles.

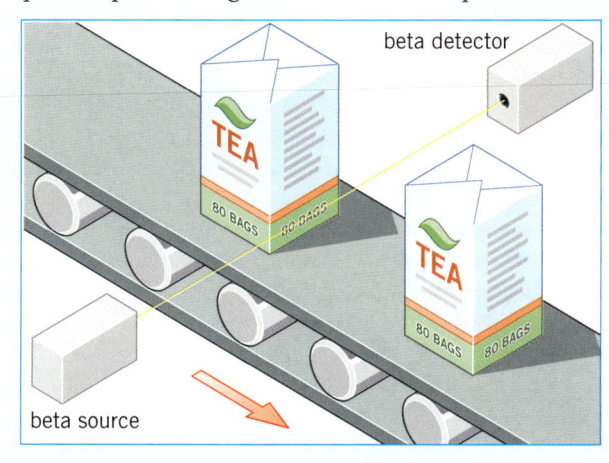

   Figure 4

   a. Explain how this set-up can be used to count the packets of tea passing along the belt.
   b. Explain how this set-up also provides a way of indicating if a packet is not filled up to the top.

Key Ideas

- Some substances produce radiation all the time, no matter what is done to them. These substances are said to be radioactive.

- There are three types of radiation emitted by radioactive sources: alpha (α), beta (β) and gamma (γ).

- Radiation can be absorbed as it passes through a material.
  - Alpha radiation is easily absorbed by a few centimetres of air or by a thin sheet of paper.
  - Beta radiation easily passes through air or paper, but is mostly absorbed by a few millimetres of a metal such as aluminium.
  - Gamma radiation is very penetrating – it requires many centimetres of lead or metres of concrete to absorb most of it.

- The absorption of radiation can be used to monitor and control the thickness of materials in an industrial process.

3. In an industrial process, which radiation would you use for controlling:
   a. the thickness of sheets of paper
   b. the thickness of metal sheets?

   Explain your answers fully.

Radioactivity

7.2 Unravelling the radioactive mystery

Ideas and Evidence

In 1897 a young Polish woman and her French husband were expecting their first child. Marie and Pierre Curie were delighted with the safe arrival of their first daughter, Irène, on September 12 – but within a couple of months Marie was looking for something else to do with her time while her recently widowed father-in-law helped out with the childcare!

The Curies were both scientists working in Paris. Pierre was the older and better known of the two, and his field of study was electricity and magnetism. Marie had also been working on magnets, but after the birth of her baby she wanted to find another area of research to get her doctorate. The accidental discovery of radioactivity by Becquerel only the year before had caught her imagination. The work on the rays produced by uranium was so new that the field of research was wide open – she felt sure that she would find out something that no-one had observed before.

Figure 1: Marie and Pierre Curie enjoyed cycling – even on their honeymoon they travelled around France by bike!

Marie was given a damp, cramped storeroom at the bottom of the School of Physics to carry out her research, but in spite of the appalling conditions she soon began to make some astonishing discoveries.

Marie Curie soon showed that the intensity of the radiation produced by uranium depended only on the amount of uranium present and was unaffected by light, temperature or the chemical state of the uranium. Then, in a rush of enthusiasm, she started to test all of the known elements to see if these new rays were unique to uranium. The hoped-for result was not long in coming – compounds of the element thorium emitted rays just like uranium. The new phenomenon needed a name – and Marie suggested the term 'radioactivity'.

Marie Curie then began to study the ores of different elements and, as she expected, the ores of uranium and thorium gave off radioactivity. However, more radioactivity was being produced than she had predicted. Her first assumption was that she had done something wrong and she repeated the experiments with painstaking care no less than twenty times – but there was no mistake. The ore contained a new source of radioactivity, more powerful than uranium or thorium. Marie had discovered a new radioactive element!

Figure 2: Marie Curie kept full records of all her work – and her working conditions. Here she recorded a temperature of only 6.25 °C followed by ten exclamation marks to show her disapproval of such a chilly environment.

At this stage, in 1898, Pierre Curie decided that the work his wife was doing was so exciting that he left his own projects to join her in her search for the new element. The couple shared observations and wrote joint papers – for them, two heads were certainly better than one. They worked using the uranium ore known as pitchblende, separating it into the various elements of which it was made, and checking each for radioactivity.

Radioactivity

Figure 3: One of the pieces of apparatus used by Marie Curie in her work on radioactivity.

To their astonishment and delight they found that, after eliminating uranium, they still had two sources of radioactivity – they had discovered not one but two new elements! They christened the first element polonium and the second radium, and this was the most stable, radioactive and useful of the two. Finally in 1902 they prepared 0.1 gram of pure radium salts. Before long Marie and Pierre discovered that this had the potential to be used as a treatment for cancer – but at the same time they were undergoing huge personal struggles with ill health and lack of money. They could have made a huge amount of money from patenting their discovery of how to extract radium from pitchblende, because it was soon in demand all over the world for cancer treatment. However, they felt that this was contrary to the scientific spirit and that the knowledge they had produced should be free to all. By doing this they saved countless lives but condemned themselves to more poverty. Then, towards the end of 1903, the Curies were awarded the Nobel prize, along with Becquerel. This brought them money – which was welcome – and fame, which was not.

Figure 4: Marie Curie – double Nobel prize winner for her work on radioactivity.

Marie and Pierre continued with their work until Pierre was tragically killed in a road accident. Marie never fully recovered from her loss, but she continued with her research, even taking over Pierre's professorship at the Sorbonne University. She separated pure radium metal for the first and only time and developed ways of measuring accurate doses of radiation for Curie therapy. In 1911 she achieved the unthinkable and was awarded a second Nobel prize. She continued working with her beloved elements for the rest of her life until she died in 1934, ironically from a disease linked to her years of working with radioactive materials.

Questions

1. a Why did Marie choose to work on radioactivity?
   b Why did Pierre choose to change the direction of his research and join his wife?
   c What factors do you think might influence the choice of research topic for a young scientist today?
2. Marie and Pierre Curie chose not to patent their method for extracting radium. Draw up a table to show what factors they might have considered in coming to that decision.

Key Ideas

- Work by the Curies on radioactivity led to the identification of the radioactive elements thorium, polonuim and radium.

Radioactivity

7.3 Radioactivity all around us

As you sit reading this book you are surrounded by radioactive materials – and there are radioactive materials inside you too!

As we shall see shortly, ionising radiation is due to changes that happen in the nuclei of atoms. Many of the chemical elements contain atoms that behave in this way and, as a result, radioactive substances are all around us – in the ground, in the air we breathe and in the building materials that make up our homes, schools and places of work. Radioactive substances are also in our food. Our bodies absorb the food and so also contain radioactive substances.

In addition to radiation from radioactive sources around us, radiation also reaches us from space, from nearby stars (especially the Sun). This radiation is often called cosmic rays. Cosmic rays together with the radiation from the radioactive substances around and inside us make up the **background radiation** to which everyone is subjected all the time, no matter who we are or where we live. Figure 2 shows the proportions of background radiation due to different sources for the UK population as a whole.

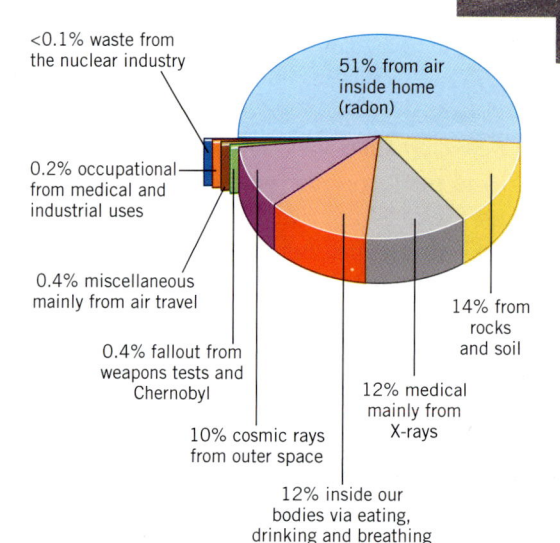

Figure 1: You can't see it, feel it, taste it or smell it – but radiation is all around you, and inside you too.

- <0.1% waste from the nuclear industry
- 0.2% occupational from medical and industrial uses
- 0.4% miscellaneous mainly from air travel
- 0.4% fallout from weapons tests and Chernobyl
- 10% cosmic rays from outer space
- 12% inside our bodies via eating, drinking and breathing
- 12% medical mainly from X-rays
- 14% from rocks and soil
- 51% from air inside home (radon)

Figure 2: About 90% of the background radiation that we receive comes from natural sources – the rest comes mainly from the X-rays we have when we go to hospital or at the dentist.

By far the greatest amount of our background radiation comes from the air, due to the radioactive gases produced by uranium and other radioactive substances in the ground. The overall amount of background radiation due to artificially produced radioactive substances is very small, and makes up about 1% of the total. Of this 1% about half comes from the 'fallout' (radioactive substances) produced by the testing of nuclear weapons in the second half of the last century and the majority of the rest comes from exposure to radioactive substances at work and in hospital investigations. Less than 0.1% of the total background radiation comes from waste produced from the production of electricity in nuclear power stations.

The amount of background radiation received depends on where you are. Flying in an aeroplane increases a person's exposure to cosmic rays, since there is less of the Earth's atmosphere above them to absorb the rays. Exposure to background radiation also increases beneath the Earth's surface, due to surrounding rocks. Some types of rock also produce a gas called radon, which is radioactive. This gas finds its way into the air, and may reach high concentrations in houses built on top of certain types of ground. To reduce exposure to radon gas, these houses must be well ventilated, and special pumped systems may be installed to ensure that the level of radon does not reach dangerous levels.

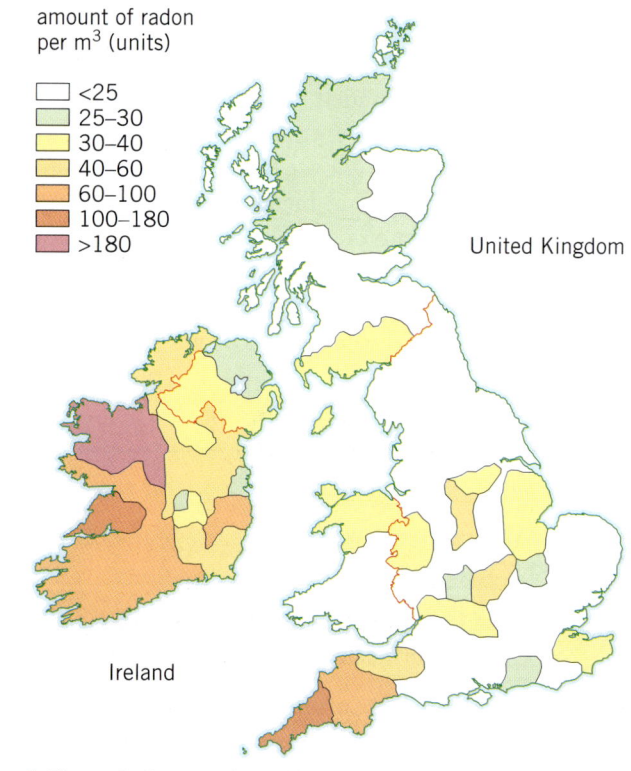

amount of radon per m³ (units)
- <25
- 25–30
- 30–40
- 40–60
- 60–100
- 100–180
- >180

Figure 3: A map of the UK showing the average dose of radon gas for different areas.

Radioactivity

Ideas and Evidence

Scientists find it hard to agree whether there is any safe level for exposure to radiation, or whether we should try to make the radiation dose received by people as low as possible. This is an especially important issue for people who work with radioactive substances, and who may receive large doses of radiation in their work.

In order to make decisions about safe levels of exposure to radiation, scientists need information about the effect of radiation on the human body. As with other areas of science, experiments have been conducted on animals to see the effect of different levels of radiation. However, it is not always easy to decide whether animal experiments provide a fair test of how humans will respond. To overcome this problem, scientists have sought data from other sources. One important source of information comes from the aftermath of the atomic bombs dropped on Hiroshima and Nagasaki in 1945, when hundreds of thousands of people were exposed to high levels of radiation. Medical studies carried out on these people have enabled a picture to be built up, and have helped provide a understanding of the likely effects of different exposures to radiation over different periods of time.

While some scientists worked to understand the effects of radiation on the unfortunate survivors of atomic warfare during the years after the Second World War, other scientists carried out radiation experiments on human beings in laboratory or hospital settings. Usually these experiments were carried out with the permission of the people involved, but not always – some records show that patients in mental hospitals were used in such experiments. Whether these patients gave their permission – or indeed were capable of giving their permission – is doubtful. Despite such doubts, some of this work has undoubtedly contributed to our present understanding of the effects of radiation on the human body.

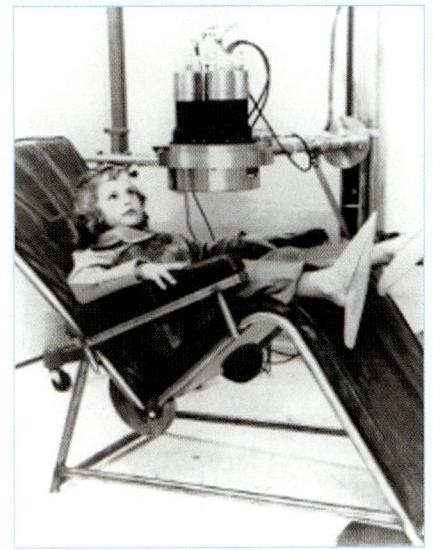

↑ **Figure 4:** Human radiation experiments were carried out during the Cold War between the USSR and the West. Can we be sure that they were always conducted with the permission of the subject – and how much was the subject told about the likely effects on them? This photograph shows an experiment to measure the amount of ionising radiation typically in the body of a child. This experiment was carried out in the 1960s.

Key Ideas

- There are radioactive substances all around us, in the air, in building materials and in food.
- Radiation also reaches us from space.
- The radiation from all these sources is called background radiation.

Questions

1 Explain why:

   a Radiation is present inside your body as well as outside it.

   b Someone who flies regularly receives a higher dose of radiation than someone who does not.

   c Where you live can affect your radiation dose.

2 Someone who lives in Cornwall might receive a dose of radiation 50% higher than someone who lives in Dorset. Redraw Figure 2 to show the make-up of this person's radiation dose.

3 Consider the issues concerned with obtaining information about the effects of radiation. Information can be obtained by studying the effects of radiation on the survivors of atomic warfare, or those people who have been affected by nuclear accidents like Chernobyl. Information can also be obtained by conducting experiments on people, or on animals. Write a short essay describing your opinions about this – if you think we need information about the likely effects of radiation, state clearly how you think we should obtain this. If you do not think that it is right to use people or animals to find out about the effects of radiation, state clearly how you think we should make decisions about the likely effects of radiation, and the safe limits that should apply when people use radiation.

Radioactivity

7.4 The effects of radiation on living things

We have already seen that radiation is absorbed by matter. The amount of radiation absorbed depends on the type of radiation, the type of material that the radiation is travelling through, and the distance that the radiation has travelled through the material. We shall now look a little more closely at how radiation is absorbed as it travels through matter.

All radiation carries energy. When radiation travels through matter, the energy it carries is slowly transferred from the radiation to the matter until there is no more energy remains to be transferred. This transfer of energy happens when the radiation collides with atoms in the matter. When alpha, beta and gamma radiations travel through matter, some collisions simply result in the atom gaining kinetic energy. However, more often the radiation has enough energy to knock one or more electrons out of the atom. When this happens the atom becomes charged, since it has different numbers of protons and electrons. A charged atom is called an **ion** – so when an atom becomes charged, this is called **ionisation**. Radiation that has enough energy to ionise atoms is called **ionising radiation**.

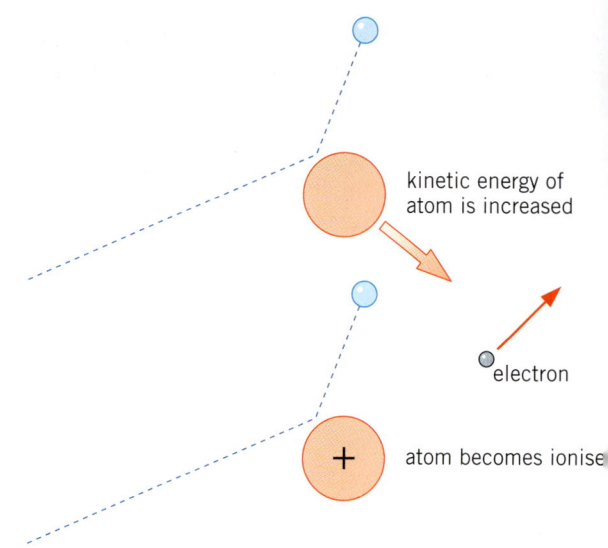

When ionising radiation travels through living tissue it forms ions in just the same way as it does when travelling through non-living matter such as aluminium or lead. However, ions that form in living tissue can cause serious damage to cells, and so ionising radiation can be very dangerous to living organisms.

When ionising radiation passes through a cell, the ions formed damage the complex molecules that are essential for the cell to work properly. Quite low doses of ionising radiation can be fatal for cells because they damage the DNA in the cell's nucleus. The DNA controls the way the cell grows and divides. When the DNA is damaged the cell may start to grow and divide uncontrollably. A cell that behaves in this way may grow into a **cancer** – a clump of cells that increases in size very rapidly. Cancers are dangerous because they grow so rapidly, causing damage to the tissue around them. The larger the dose of radiation received by a cell, the more likely it is to cause damage that can lead to cancer. However, even quite low doses of radiation can cause cancers to develop, and scientists do not all agree whether there is a safe limit to radiation exposure, below which no significant damage occurs.

↑ **Figure 1:** Energy is transferred from radiation to matter as the radiation collides with atoms. Sometimes this may simply increase an atom's kinetic energy, but more often it ionises it.

↑ **Figure 2:** The symbol for a radiation hazard. Great care is needed in handling radiation sources to ensure that no damage to living tissue can occur.

↓ **Figure 3:** The chain of events leading to the development of cancer due to exposure to radiation.

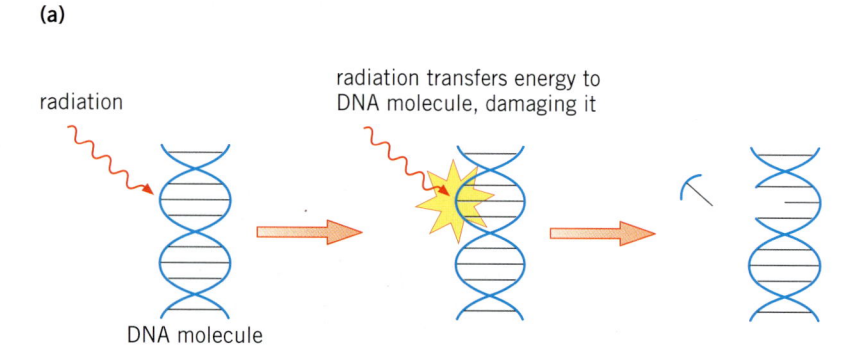

(a)

Radiation damages the cell's DNA.
As a result of the damaged DNA the cell cannot function properly.

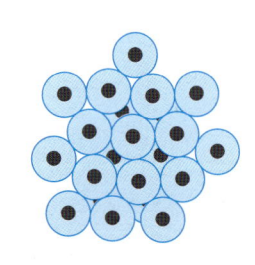

(b)

The cell starts to grow and divide uncontrollably.

124 Radioactivity

While lower doses of ionising radiation cause long-term damage to cells, very high doses of radiation cause so much damage that the cell dies very quickly. This happens because essential molecules like enzymes are badly damaged by the radiation. Uncontrolled large doses of radiation lead to radiation sickness, which is usually fatal within days. Controlled large doses of radiation can be used to kill cancerous cells, which are usually more sensitive to radiation than healthy cells. To treat a cancer a beam of radiation is carefully directed at it, using just the right dose to kill the cancer cells and to damage the surrounding healthy cells as little as possible. Even with the greatest care, however, some damage is inevitably done to healthy tissue and this makes the patient feel very unwell.

Because ionising radiation is so damaging to cells, it can be used to kill unwanted or dangerous micro-organisms. Medical instruments and other supplies can be sterilised by irradiating them with ionising radiation, rather than using very hot steam. This is especially useful where it is necessary to sterilise items made of plastic or other materials that would not withstand very high temperatures.

Ionising radiation can also be used to kill micro-organisms on or in food. These micro-organisms are responsible for making the food go 'off', so irradiated food stays fresh for longer. Food exposed to ionising radiation *cannot* become radioactive, and anyone eating the food is not exposed to ionising radiation.

Figure 4: Using radiation to treat a cancer.

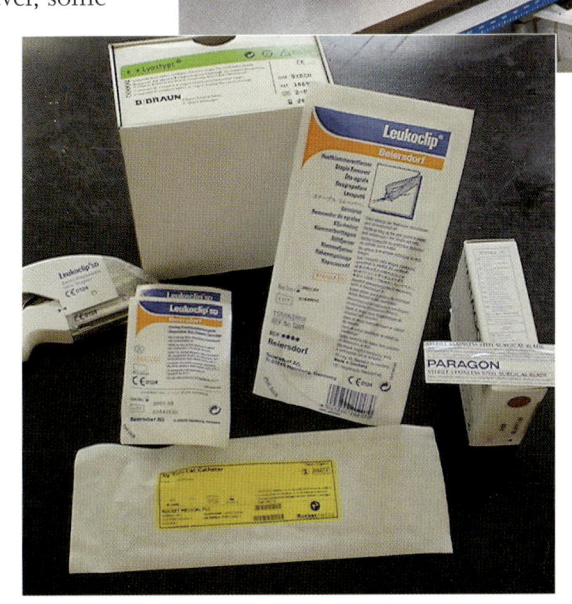

Figure 5: Ionising radiation has been used to sterilise this veterinary equipment.

Key Ideas

- When radiation from radioactive materials collides with neutral atoms or molecules these may become charged (ionised).
- When radiation ionises molecules in living cells it can cause damage, including cancer.
- The larger the dose of radiation, the greater is the risk of cancer.
- Higher doses of ionising radiation can kill cells; they are used to kill cancer cells and harmful micro-organisms.

Questions

1. Why are alpha, beta and gamma radiations called **ionising radiation**?
2. Why must the beam of radiation used to treat cancer be targeted very carefully?
3. Alpha radiation is more readily absorbed by matter than beta radiation. Gamma radiation is less readily absorbed by matter than either alpha or beta radiation.

   a What does this tell you about the number of ions produced by alpha, beta and gamma radiations as they travel through matter?

   b Which radiation is likely to be most damaging to cells – alpha, beta or gamma radiation?

4. Produce a poster for a supermarket to explain how irradiated food has been treated to make it last longer.

7.5 Working with radiation

Ionising radiation has many uses. However, like any other useful tool, radiation must be handled carefully and treated with respect if it is not to cause unwanted damage – particularly to people.

Radiation sources are usually made by placing a substance inside a special kind of nuclear reactor. Inside the reactor the substance is bombarded with neutrons, and it becomes radioactive. For example, radioactive iodine is used to help diagnose and treat problems with the thyroid gland. It is made by placing the element tellurium inside a nuclear reactor, where it becomes radioactive iodine:

$$\text{tellurium} \xrightarrow{\text{bombard with neutrons inside a nuclear reactor}} \text{radioactive iodine}$$

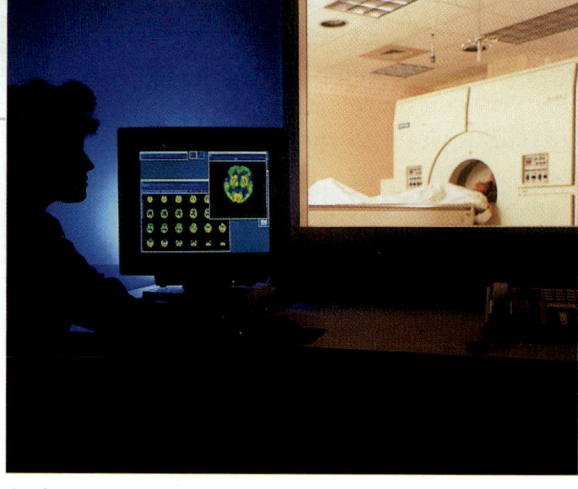

Figure 1: Protecting a radiographer from ionising radiation using a glass screen.

Handling and storing radioactive materials must be done in such a way that people are not exposed to unnecessary risks to their health. To do this, a good understanding of the properties of the three types of radiation given off by radioactive sources is needed.

The hazard that a radiation source poses depends on where it is. Because alpha radiation is very strongly absorbed by matter, when it is outside the body it is unlikely to be dangerous. If it is more than a few centimetres distant it will be absorbed by the air before it ever reaches the body. Even if it is close enough to reach the body it will be absorbed by a person's clothing, or by the layer of dead skin cells on the surface of the body – so it cannot do any damage. Beta and gamma radiations are a different story, however, since they are sufficiently penetrating to reach the body and to travel through it to reach the internal organs where they may cause damage.

When we think about protecting people from ionising radiation, we can also consider X-rays as well as alpha, beta and gamma radiation. X-rays are very similar to gamma radiation, although they are not produced by radioactive substances. The principles of protecting someone from all types of ionising radiation are exactly the same, no matter what the source.

Protecting people from ionising radiation outside the body involves stopping the radiation reaching them. This can be done in two ways. The first of these is to make sure that the person is kept as far away from the radioactive source as possible. If this alone is not enough to reduce the exposure to radiation to a safe level, then a protective screen must be used.

Where people have to handle radioactive sources, they are screened from the radiation, and use special apparatus that manipulates the radioactive material using remotely controlled tongs (Figure 2).

It is important to have accurate information about the dose of radiation that a person working with radiation has received. One way of doing this is to use a radiation badge (which has the proper name of **film badge dosimeter**). This is worn by all staff who may be exposed to ionising radiation – for example, staff making and handling radioactive sources like radioactive iodine. The badge is a small container, which is easily worn by pinning it to a lab coat or other item of clothing. Inside the badge is a special photographic film. When this film is exposed to ionising radiation it

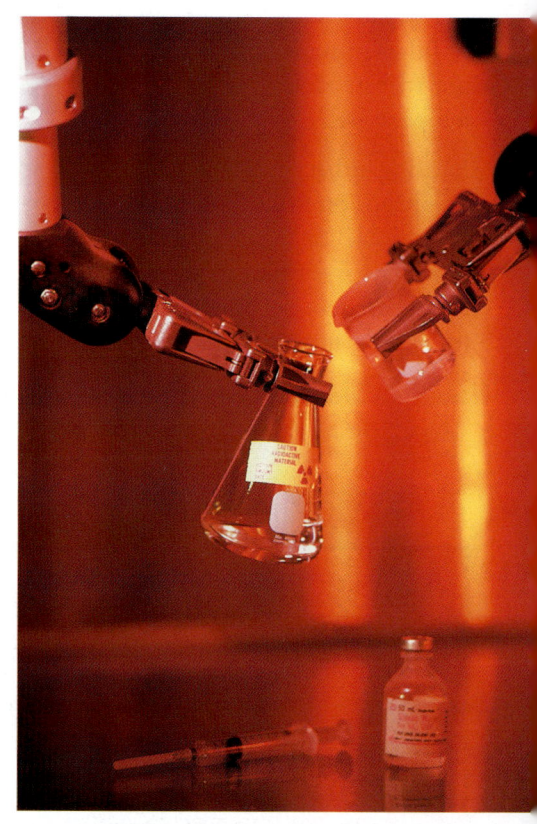

Figure 2: The handling of highly radioactive sources requires special equipment to protect the operator.

darkens. At fixed intervals, each person's badge is removed and the film developed – the amount of darkening depends on the dose of radiation that the badge has received. As the badge is worn by a person, it effectively measures the dose of radiation received by that person.

A code of practice is always followed when people are working with ionising radiation. In general:

- Areas where ionising radiation is used are clearly marked. Access to these areas is limited by signs, and possibly by security measures (such as locked doors) too.
- All equipment used to work with ionising radiation is regularly checked.
- Radiation monitoring equipment (such as film badges) are worn by all personnel who work with ionising radiation or who may be exposed to it during the course of their work.
- Personnel keep as much distance as possible between themselves and the source of the radiation, in order to minimise their exposure to it.

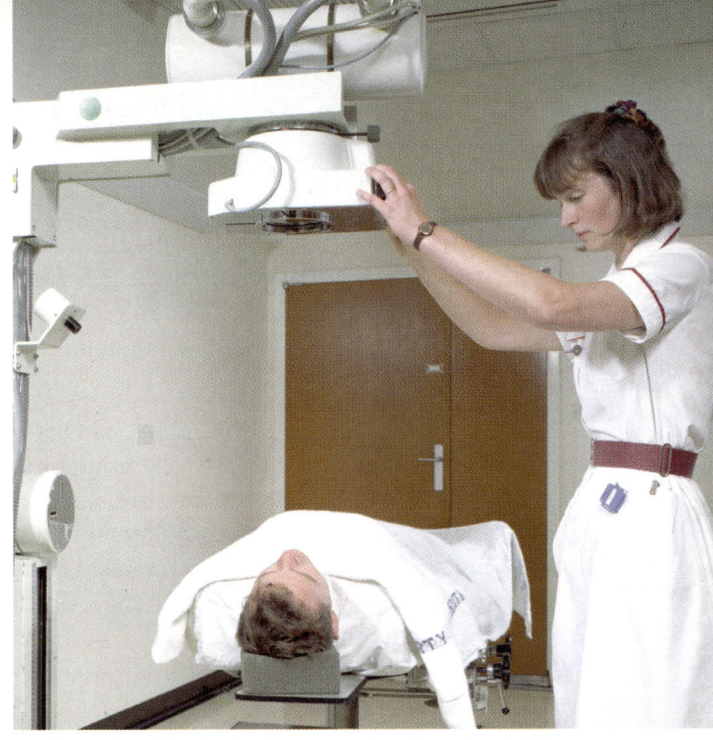

Figure 3: A film badge is worn pinned to the clothing of the person who is being monitored.

Key Ideas

- When sources of radiation are outside the body:
  - Beta and gamma radiation are the most dangerous because they can reach the cells of the organs and may be absorbed by them.
  - Alpha radiation is least dangerous because it is unlikely to reach living cells.
- Workers who are at risk from radiation often wear a radiation badge to monitor the amount of radiation they have been exposed to over a period of time.
- A radiation badge is a small packet containing photographic film. The more radiation a worker has been exposed to, the darker the film is when it has been developed.

Questions

1. Figure 4 shows a simplified diagram of a radiation badge.
   a. Which area of the badge measures the total dose of radiation?
   b. What dose of radiation will be measured by the film under the plastic filters?
   c. What dose of radiation will be measured by the film under the metal filters?
   d. How is the dose of alpha radiation calculated?

2. This is the safety advice on a radioactive source: *This substance gives off a type of ionising radiation called **alpha radiation**. Whilst relatively harmless outside the body, this substance may be dangerous if swallowed.*
   a. What is meant by **ionising radiation**?
   b. Why is the substance likely to be 'relatively harmless outside the body'?
   c. Would this safety notice apply to a substance emitting gamma radiation? Explain your answer.

← Figure 4

Radioactivity

7.6 Radioactivity and medicine

Sometimes a source of ionising radiation is used inside the body. In order to treat certain cancers, a radioactive source may be implanted in a patient's body immediately next to the cancer. This makes the amount of radiation received by the cancer as large as possible, while keeping the exposure of the rest of the body as low as possible.

When a source of ionising radiation is inside the body, alpha radiation from the source is strongly absorbed by the cells around it, causing a great deal of damage. In contrast, beta and gamma radiation are much less strongly absorbed, so cause a lot less damage to the cells around the source. As with sources outside the body used to treat cancers, sources inside the body must be chosen and placed carefully in order to provide a dose that will kill the cancer cells, while minimising the damage to healthy cells.

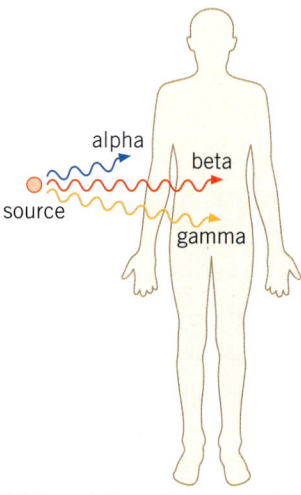

← **Figure 1:** The relative dangers of ionising radiation inside and outside the body.

(a) Any alpha radiation not absorbed by the air between the source and the body will be absorbed by the clothing or by the layer of dead skin cells on the surface of the body. Beta and gamma radiations may enter the body and damage cells inside.

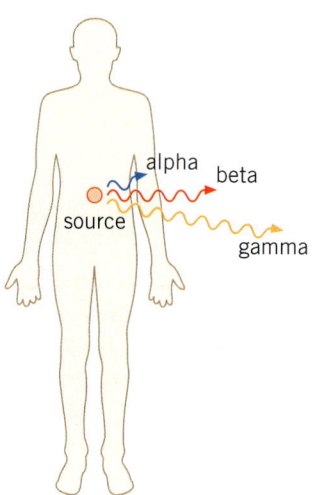

(b) Alpha radiation is strongly absorbed by cells around the source, causing much damage. Beta and gamma radiations are much less strongly absorbed, and can travel through the body tissues, leaving the body through the skin.

Sometimes a source of radiation may be used inside the body in order to find out what is wrong with a patient. The patient swallows or is injected with a special substance that consists of molecules that contain a radioactive element which emits gamma radiation – called a **radioactive tracer**. The body's natural systems transport these molecules it to the part of the body under investigation (for example, the kidneys). Once there, special imaging equipment called a **gamma camera** records the gamma radiation coming from the patient's body. The gamma camera builds up a visible picture of this radiation, from which doctors can get information to help them to decide what may be wrong with the patient.

The image in Figure 3 shows a gamma camera image of a patient's

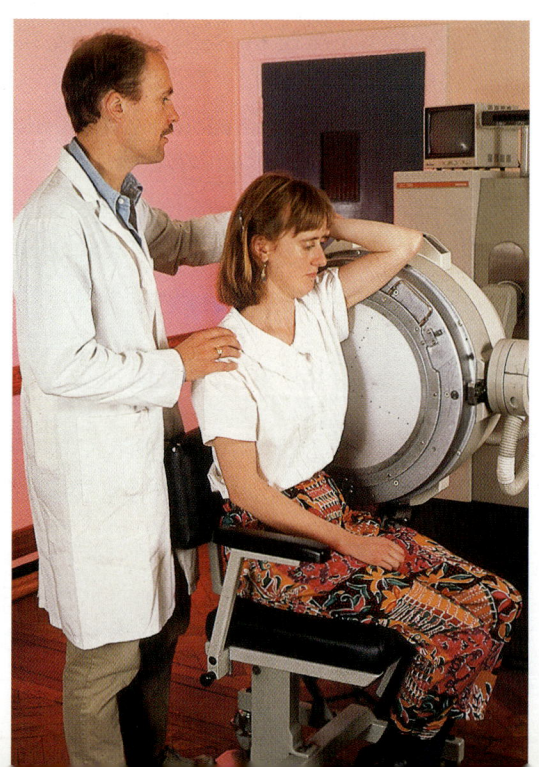

→ **Figure 2:** A gamma camera, used to help doctors understand what is happening inside a patient's body.

Radioactivity

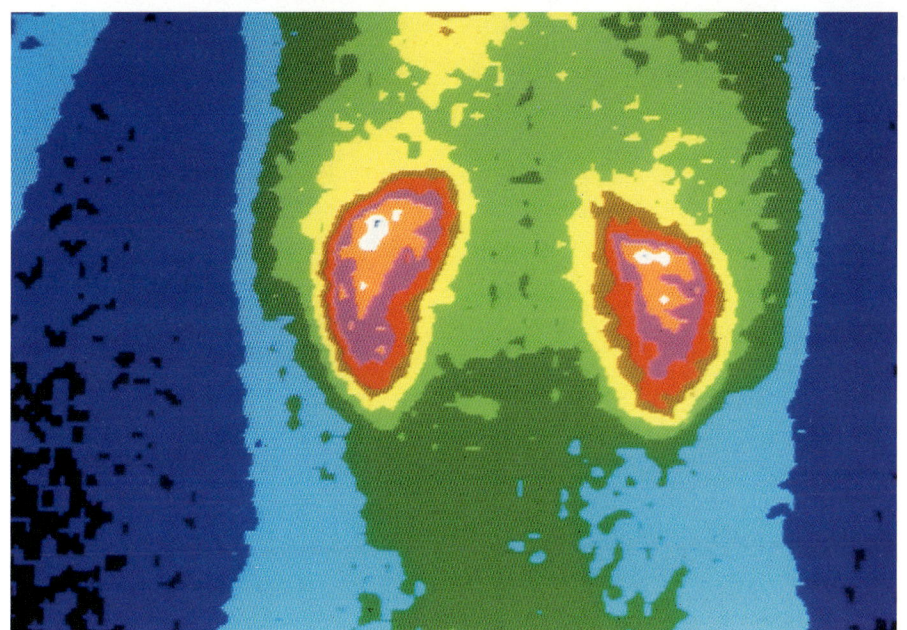

← **Figure 3:** A gamma camera image of a patient's kidneys.

Key Ideas

- When sources of radiation are inside the body:
  - Alpha radiation is the most dangerous because it is so strongly absorbed by cells.
  - Beta and gamma radiations are less dangerous because cells are less likely to absorb the radiation.
- When external sources of radiation are used in medicine both patients and health workers need to be protected. This is achieved by making the distance between the source of ionising radiation and the people likely to be affected by it as large as possible. Where this is not possible, screens may be used to absorb the radiation – these usually contain a high proportion of lead, which absorbs ionising radiation strongly.

kidneys. The right kidney is giving off much less radiation than the left kidney, showing that it has absorbed much less of the radioactive tracer. There may be several reasons for this – the doctors will need to carry out further tests to decide what is wrong.

X-rays are used widely for medical diagnosis. Although X-rays are produced artificially, they behave in a very similar way to gamma rays and therefore the same precautions must be taken. Someone having an X-ray photograph taken of their arm may be asked to wear a lead 'apron' to protect the rest of their body. In some cases it is important that the protective screen is transparent, so that someone can see through it. Figure 1 on page 126 shows how a radiographer is protected from X-rays. Notice how the thick glass screen provides the protection from the radiation. This glass contains lead to make it absorb the radiation more strongly.

Questions

1. Describe **two** ways in which a person's exposure to ionising radiation can be decreased.

2. Explain why a source emitting alpha radiation poses very little danger when outside the body but would be very dangerous if swallowed.

3. A newspaper report says: *The patient will swallow a radioactive substance that emits alpha radiation. This radiation will be picked up by a camera, which produces a picture of the inside of the patient.*

   Give **two** reasons why alpha radiation would not be used in this way.

4. Figure 4 is a graph showing the amount of gamma radiation coming from a patient's lungs immediately after they have breathed in a gas that emits gamma radiation. Explain what this graph may tell a doctor.

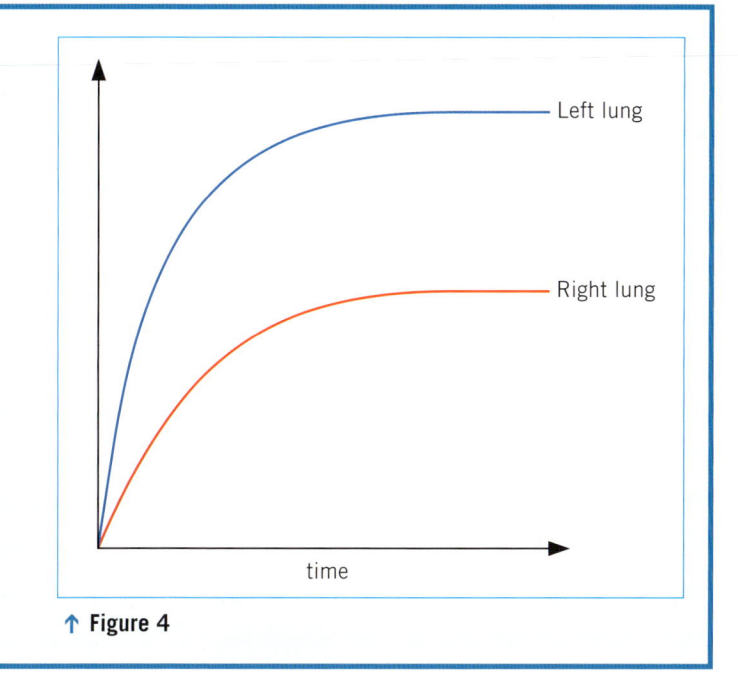

↑ **Figure 4**

Radioactivity 129

7.7 How long?

When a radioactive substance gives off ionising radiation, unstable atoms in the substance change into a different kind of atom. This process is called **radioactive decay.**

The radioactive decay of a substance can be measured by the amount of radiation emitted from it using a Geiger counter. This counts the number of alpha particles, beta particles and gamma rays reaching the counter each second, which is called the **count rate**. If the count rate for a sample of the radioactive gas radon is measured and plotted on a graph, it looks like the graph in Figure 1. This is called a **decay curve.**

The decay curve for any radioactive substance always looks like this. The time taken for the count rate to fall by half is called the **half-life.** The decay curve for radon in Figure 1 shows how it always takes about 50 seconds for the count rate to halve. The half-life for a particular atom is always the same, no matter what chemical compound it is in. Half-life is not affected by temperature or pressure either, although the half-lives of different atoms can be very, very different. As an example, the half-life of radioactive helium atoms is under one second, while the half-life of one type of uranium atom is nearly one thousand million years!

Because ionising radiation is given off by a substance when unstable atoms decay, the half-life of a substance can also be thought of as the time taken for the number of radioactive atoms to halve. Because the number of radioactive atoms halves in one half-life, the **mass** of radioactive substance present halves too.

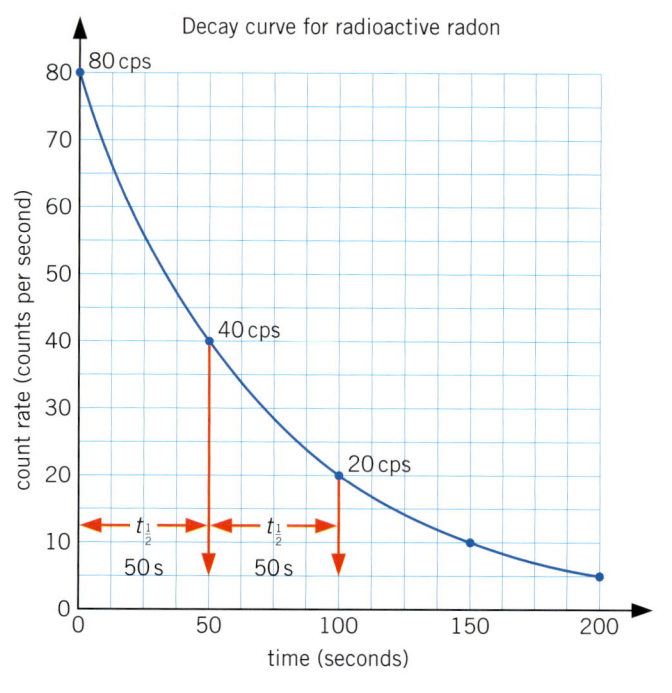

Figure 1: The decay in radioactivity for a sample of radon gas.

Figure 2: In one half-life three important things happen to a sample of a radioactive substance.

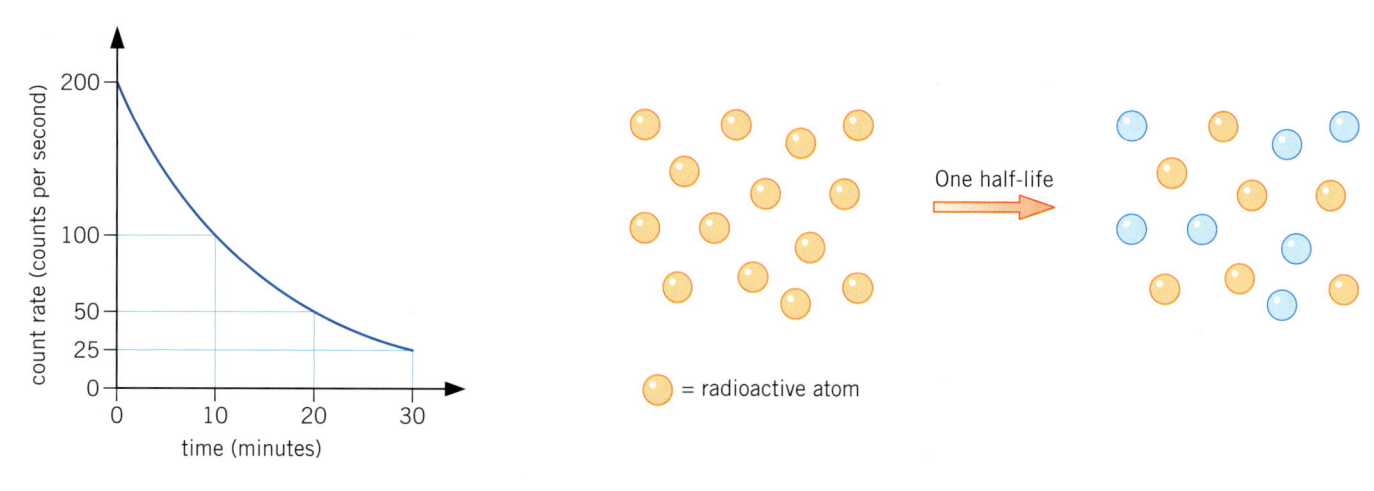

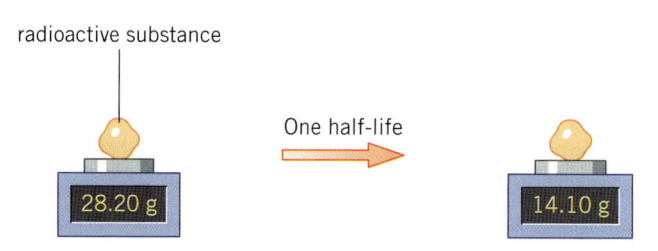

130 Radioactivity

Example

The half-life of a radioactive substance is 10 minutes. A mass of 5 grams of the substance produces a count rate of 200 counts per second.

a What will the count rate produced by the substance be after 30 minutes?

b What mass of substance will be left after this time?

a The half-life of the substance is 10 minutes, which tells us that it takes 10 minutes for the count rate to halve. This means that the count rate decreases as follows:

Time (minutes)	Count rate (counts per second)
0	200
10	$\frac{1}{2} \times 200 = 100$
20	$\frac{1}{2} \times 100 = 50$
30	$\frac{1}{2} \times 50 = 25$

After 30 minutes the count rate will have fallen to 25 counts per second.

b In one half-life exactly half of the unstable atoms in the substance will decay, leaving half undecayed. This means that the mass of unstable atoms remaining undecayed after one half-life will be exactly half of the original mass. The mass of substance remaining can be calculated in just the same way as the count rate:

Time (minutes)	Mass of radioactive substance remaining (grams)
0	5
10	$\frac{1}{2} \times 5 = 2.5$
20	$\frac{1}{2} \times 2.5 = 1.25$
30	$\frac{1}{2} \times 1.25 = 0.625$

After 30 minutes the mass of the radioactive substance will have decreased to 0·625 grams.

Key Ideas

- The half-life of a radioactive substance is:
  - the time it takes for the number of radioactive atoms in a sample to halve
  - the time it takes for the count rate from the original substance to fall to half its initial level.

Questions

1 A radioactive element has a half-life of 24 days. A detector placed next to a sample of the element registers a count rate of 2000 counts per second. What count rate would be registered after:

  a 24 days

  b 48 days

  c 96 days?

2 A radioactive gas has a half-life of 0·8 seconds. A sample of the gas with a mass of 1.0 gram is put into a sealed container. What mass of the gas would be left after:

  a 0·8 seconds

  b 1·6 seconds

  c 4·0 seconds?

3 The count rate from a radioactive substance is shown in the table.

Time (minutes)	0	2	4	6	8
Count rate (counts per second)	120	69	40	23	13

  a Plot a graph of these results.

  b From your graph calculate the half-life of the substance.

  c Predict the count rate at 10 minutes. Comment on your answer.

7.8 Using radioactivity H

The right radioactive substance for the job

Ionising radiation has many uses – in medicine, in industry and in scientific research. Wherever ionising radiation is used, careful thought must be given to safety, and the practical implications must be considered too. Both the type of radiation and the half-life of a particular source are important. The two examples here explain this further.

Controlling thickness

We saw on page 118 how ionising radiation can be used to control the thickness of plastic sheeting produced when hot plastic is squeezed between two metal rollers. As the thickness of the plastic decreases, it absorbs less of the ionising radiation passing through it so more radiation reaches the detector. The reverse is true as the thickness of the plastic increases. This change can be used to control the pressure on the rollers, thus keeping the thickness of the plastic sheeting produced constant.

Obviously we must choose ionising radiation that is able to pass through the plastic sheeting, otherwise the control system would not work. This rules out alpha radiation. Similarly, gamma radiation is ruled out, since it would pass through the sheeting with very little radiation being absorbed, which would make control very difficult. For this reason, beta radiation is the obvious choice here. Beta radiation is a good choice for safety reasons too, since it is easier to protect people from it than from gamma radiation.

↑ **Figure 1:** Using radioactivity to control the thickness of paper in a paper mill.

For a use like this the radioactive source producing the beta radiation should have a reasonably long half-life so that it is not necessary to recalibrate the equipment constantly because the amount of radiation produced by the source falls too quickly.

Medical diagnosis

Safety considerations are obviously vital when radioactive substances are used in medicine. We have already seen that when a radioactive tracer is used to help diagnose what is wrong with a patient the substance chosen usually emits gamma radiation, which is much less strongly absorbed by the cells of the body than alpha radiation. This reduces the likely damage to the cells, and makes it possible to detect the radiation outside the body.

As well as thinking about the radiation itself, medical physicists also choose the radioactive tracer very carefully so that it has an appropriate half-life. This needs to be long enough to enable doctors to make the measurements needed for diagnosis, but short enough to ensure that the patient is exposed to ionising radiation for the shortest possible time.

Radioactivity

One radioactive substance that is very commonly used in hospitals is called technetium-99m. This emits only gamma rays and has a half-life of 6 hours, both of which help to minimise the exposure of patients to radiation. In addition technetium atoms are easily combined with chemicals that are absorbed by particular parts of the body, allowing doctors to 'target' specific organs.

↓ **Figure 3:** Radiation is also used by veterinary surgeons to treat sick animals.

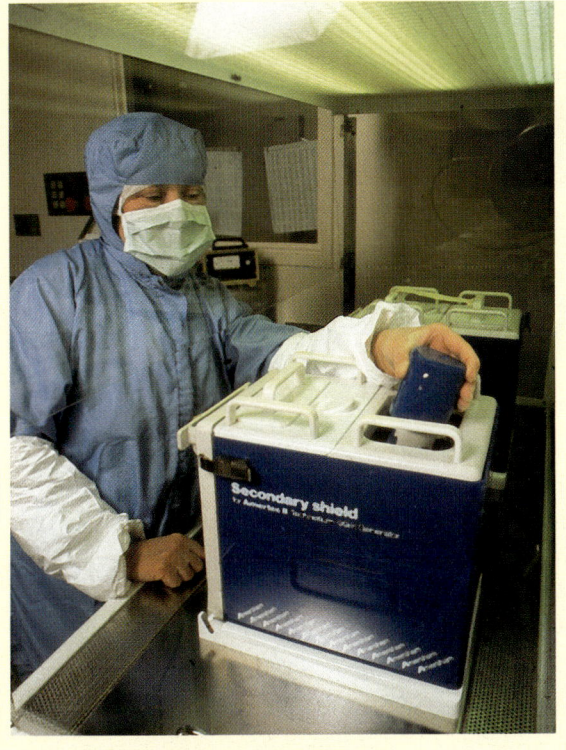

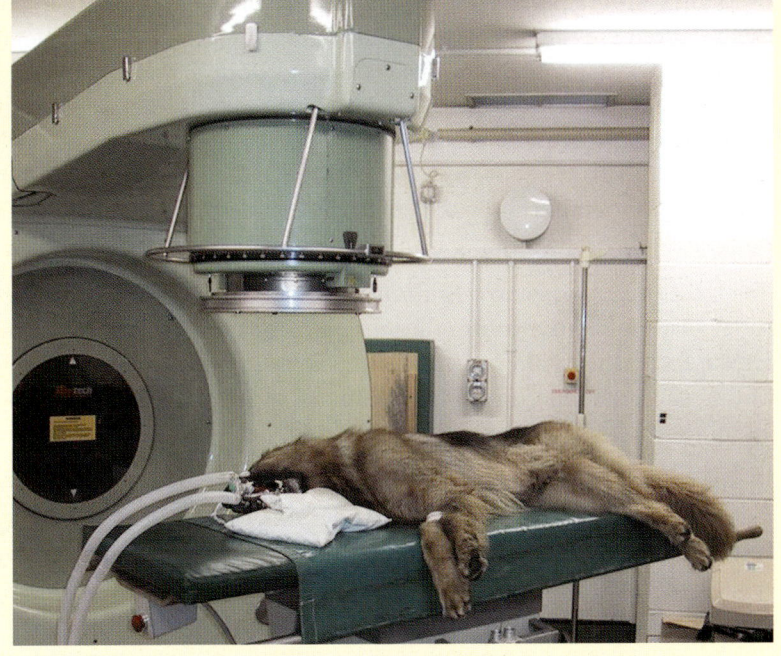

← **Figure 2:** In a hospital medical physics department a technician 'milks' the technetium 'cow', obtaining the radioactive technetium needed for the day's examinations.

Questions

1 Gamma radiation can be used to treat cancerous tumours deep inside a person's body, using a source of gamma radiation outside the patient's body. When this is done, the source of gamma radiation may be rotated around the patient, so that the beam of gamma radiation passes through the tumour from directions 360° around the patient. Figure 4 shows this happening.

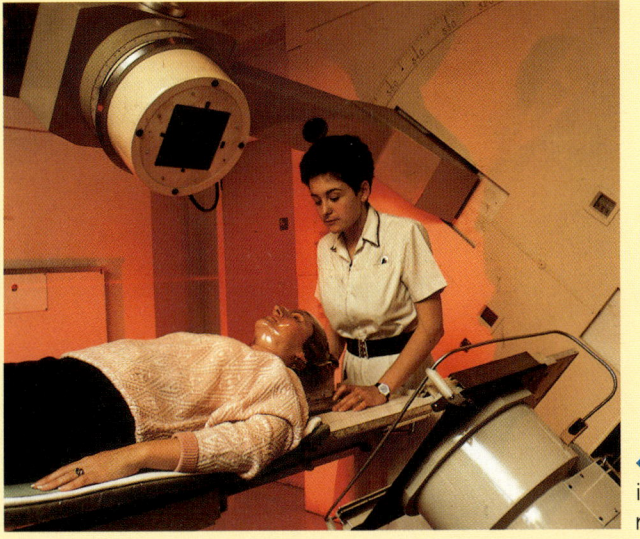

Key Ideas

- The type of radiation emitted and the half-life of the radioactive substance emitting it need to be considered when thinking about which radioactive source to use for a particular application.

a Why is gamma radiation used to treat tumours in this way rather than alpha and beta radiation?

b Why should the source of gamma radiation used have a long half-life?

c How does rotating the source of gamma radiation around the patient affect the dose of radiation they receive?

← **Figure 4:** Cancer therapy using ionising radiation. The source of radiation is rotated around the patient.

Radioactivity

7.9 The structure of atoms

Everything around us is made of atoms. These are so small that the number of them in even the tiniest object is almost unimaginable. For example, fifty million atoms would fit across the diameter of the full stop at the end of this sentence! Even more difficult to imagine, atoms are made up of even tinier particles called **protons**, **neutrons** and **electrons**. In the middle of an atom is a small nucleus that contains two types of particles, called protons and neutrons. A third type of particle is found orbiting the nucleus – the electron. Any atom has the same number of electrons orbiting its nucleus as it has protons in the nucleus.

The mass of a proton and a neutron are the same. Another way of putting this is to say that the **relative mass** of a neutron compared to a proton is one. Electrons are far, far smaller than protons and neutrons – their mass is negligible. Because of this, the mass of an atom is concentrated in its nucleus – the electrons in an atom just do not matter when it comes to thinking about its mass!

However, the electrons *are* important when it comes to thinking about charge. Protons have a positive charge while neutrons have no charge – they are neutral – so the nucleus itself has an overall positive charge. The electrons orbiting the nucleus are negatively charged. The size of the negative charge on an electron is exactly the same as the size of the positive charge on a proton. (In other words, the **relative charge** on a proton is +1, while the relative charge on an electron is −1.) Because any neutral atom contains equal numbers of protons and electrons, the overall charge on any atom is exactly zero. For example, a carbon atom has 6 protons, so we know it also has 6 electrons. Similarly oxygen has 8 protons and therefore 8 electrons.

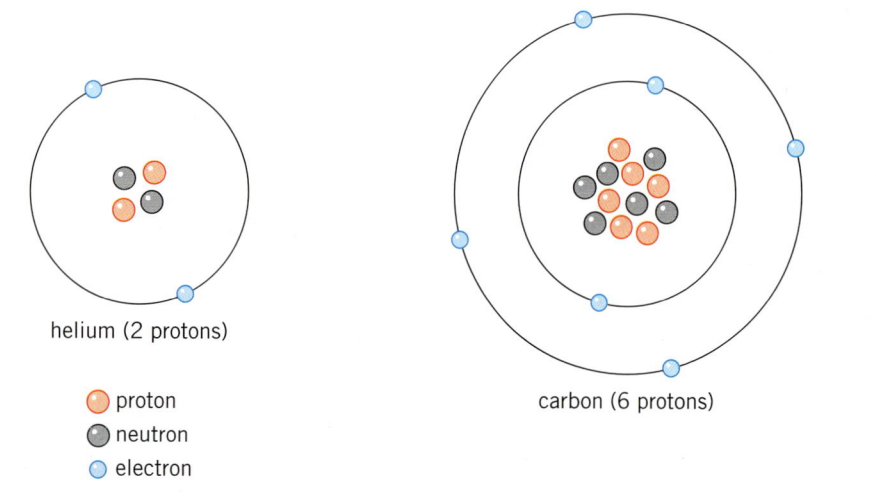

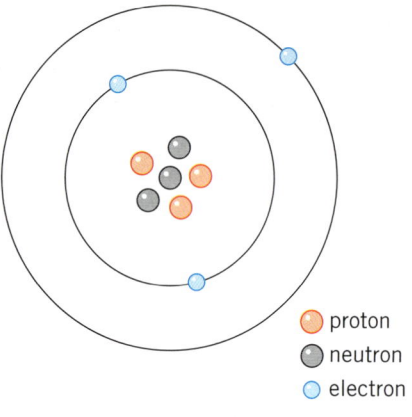

○ proton
● neutron
○ electron

↑ **Figure 1:** A simple model of the atom.

Type of sub-atomic particle	Relative mass	Relative charge
proton	1	+1
neutron	1	0
electron	negligible	−1

All the atoms of a particular element have the same number of protons – for example, boron atoms always have five protons in their nuclei. Atoms of different elements have different numbers of protons in their nuclei.

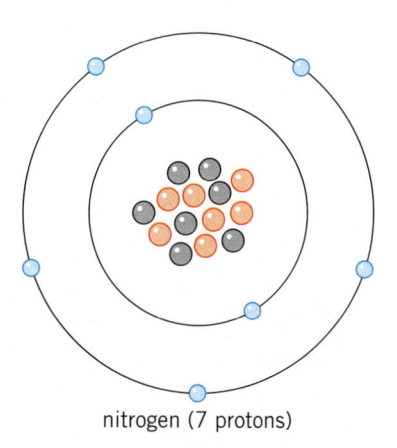

helium (2 protons)

○ proton
● neutron
○ electron

carbon (6 protons)

nitrogen (7 protons)

↖ **Figure 2:** Different elements, different numbers of protons.

Radioactivity

The total number of protons and neutrons in an atom is known as the **mass number** or **nucleon number**. Although all the atoms of the same element always have the same number of protons, they do not always have the same number of neutrons. Atoms of the same element that have different numbers of neutrons are known as **isotopes**. For example, lithium has four isotopes, one with three neutrons in the nucleus, another with four neutrons, a third with five neutrons and the fourth isotope with six neutrons. All four isotopes have three protons in the nuclei of their atoms – otherwise the atoms would not be atoms of lithium but atoms of another element.

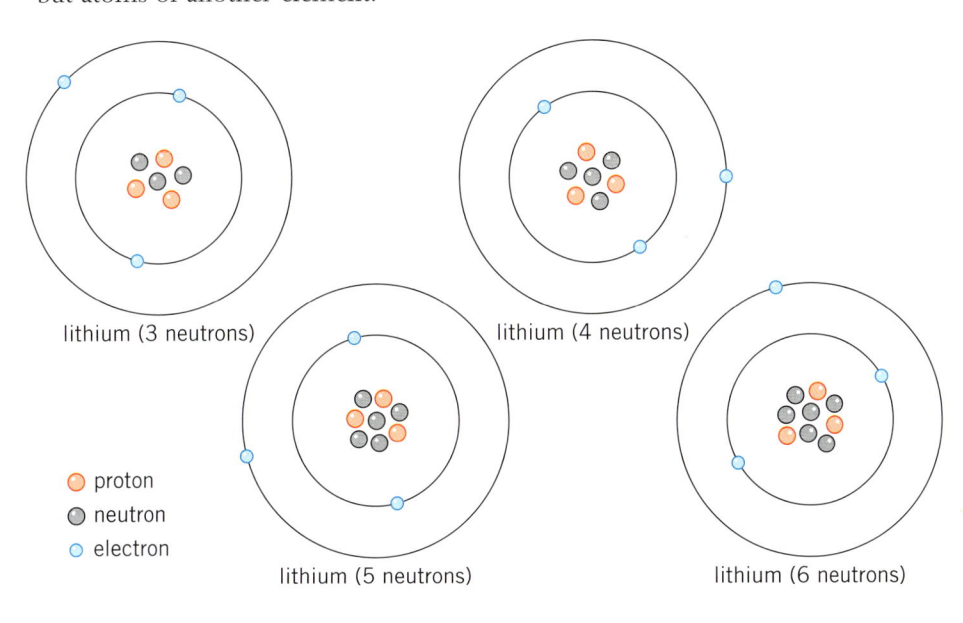

← **Figure 3:** Same element – same number of protons but different numbers of neutrons.

lithium (3 neutrons)
lithium (4 neutrons)
lithium (5 neutrons)
lithium (6 neutrons)

○ proton
○ neutron
○ electron

Key Ideas

- Atoms have a small central nucleus made up of protons and neutrons around which there are electrons.
- The relative masses of protons, neutrons and electrons and their relative charges are as shown in the table on page 134.
- In an atom, the number of electrons is equal to the number of protons in the nucleus. All atoms of a particular element have the same number of protons, while all atoms of different elements have different numbers of protons.
- The total number of protons and neutrons (nucleons) in an atom is called its mass number or its nucleon number.
- Atoms of the same element that have different numbers of neutrons are called isotopes.
- The atom as a whole has no electrical charge (it is electrically neutral).

? Questions

1. How many electrons do the following atoms have?
   a. A hydrogen atom, with 1 proton in its nucleus
   b. A potassium atom, with 21 protons in its nucleus
   c. A uranium atom, with 92 protons in its nucleus

2. What would be the effect on the overall charge of an atom if it:
   a. loses an electron
   b. gains an electron
   c. loses a proton?

3. The stable isotope of sodium has 11 protons in its nucleus. Sodium also has a radioisotope with 13 neutrons in its nucleus – how many protons are in the nucleus of this radioisotope? Explain your answer.

4. Copy and complete the table.

Element	He	C	N	K	Br	Pb	U	No
Proton number	2	6	7	19	35	82	92	102
Mass number	4	12		40			238	
Number of neutrons			7		44	126		153
Number of protons								
Number of electrons								

Radioactivity 135

7.10 Developing a model of the atom

Ideas and Evidence

The basic model of the atom still used by scientists today was developed nearly 100 years ago. The story of the atomic model starts around 150 years ago, in the middle of the 19th century.

In 1855 a physicist called William Crookes was investigating the conduction of electricity in gases. He found that if a piece of heated metal in a vacuum was given a negative charge it emitted a stream of radiation or rays of some kind that caused gases at low pressure to give off a mysterious glow. The negative electrode in a vacuum tube is called the cathode – so these rays were called **cathode rays**. Debates raged in the next forty years – some physicists thought that cathode rays must be waves, like electromagnetic waves, while others thought that they must be particles. An Irish physicist called George Stoney was so convinced that cathode rays must be particles that he gave the particle a name – electron. By the middle of the 1890s enough work had been done to show that cathode rays carried a negative charge. Two different ideas for the atom were then proposed. In England, Joseph John Thomson thought that the atom was best described using 'the plum pudding model'. In this model, tiny negatively charged electrons were contained in a 'sphere of positive charge' – just like the plums in a pudding (Figure 1). Directly opposing this idea, the Japanese physicist Hantaro Nagaoka described the atom like the planet Saturn, with a positively charged nucleus surrounded by circling electrons (Figure 2). The problem for physicists lay in deciding which of these two models was the correct one – or whether neither was right.

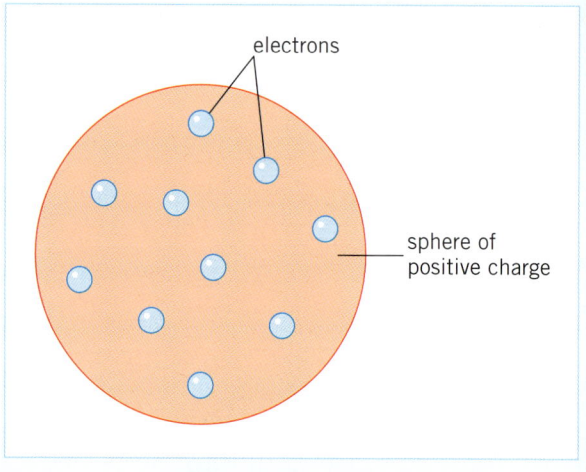

↑ **Figure 1:** Plum pudding was popular in Victorian times – and gave its name to Thomson's model of the atom.

↓ **Figure 2:** Nagaoka's model of the atom was inspired by the structure of the planet Saturn.

Radioactivity

The conclusive evidence for the structure of the atom came in just over ten years. In Cambridge, a physicist called Ernest Rutherford was working with two of his research assistants, Hans Geiger and Ernst Marsden. Two years earlier, Rutherford had shown that alpha radiation consists of streams of massive positively charged particles. The three physicists now took a radioactive substance that emitted alpha radiation, and used it to fire beams of alpha radiation at a very thin sheet of gold foil. To their surprise, most of the alpha particles went straight through the foil, while a tiny proportion bounced back in the direction in which they had come!

Rutherford quickly realised that the results of their experiments must mean that most of the atom is simply empty space, and that the truth lay much closer to Hantaro's model than to Thomson's. In 1911 he published a paper in which he described a model of the atom along the lines of the Solar System, with negatively charged electrons orbiting a positively charged nucleus in much the same way as planets orbit the Sun. Calculations based on his results showed that the diameter of the atom was about 10 000 times greater than the diameter of the nucleus, explaining why so many alpha particles could pass through the sheet of gold foil, and why so few bounced back.

While the details of Rutherford's model continued to change over the next ten years or so, his basic model of the atom remains as good today as it was nearly one hundred years ago – a model inspired by the heavens rather than an item on a Victorian dinner table.

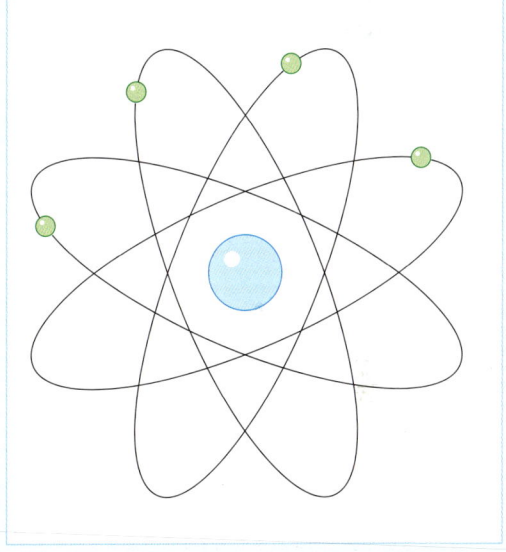

↓ **Figure 3:** Rutherford's alpha particle scattering experiment.

Most alpha particles go straight through.

Some alpha particles bounce back in the direction from which they have come.

↑ **Figure 4:** Rutherford's model – the similarity to the Solar System is very clear from this diagram.

Questions

1 Imagine that you are a newspaper reporter working in 1911. Write a report for your paper explaining Rutherford's experiment and what it tells us about the structure of the atom. Remember to use language that people will be able to understand, even if they have not studied science – you may find it helpful to include diagrams.

Key Ideas

- The model of the atom that we use today has evolved over the past 150 years as a result of 'thought experiments' and experimentation.

Radioactivity

7.11 Atoms and radioactivity

The isotopes of some elements are made up of nuclei that are unstable. In order to become more stable a nucleus may break apart or **disintegrate**. When this happens the nucleus emits ionising radiation, and an atom of a different element is formed. Isotopes that behave like this are called **radioisotopes** or **radionuclides**. One common element with a radioisotope is carbon. The most common isotope of carbon has 6 protons and 6 neutrons in its nucleus – this nucleus is perfectly stable. Another isotope of carbon has 6 protons and 8 neutrons in its nucleus. The nucleus of this isotope is unstable, and decays by emitting beta radiation. When it does this, the carbon atom becomes a nitrogen atom, with a stable nucleus.

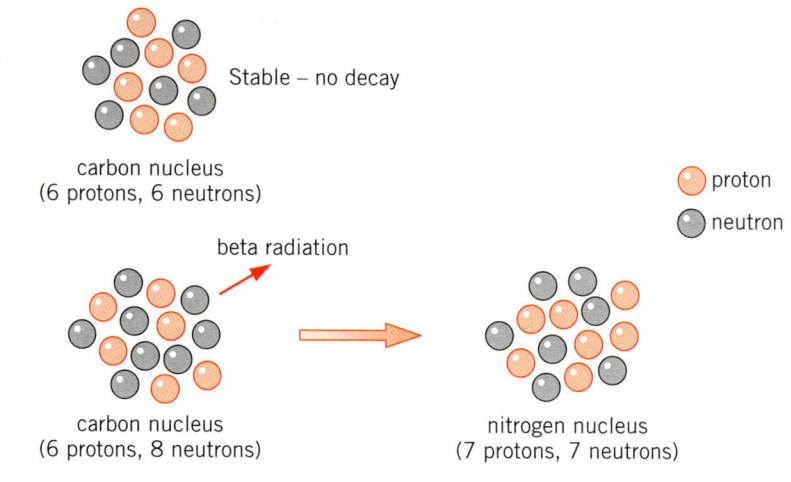

↑ **Figure 1:** The unstable nucleus of a carbon atom emits beta radiation and becomes the stable nucleus of a nitrogen atom.

H Careful observation of the radiation given off by radioactive substances shows that the three types of radiation are made up in different ways, which explains their very different properties.

For example, alpha radiation is actually the nuclei of helium atoms, composed of two protons and two neutrons held tightly together. In contrast, beta radiation is made up of high-energy electrons given off when a neutron in the nucleus of an unstable atom turns into a proton.

Sometimes the nucleus that is produced as a result of alpha and beta decay may still be unstable. When this happens, the nucleus may become more stable by emitting gamma radiation. This is electromagnetic radiation with a very short wavelength. Emitting gamma radiation does not change the number of protons or neutrons in the nucleus. The thorium nucleus and the fluorine nucleus produced in the radioactive decays shown in Figures 2 and 3 both give off gamma radiation in order to become more stable.

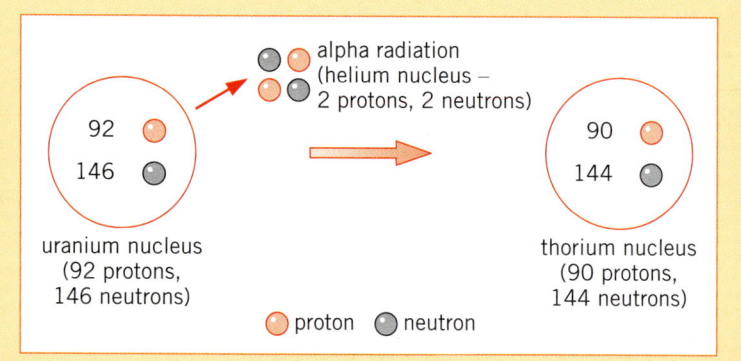

↑ **Figure 2:** A uranium nucleus decays by giving out alpha radiation, producing a thorium nucleus.

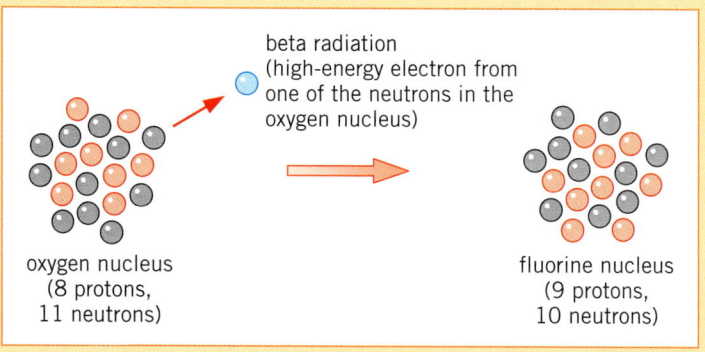

↑ **Figure 3:** An oxygen nucleus decays by giving out beta radiation, producing a fluorine nucleus.

The nature of the three types of radiation explains their very different behaviours. Alpha radiation consists of massive particles carrying two positive charges. These particles interact strongly with matter as they pass through it, smashing past atoms and ionising them. This quickly absorbs their energy, and they can penetrate only a very short distance through air. Beta radiation consists of particles which are many times less massive than alpha particles, and which carry only a single negative charge. These interact much less strongly with matter, and so the radiation is much less quickly absorbed as they travel through matter – so they can travel through thin sheets of aluminium. Being short wavelength electromagnetic waves, gamma radiation is not strongly absorbed by matter at all, and it is therefore the most penetrating of all three radiations.

Radioactivity

Science people

Enrico Fermi

Enrico Fermi was born in Rome in 1901, and became professor of theoretical physics at the University of Rome when he was only 25 years old. He quickly gathered a small team of young researchers around him, and began work on various problems in radioactivity, including beta decay and the production of artificial radioactivity by bombarding elements with neutrons. In 1938 he was awarded the Nobel Prize in physics for this work. When travelling with his family to Sweden, Fermi took the opportunity to travel on to the United States rather than returning to Italy. Fermi's wife was Jewish, and life under the Fascist regime at that time was becoming increasingly difficult for them.

Fermi settled in the USA and worked to produce atomic energy, first at the University of Chicago and then on the Manhattan Project, which produced the atomic bombs dropped on Hiroshima and Nagasaki in 1945. Despite this work, Fermi became a firm opponent of the development of the hydrogen bomb in the years after the war. He died from stomach cancer in November 1954.

Figure 4: A painting of the first controlled nuclear fission chain reaction, under the direction of Enrico Fermi, in December 1942.

Key Ideas

- Radioactive isotopes (radioisotopes or radionuclides) are atoms with unstable nuclei.
- When an unstable nucleus splits up (disintegrates):
  - it emits radiation
  - a different atom, with a different number of protons, is formed.
- Alpha radiation consists of helium nuclei – particles made up of two protons and two neutrons.
- Beta radiation consists of high-energy electrons emitted from the nuclei of atoms. For each electron emitted, a neutron in the nucleus splits to become a proton and an electron.
- Gamma radiation is very short wavelength electromagnetic radiation.

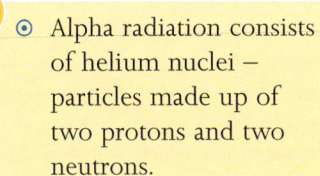

Questions

1. Copy and complete the table.

Starting atom	Decay	Final atom
mass number = 32 proton number = 15	beta	
	alpha	mass number = 236 proton number = 92
mass number = 90 proton number = 36		mass number = 90 proton number = 37
mass number = 214 proton number = 82		mass number = 214 proton number = 82
mass number = 212 proton number = 84	alpha	

2. Fermi's work contributed to the production of the first atomic bomb. Many scientists working on the Manhattan Project were very worried that if they did not develop the atomic bomb the enemy might do so first, and then the war would be lost. Is it right for scientists to use their talents to produce new weapons? Imagine that you are a scientist who has been invited to join a team working on a new weapon. Draw up a list of arguments for and against joining the team – what decision do you think you might make?

Radioactivity

7.12 Using radioactive decay

As radioactive substances decay the amount of radiation they emit decreases. This means that we can use radioactive decay to help us to date things.

One very important dating technique using radioactivity is **carbon dating**. High up in the Earth's atmosphere, molecules of carbon dioxide are bombarded by streams of radiation from space. This radiation converts some of the stable carbon atoms in these molecules to radioactive carbon atoms. As the carbon dioxide molecules diffuse through the atmosphere, many of them are taken up by plants and incorporated into the plant matter during photosynthesis. This radioactive carbon also finds it way into the bodies of animals as they eat plants. When a plant or animal dies, the amount of radioactive carbon in it slowly decreases, through radioactive decay. The age of the remains of the plant or animal can be calculated from the amount of radioactive carbon left in it.

Carbon dating provides archaeologists with a valuable tool for calculating the age of remains that they discover. It has been used to work out the age of the shroud of Turin – a piece of cloth said to be the burial cloth in which Christ was wrapped following his crucifixion. Using this technique on a small piece of the shroud suggests that the cloth was made at some time between 1260 and 1390 AD. Methods like this can also be used to measure the age of rocks, based on the amount of radiation they emit.

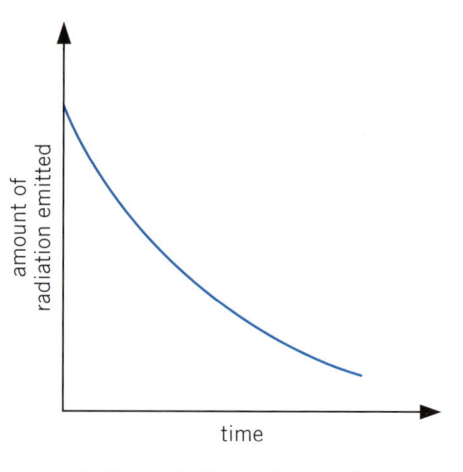

↑ **Figure 1:** The older a radioisotope, the less radiation it emits.

H There are two important ways in which the age of rocks can be measured based on radioactive decay. The **uranium-lead method** uses the fact that uranium nuclei decay through a series of relatively short-lived radioisotopes to produce a stable isotope of lead. By measuring the relative proportions of uranium and lead isotopes in the rock, an age for the rock can be calculated.

Another method is based on the decay of the radioactive isotope potassium-40, which produces argon gas. This does not decay any further. This decay can be used to date a lot of rocks, since many types of rocks contain potassium atoms. The age of the rock is found by measuring the amount of argon gas trapped in it, and calculating the relative proportions of argon and potassium atoms in the rock. This method relies on gas being trapped in the rock, and therefore works only for igneous rocks, which are impermeable to gas.

↑ **Figure 2:** Radioactivity can also be used to measure the age of rocks.

Example

A sample of rock is examined. Argon gas is found trapped inside the rock, formed through the radioactive decay of potassium-40 atoms. For every three atoms of argon gas trapped in the rock there is one atom of potassium in the rock. Estimate the age of the rock of the half-life of potassium-40 is 1300 million years.

When the rock formed:
There are no argon atoms present in the rock so, for every four potassium atoms in the rock there are zero argon atoms.

The ratio, potassium atoms : argon atoms = 4 : 0.

After one half-life:
Half of the potassium atoms have decayed to form argon atoms – so for every four potassium atoms that were present in the rock when it formed, two will have decayed to produce argon atoms.

The ratio, potassium atoms : argon atoms = 2 : 2 (= 1 : 1).

After two half-lives:
A further half of the potassium atoms have decayed to form argon atoms – so for every two potassium atoms present in the rock after one half-life, one will have decayed to produce an argon atom. This means that three out of the four of the potassium atoms present in the rock when it formed have now decayed to produce argon atoms.

The ratio, potassium atoms : argon atoms = 1 : 3 – there are three times as many argon atoms as potassium atoms.

This means that the rock is two half-lives old. Since the half-life of potassium-40 is 1300 million years, this makes the rock 2 × 1 300 million years old = **2600 million years**.

Questions

1 Geologists are investigating a volcano that is known to have erupted several times over the last thousand years. They measure the amount of radioactive material in the cooled lava lying on the slopes of the volcano – explain how measurements like this can help to decide when the volcano erupted.

2 The table shows data for the decay of radioactive carbon.

Time (years)	0	2000	4000	6000	8000	10 000	12 000	14 000
% carbon-14 remaining	100	94	73	58	45	36	28	22

a Use the data in the table to plot a graph for this decay.

Archaeologists investigating an ancient burial site find some wood. They measure the amount of radioactive carbon-14 atoms in this wood, and find that there is only 75% as much radioactive carbon in the wood as there is in a modern piece of wood.

b Use your graph from part (a) to estimate the age of the wood. Explain how you arrive at your answer.

H 3 A sample of rock contains fifteen times as many lead atoms as it does uranium atoms. If the half-life for uranium to decay into lead is 713 million years, estimate the age of the rock.

Key Ideas

- The older a particular radioactive material, the less radiation it emits. This idea can be used to date materials, including rocks.
- H The relative proportions of uranium and lead isotopes in a sample of rock can be used to estimate its age.
- The proportions of the radioisotope potassium-40 and its stable decay product argon can be used to estimate the age of igneous rocks from which argon has been unable to escape.

Radioactivity 141

7.13 Nuclear power (H)

An atom with an unstable nucleus may become more stable through radioactive decay – emitting alpha, beta or gamma radiation. Some atoms with very large nuclei can also become more stable when their nucleus splits into two smaller parts. This is called nuclear fission. For example, the nucleus of a uranium atom may split when struck by a neutron. The nucleus splits into two smaller nuclei, and two more neutrons and a great deal of energy are also released in this process.

The energy released when a large nucleus splits (or **fissions**) into two smaller nuclei is very large – much larger than the amount of energy released when a chemical bond is formed. The energy released when chemical bonds form is used in power stations that burn fossil fuels. (The furnace of a fossil fuel power station breaks carbon-carbon and carbon-hydrogen bonds, and forms carbon-oxygen and hydrogen-oxygen bonds as hydrocarbons are burnt in air.) In contrast, nuclear fission is concerned with the bonds that hold a nucleus together, rather than chemical bonds. This means that nuclear fission can be a very valuable way to obtain energy, since quite small amounts of material can be used to release very large amounts of energy. For example, fissioning 1 kg of uranium releases as much energy as burning more than $2\frac{1}{2}$ thousand tonnes of coal!

A uranium nucleus produces two neutrons when it fissions. Each of these neutrons can fission another uranium nucleus – which will produce a total of four (2 × 2) more neutrons. These four neutrons can fission four more uranium nuclei, producing eight (2 × 4) more neutrons and so on. This is called a **chain reaction**. In a chain reaction the rate at which uranium atoms fission increases rapidly, and enormous amounts of energy are released very quickly. Figure 3 shows this happening.

There is a big challenge when we want to use nuclear fission to produce energy in a controlled way (for example, in a nuclear power station). This is to ensure that a chain reaction cannot happen. Nuclear scientists and engineers designing reactors do this by controlling the amount of neutrons that are allowed to fission uranium atoms. This ensures that only one of the two neutrons produced when a uranium atom splits is allowed to split another uranium nucleus.

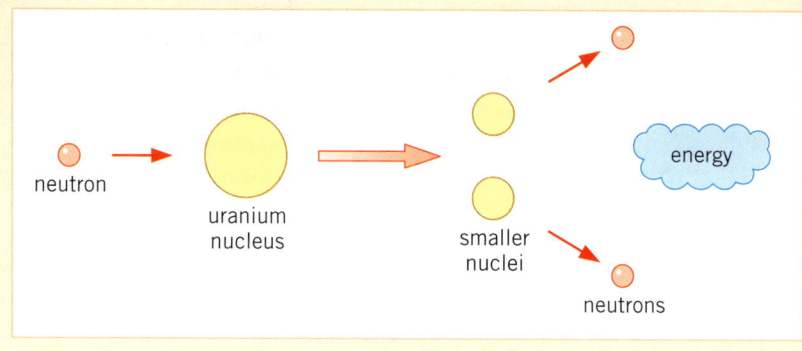

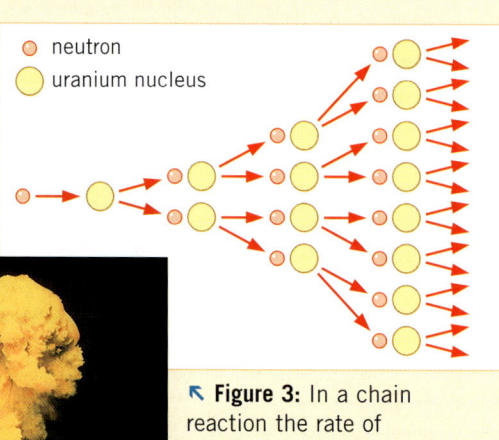

↑ **Figure 1:** When a uranium nucleus is hit by a neutron, it may split into two smaller nuclei. This process of nuclear fission also produces two more neutrons and a lot of energy.

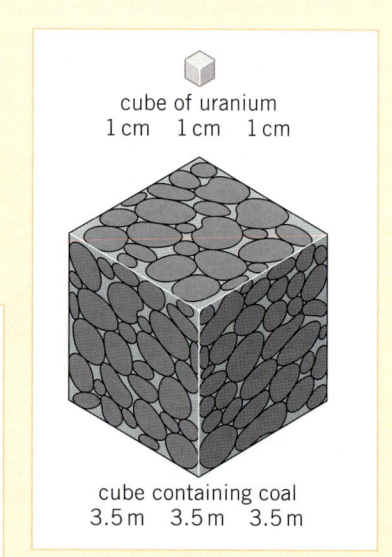

↑ **Figure 2:** Nuclear fission releases an amazing amount of energy – a cube of uranium 1 cm × 1 cm × 1 cm can produce as much energy as a heap of coal which would fit in a cube measuring 3.5 m × 3.5 m × 3.5 m.

↖ **Figure 3:** In a chain reaction the rate of nuclear fission increases rapidly. This releases vast amounts of energy very quickly – a fact exploited in an atomic bomb.

↓ **Figure 4:** The rate at which uranium atoms in a nuclear reactor are allowed to fission is controlled so that each nucleus that fissions causes one other nucleus to fission, and no more.

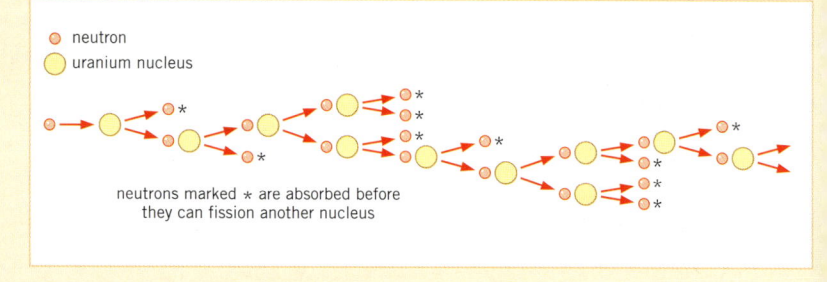

neutrons marked * are absorbed before they can fission another nucleus

Radioactivity

The nuclei produced when large nuclei break up are also unstable, and are radioactive. This presents a problem when nuclear fission is used to generate electricity – once all of the uranium (sometimes called **nuclear fuel**) in a nuclear reactor has been fissioned it must be removed and replaced with new uranium. The 'spent' nuclear fuel removed from the reactor is highly radioactive, and many of the radionuclides it contains have very long half-lives. This **radioactive waste** must be stored carefully until it is no longer a hazard, something that may take many tens of thousands of years.

↑ **Figure 5:** An underground storage cavern for radioactive waste. The waste will need to be stored here for thousands of years until the level of radioactivity has fallen to safe levels.

Ideas and Evidence

Should we or shouldn't we use nuclear power?

The issues concerned with using the energy released by nuclear fission to generate electricity are complicated. Here are some of the arguments on both sides:

Arguments for nuclear power	Arguments against nuclear power
• Generating electricity using nuclear energy does not release carbon dioxide into the atmosphere. • Amounts of fossil fuels are very limited – there is enough nuclear fuel to produce electricity for many years to come. • Nuclear power stations are small and unobtrusive nuclear compared to alternative energy sources like wind power. • Britain's nuclear industry makes money for the country by storing and reprocessing our own and other country's nuclear waste.	• Generating electricity using nuclear energy produces radioactive waste that must be stored for thousands of years. • Amounts of fossil fuels are very limited – it would be better to use renewable sources to generate electricity. • Although supporters of nuclear power say that power stations are very safe, the devastating consequences of an accident make it not worth the risk. • Why should we take the risks involved in importing and dealing with other countries' waste?

↓ **Figure 6:** Feelings can run high when nuclear power is discussed.

Questions

1. A coal-fired power station burns 30 tonnes of coal a minute. If 1 kg of uranium produces as much energy when fissioned as 2700 tonnes of coal, how much uranium would have to be fissioned each minute in order to supply the same amount of electricity, using uranium instead of coal?

2. Starting with the list of arguments for and against nuclear power, write down the questions that you think you would need answered before you could make a decision about whether or not we should generate more of our electricity using nuclear energy.

Key Ideas

- When an atom with a very large nucleus is bombarded with neutrons the nucleus splits (**fissions**) into two smaller nuclei.
- When a nucleus fissions it produces further neutrons that may cause further nuclear fission, causing a **chain reaction**.
- The new nuclei formed as a result of nuclear fission are themselves radioactive.
- The energy released by an atom during nuclear fission is very large compared to the energy released when a chemical bond is made between two atoms.

Radioactivity

7.14 End of chapter questions

1 a Copy and complete the table below to show the relative mass and charge of a neutron and an electron. The relative mass and charge of a proton have already been done for you.

Particle	Relative Mass	Relative Charge
proton	1	+1
neutron		
electron		

(2 marks)

b The diagrams below show the nuclei of four different atoms **A**, **B**, **C** and **D**.

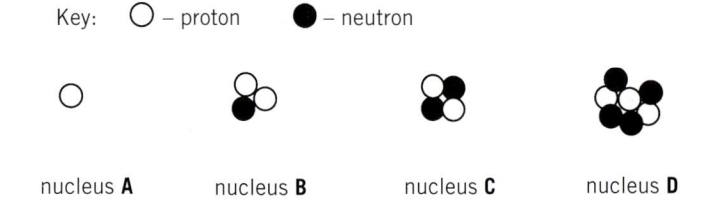

Key: ○ – proton ● – neutron

nucleus **A**   nucleus **B**   nucleus **C**   nucleus **D**

  i State the mass number of **C**. (1 mark)

  ii Which two are isotopes of the same element? (1 mark)

   Explain your answer. (2 marks)

(Total 6 marks)
AQA specimen question

2 The radioactive isotope, carbon-14, decays by beta (β) particle emission.

a Plants absorb carbon-14 from the atmosphere. The graph shows the decay curve for 1 g of carbon-14 taken from a flax plant.

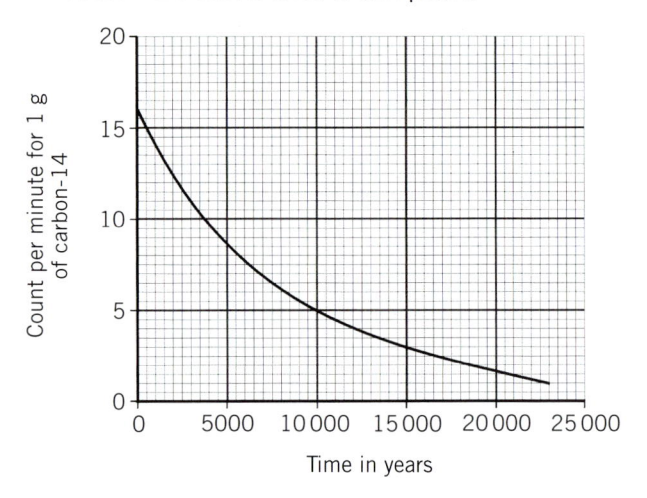

Use the graph to find the half-life of carbon-14. You should show clearly on your graph how you obtain your answer. (2 marks)

b Linen in a cloth made from the flax plant. A recent exhibition included part of a linen shirt, believed to have belonged to St Thomas à Becket, who died in 1162. Extracting carbon-14 from the cloth would allow the age of the shirt to be verified.

If 1 g of carbon-14 extracted from the cloth were to give 870 counts in 1 hour, would it be possible for the shirt to have once belonged to St Thomas à Becket? You must show clearly the steps used and reason for your decision.

(3 marks)

(Total 5 marks)
AQA specimen question

Radioactivity

3 At the beginning of the 20th century, a team of scientists carried out an experiment which led to the idea that atoms contain a positively charged nucleus which contains virtually all of the mass of the atom.

  a Outline the way that this experiment was done, and show how the results led to the idea of the nuclear atom. (4 marks)

  b We now know that the nucleus of an atom contains positively charged protons and uncharged neutrons. The neutron was discovered much later than the proton. Suggest why neutrons were much harder to detect than protons. (2 marks)

  (Total 6 marks)

4 A company wishes to check the level of coffee in packets passing along a conveyer belt. They wish to do this by placing a radioactive source on one side of the belt and a detector on the other, as shown in the figure.

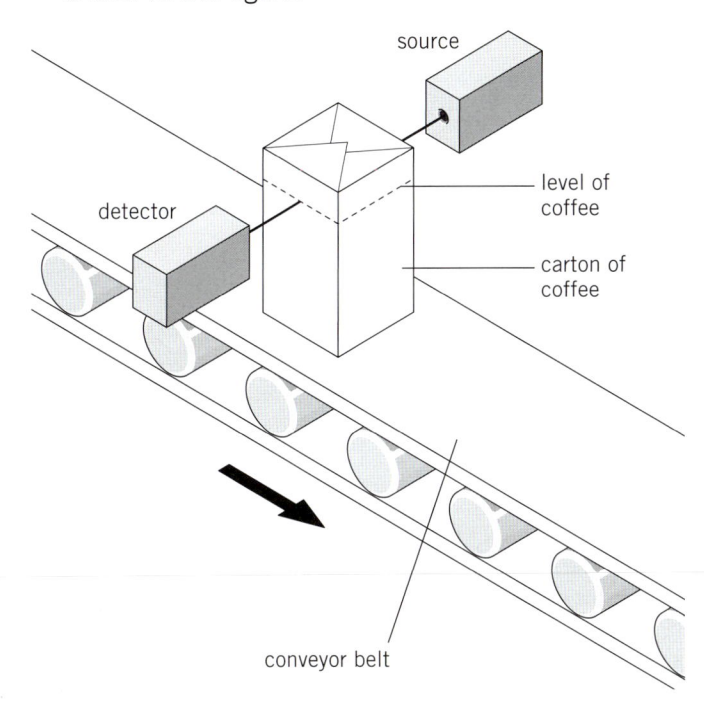

Possible radioactive sources that could be used for this purpose are shown in the table.

Source	Radiation emitted	Half-life
A	alpha	30 000 years
B	beta	30 years
C	beta	5 minutes
D	alpha and gamma	20 years
E	gamma	500 years

  a Which type of radiation is most suitable for this application? Explain your answer clearly. (2 marks)

  b How does the half-life of a source affect the choice of source for this application? (2 marks)

  c Which source in the table would you recommend the company to use and why? (2 marks)

  d Explain how the system could be used to alert the production line staff to the fact that one of the packets does not contain enough coffee. (2 marks)

  e What precautions should the company take to protect their staff from the radiation from the source used? (2 marks)

Radioactivity 145

Data sheets

This list shows the formulae for quantitative relationships in the Physical Processes section of the specification which candidates will be expected to recall (N.B. for convenience, formulae are also given here in symbolic form even though this form is not required by the specification).

FT and HT

potential difference = current × resistance $V = IR$
(volt, V) (ampere, A) (ohm, Ω)

power = potential difference × current $P = VI$
(watt, W) (volt, V) (ampere, A)

energy transferred = power × time $E = Pt$
(kilowatt hour, kWh) (kilowatt, W) (hour, h)

total cost = number of Units × cost per Unit

energy transferred = power × time $E = Pt$
(joule, J) (watt, W) (second, s)

$$\text{acceleration} \atop (\text{metre/second squared, m/s}^2) = \frac{\text{change in velocity (metre/second m/s)}}{\text{time taken for change (second, s)}} \qquad a = \frac{v - u}{t}$$

wave speed = frequency × wavelength
(metre/second, m/s) (hertz, Hz) (metre, m)

$$\text{efficiency} = \frac{\text{useful energy transferred by device}}{\text{total energy supplied to device}}$$

work done = energy transferred

work done = force applied × distance moved in direction of force $W = Fs$
(joule, J) (newton, N) (metre, m)

$$\text{power (watt, W)} = \frac{\text{work done (joule, J)}}{\text{time taken (second, s)}} \qquad P = \frac{W}{t}$$

weight = mass × gravitational field strength $\quad w = mg$
(newton, N) (kilogram, kg) (newton/kilogram, N/kg)

change in gravitational = weight × change in vertical height $\quad gpe = mg\Delta h$
potential energy (joule, J) (newton, N) (metre, m)

kinetic energy = ½ × mass × speed² $\quad ke = \tfrac{1}{2}mv^2$
(joule, J) (kilogram, kg) [(metre/second)², (m/s)²]

HT

energy transferred = potential difference × charge $\quad E = VQ$
(joule, J) (volt, V) (coulomb, C)

charge = current × time $\quad Q = It$
(coulomb, C) (ampere, A) (second, s)

force = mass × acceleration $\quad F = ma$
(newton, N) (kilogram, kg) (metre/second squared, m/s²)

$\dfrac{\text{voltage across primary (volt, V)}}{\text{voltage across secondary (volt, V)}} = \dfrac{\text{number of turns on primary}}{\text{number of turns on secondary}} \quad \dfrac{V_p}{V_s} = \dfrac{N_p}{N_s}$

Index

A
absorption of radiation 118–19
acceleration 28–9
   force, mass and 32–3
acid rain 96
aircraft refuelling 21
alpha particle scattering
   experiment 137
alpha radiation 118, 126, 128, 138
alternating current (a.c.) 12
   comparing alternating currents 12–13
   and electricity supply 110, 111, 115
ammeter 2–3
amperes (amps) 2
amplitude 41
amplitude modulation (AM) 52
analogue signals 52–3
argon gas 140–41
astronomical satellites 68, 69
atoms
   model of the atom 136–7
   and radioactivity 138–9
   structure 134–5
   vibrating and conduction 84
attractive forces 20
average speed 28

B
background radiation 122–3
beta radiation 118, 126, 128, 138
big bang 74–5
big crunch 75
black holes 71
bonding cable 21
Brahe, Tycho 65
brakes 34
braking distance 34–5
brushes 112

C
cable, electric 16
cancer 124–5
carbon dating 140
carbon dioxide 96
carrier wave 52
catapult effect 104
cathode rays 136
cavity wall insulation 80–81

cells, electric 10
   polarity 2–3
   in series 6
cells, living *see* living cells
chain reaction 142
charge
   charging by rubbing 20
   in circuits 10–11
   discharging 21
   electrons, protons and neutrons 134
   electrostatic 20–23
   positive and negative 20
chemical energy 10
chemical evidence of life 73
circuit breakers 18, 106–7
circuits, electric 2–5
   energy in 10–11
comets 64, 65
communications 52–3
communications satellites 68
commutator 106
conduction 78, 80–81, 84
conductors 19
constellations of stars 64
continental drift 58–9
convection 78, 80–81, 84–5
convection currents 58, 85
core, Earth's 56, 92
cosmic rays 122
coulombs 11
count rate 130
critical angle 46
crust (lithosphere) 56
Curie, Marie 120–21
Curie, Pierre 120–21
current 2–3, 6, 19
   alternating current *see* alternating current
   direct current 12, 114–15
   induced 108
   magnetic effects 104–5
current-voltage relationships 8–9

D
dating techniques 140–41
day and night 64
decay curve 130
density 84–5
diffraction 44, 47
digital signals 52–3
diode 8–9
direct current (d.c.) 12, 114–15
distance 28–9
distance–time graphs 28
Doppler effect 74
double glazing 81
drag forces 36

E
Earth 64
   magnetic field 61
   structure of 56
earth-sheltered houses 83
earth wire 17
earthquakes 59, 60
Edison, Thomas Alva 114
efficiency 86–7
   power stations 89
Einstein, Albert 67
elastic potential energy 101
electric chair 115
electric circuits *see* circuits, electric
electric fences 7
electric motors 106
electrical energy 10–11, 14–15
electricity 2–27
   a.c. vs d.c. for supply 114–15
   circuits 2–5, 10–11
   current, voltage and resistance 6–9
   distribution 110–13
   energy resources *see* energy resources
   generators 108–9, 112
   induced current 108
   mains electricity 12–13, 16–17
   safety 16–19
   sources and meeting demand 94–5
   static 20–23
electrodes 24
electrolysis 24–5

electromagnetic waves 48–53
   and communication 52–3
   effect on living cells 50–51
   spectrum 48–9
electromagnets 104–7
electrons 19, 84, 134, 136
electrostatic charge 20–23
ellipses 64
endoscopes 47
energy
   chemical energy 10
   electrical energy 10–11, 14–15
   kinetic energy 101
   losses in transmission of
     electricity 110, 112–13
   nuclear energy 142–3
   potential energy 100–101
energy-efficient buildings 80–83
energy resources 88–99
   and the environment 96–7
   fuels 88–9, 91, 94, 96
   geothermal energy 92
   hydroelectric energy 90, 94, 97
   meeting electricity demand 94–5
   solar energy 92–3, 95
   tidal energy 91, 95, 97, 98–9
   wind energy 90, 94–5, 97
energy transfer 78–87
   calculations 100–101
   electrical energy 10–11, 14–15
   heat energy 78–9, 84–5
   useful and useless transfers 86–7
   waves 44
environment 96–7
expanding Universe 74–5

F
Faraday, Michael 105
Fermi, Enrico 139
filament lamp 8
film badge dosimeter 126–7
fission, nuclear 142–3
forced convection 85
forces 30
   attractive and repulsive 20
   balanced and unbalanced 30–31
   drag forces 36
   frictional 34–5, 36
   due to gravity 64, 66–7
   magnetic 104
   mass, acceleration and 32–3

fossil fuels 88–9, 94, 96
Franklin, Benjamin 21
free fall 36–7
frequency 12, 41
frequency modulation (FM) 52
frictional forces 34–5, 36
fuels 88–9, 91, 94, 96
fuses 3, 16–17
   resettable 106
fusion, nuclear 71

G
galaxies 70
gamma camera 128–9
gamma radiation 48, 50, 118,
   126, 128, 138
gases 84–5
generators 108–9, 112
geostationary orbits 68
geothermal energy 92
global warming 96
gravitational potential energy 100
gravity 64, 66–7

H
half-life 130–31, 132–3
Halley's comet 65
heat energy 78–9, 84–5
   energy-efficient buildings 80–83
Henry, Joseph 105
human radiation experiments 123
hydroelectric energy 90, 94, 97

I
induced current 108
induced voltage 108
infra-red radiation 48, 50, 78–9
inkjet printer 23
insulators 19, 20, 111
ionising radiation 124–5
   see also radioactivity
ions 24
isotopes 135
   radioisotopes 138

K
kilowatt hours 14–15
kinetic energy 101

L
laser printer 23
left-hand rule 104
life elsewhere in the Universe
   72–3
light
   red shift of light from distant
     galaxies 74
   reflection 42
   wave-particle duality 45
   waves 46–7
light-dependent resistor 9
light pipe 47
lightning conductor 21
liquids 84–5
lithosphere 56
living cells
   effects of electromagnetic waves
     50–1
   effects of ionising radiation
     124–5
local group 70
longitudinal waves 40–41
low polar orbit 68

M
magnetic field 104–5
   Earth's 61
magnetism 104–9
   catapult effect 104
   electromagnets 104–7
   induced current and voltage
     108–9
main sequence stars 71
mains electricity 12–13, 16–17
mantle 56
Marconi, Guglielmo 49
Mars, life on 72
Marshmead School, Australia 82
mass 32–3, 36
   electrons, protons and neutrons
     134
   radioactive decay 130
mass number 135
medicine 128–9, 132–3
metals 84
meteorites 72
microwaves 48, 50
mid-ocean ridges 61
Milky Way 70
mobile phones 51
models 4–5
moons 68
Morse code 52

Index 149

motion 28–39
  changing 30–31
  distance, speed and time 28–9
  force, mass and acceleration 32–3
  free fall 36–7
motors, electric 106

N
National Grid 110–11
negative charge 20
neutron stars 71
neutrons 134–5
Newton, Isaac 65, 66
newtons 30, 32
Newton's laws of motion
  second 32
  third 30
night and day 64
non-renewable energy resources 88, 90, 94, 96
normal rays 42
nuclear energy 142–3
nuclear fission 142–3
nuclear fuels 89, 96
nuclear fusion 71
nuclear power stations 89, 94, 143
nucleon number 135
nucleus, atomic 134
  unstable and radioactivity 138

O
ohms 6
optical fibres 47
orbits 66
  planets and comets 64
  satellites 68
oscilloscope 12–13, 54

P
P waves 56–7
photocopier 22
photovoltaic cells 93, 95
pickups 94
planets 64, 66–7
plastic sheet thickness 118–19, 132
plate tectonics 58–61
plugs, electric 13, 16
plum pudding model of the atom 136
polarity of a battery 2–3
polonium 120–21
positive charge 20
potassium-40 dating method 140–41

potential difference see voltage
potential energy 100–101
  elastic 101
  gravitational 100
power 100
  electrical 10, 14, 112–13
power stations 88–9, 110
  and the environment 96–7
  meeting demand 94–5
  nuclear 89, 94, 143
  see also energy resources
primary coil 113
prisms 46, 48
protons 134–5
pumped storage 94

R
radiation 78–9, 81, 85
radiation badge 126–7
radio signals from space 73
radio waves 48, 49
radiaoctive decay 130–31
  using 140–41
radioactive tracers 128, 132
radioactive waste 96, 143
radioactivity 118–45
  absorption of radiation 118–19
  atoms and 138–9
  background radiation 122–3
  effects on living things 124–5
  half-life 130–31, 132–3
  handling radioactive sources 126–7
  and medicine 128–9, 132–3
  uses 118–19, 132–3
radioisotopes (radionuclides) 138
radium 120–21
radon gas 122
reaction forces 30
red giants 71
red shift 74
reflection 42
  total internal reflection 46–7
refraction 43, 46, 57
relative charge 134
relative mass 134
remote-sensing satellites 68
renewable energy resources 90–93, 94–5, 97
repulsive forces 20
resettable fuses 106
residual current devices (RCDs) 106–7

resistance 4, 5, 6, 112
resistors 8
  in parallel 6
  in series 5
ripple tank 40, 42, 43, 44
robotic probes 72
rocks, age of 140–41
rubbing, charging by 20
Rutherford model of the atom 137
Rutherford's alpha particle scattering experiment 137

S
S waves 56–7
safety
  electricity and 16–19
  working with radiation 126–7
satellites, artificial 68–9
sea floor ridges 61
secondary coil 113
seismic waves 56–7
SETI project (Search for Extra-Terrestrial Intelligence) 73
Severn barrage 98–9
shock waves 40
slip rings 112
sockets, electric 16
solar cells 93, 95
Solar System 64–7
solar thermal electricity 92–3, 95
sound waves 54–5
sparks 21
spectrum 48
speed 28
  wave speed 41
stars 64, 70–71
static electricity 20–23
step-down transformers 110, 113
step-up transformers 110, 113
stopping distance 34–5
subduction 60
sulphur dioxide 96
Sun 70
  see also Solar System; solar thermal electricity
supernovae 71

Index

T

technetium-99m 133
tectonic plates 58–61
terminal velocity 36
Tesla, Nikola 114–15
theories 75
thermistor 9
thickness, controlling 118–19, 132
thinking distance 34–5
thorium 120
thought experiments 67
ticker-tape timer 32
tidal energy 91, 95, 97, 98–9
total internal reflection 46–7
tracers, radioactive 128, 132
transformers 110, 113
transverse waves 40–41

U

ultrasonic waves 54–5
ultrasound scanning 55
ultraviolet radiation 48, 50
undergound houses 83
Universe 64, 70–75
   life apart from on Earth 72–3
   origins 74–5
uranium 120, 142
uranium-lead dating method 140

V

velocity 28
velocity-time graphs 28, 29, 32
visible light 48
volcanoes 59, 60
voltage (potential difference) 2, 4, 6
   current-voltage relationships 8–9
   mains supply 13
voltmeter 2–3
volts 2

W

waste, radioactive 96, 143
water circuit 4–5
watts 10
wave energy 91, 95
wave-particle duality 45
wave speed 41
wavefronts 41
wavelength 41
waves 40–63
   behaviour 40–45
   electromagnetic 48–53
   light waves 46–7
   seismic waves 56–7
   sound waves 54–5
Wegener, Alfred 59
weight 36
white dwarfs 71
wind energy 90, 94–5, 97
work done 100

X

X-rays 48, 50, 126, 129